This book is dedicated to my family and friends. They tolerated me before I ran for statewide office, and they seem to be tolerating me just fine now.

As for one friend in particular, Judge Betsy Lambeth, district judge for Williamson County, I hereby except and exclude her from any disparaging remarks I might make about politicians, even Republican politicians. Betsy is simply terrific!

Contents

Prologue

I'm not the only Texan who drinks cold beer at Mexican restaurants! But when you're running for the office of Texas lieutenant governor, you've got to worry about appearances.

Now, I love Mexican food, beer, and Suzanne. And after eighteen months of nonstop campaigning, Suzanne and I found an evening to celebrate our twenty-ninth anniversary at Chachi's, our favorite Mexican restaurant near our home in Kingwood. No campaign staff, no reporters. Just me and Suzanne and the waitstaff, who know us by name. And I was hoping no one else there that night would figure out who I was.

Kingwood is ultra-Republican, so I hadn't done much campaigning there. Only a few of our friends and the Kingwood Democrats (a small club I joined in 2011 when I was thinking about leaving the Republican Party) knew what I was up to.

As Suzanne and I stood behind the bar waiting for our table, we started talking with a woman who was waiting for some friends. We were having fun getting to know each other when, out of nowhere, she asked, "So, what do you do?"

Uh oh, I thought. *Better find a way to change the subject; if she figures out I'm running for office, we'll end up talking politics. Why ruin a perfectly good evening?*

I smiled at the woman and simply said, "It's a secret."

What a mistake! She almost squealed with delight. "Well, now you HAVE to tell me! What do you do?"

I turned to the hostess across the room and mouthed, *Is our table ready?* She shook her head *no*. I playfully mouthed the words, *Help me!* The hostess only smiled. That's when Suzanne nudged me and said with a laugh, "Go on, Mike, tell the nice lady what you do!"

"OK," I said, pausing for dramatic effect. I cleared my throat and declared, "I am an accountant!"

That should end the inquiry (it usually does).

"An accountant? So am I! That's cool. Who do you work for?"

There's no escape. I turned to Suzanne, who was still laughing. "Do we have to do this?"

"Oh, Mike—just tell her and get it over with."

OK. Here we go. I turned and faced the woman directly. I slowly leaned in. Our eyes were very close. She could see I was about to reveal something provocative.

"Well, ma'am—I am a DEMOCRAT!"

Provocative indeed! Her reaction was hilarious. Her eyes shot wide open. Her chin seemed to hit the floor. She gasped, then stared, motionless. This woman had never seen a Democrat before! I could almost hear her thinking: "He's a good guy, friendly, looks Republican. But a *Democrat?* What's happening here!"

I leaned in even closer and whispered my secret: "And I am running for lieutenant governor, against Dan Patrick."

The woman rocked back in her chair and virtually exploded. "You're joking, right? You're running against Dan Patrick? I HATE Dan Patrick! Tell me your name. Can I have a yard sign? Let's take a selfie. My friends won't believe this. They hate Dan Patrick too. This is so cool!"

She and her friends don't really hate Dan Patrick, I thought. *It's just an expression. I'm sure plenty of people hate me, too; you know, the way people hate politicians.*

But then the woman told me something I'd heard everywhere on the campaign trail. With a sly grin, as though she were being naughty, she said, "I'm a lifelong Republican, but I'm going to vote for YOU!"

My response surprised her. "Can I put you in my book?"

She looked confused. "Your what? I thought you said you were running for . . ."

"That's right. I'm running for lieutenant governor. But in 2014 I ran for comptroller, and I wrote a book about it called *Out of Comptrol: A Converted Democrat's Improbable Quest to Save Texas Politics*. After the campaign, I'm going to update it."

"Ooh, I love the title!" (An accountant would.) "But why do you call yourself a 'converted' Democrat?"

"Because I used to be a Republican."

"That explains it! Why did you switch?"

"Because the Republicans wouldn't help me."

About then, the hostess signaled our table was ready, so I figured I better wrap things up. "I wish I had time to explain, but if you really want to know, it's all in the book. After you read it, maybe you'll become a Democrat too."

"NEVER!"

She said it with a big smile, so I figured she didn't mean that either. The conversation had been fun, and she didn't seem to mind that the Democratic nominee for Texas lieutenant governor was drinking beer when he was supposed to be out campaigning. I'll never know if she bought the book. But I'll bet she—and her friends—voted for me.

Fact is, a lot of Texans crossed party lines and voted for me for lieutenant governor, in a way they didn't when I ran for comptroller four years earlier. I lost that race by a whopping twenty points (ouch!). But I lost the lieutenant governor race by only five. Sure, that kid from El Paso, the one who ran for Texas Senate, had a lot to do with Democrats turning out in record numbers. But voters stuck around and voted for me, too, despite the fact that Mr. Patrick spent $17 million promoting his candidacy. They did it because the problems we face in Texas are piling up, just as I predicted they would. And when Texans realize Republicans can't lead, they're going to stop voting Republican. Based on the 2018 election result, that day is fast approaching.

In 2014 I quit the Republican Party for good. I sought the Democratic nomination for Texas comptroller because I could see the reckoning coming. Republicans hadn't faced serious competition in a long time, and politics in the Lone Star State had become a Republican versus Republican affair; the only elections that mattered were primaries. Candidates began using false bravado and fearmongering (two ingredients the Far Right finds irresistible) to win primaries. But they refused to actually govern.

Want some examples of false bravado? We're told that Texas creates more jobs than any other state in America. What we're not told is that Texas lags on unemployment. The fact is, our unemployment rate is worse than average, which means more Texans are looking for work than in most other states.

Here's another whopper we hear all the time from Republicans: Texas always balances its budget. The truth is, Texas hasn't balanced its budget in decades! We owe more than $100 billion—and that's at the state level. School districts owe $120 billion; cities and counties owe billions more. We're so deeply in debt that Wall Street has started hinting at a credit downgrade.

How about this one: Texas is a low-tax state. In truth, Texas is only a low-tax state if you happen to be affluent. Those earning a median income—half of all workers in Texas—pay a higher percentage of their income in state and local taxes than workers in twenty-seven other states! We are NOT a low-tax state.

The amount of hooey that comes out of politicians' mouths in Texas can be staggering. And lack of political competition makes this possible.

Want to talk about fearmongering? Probably the best, if not most comical, example is Governor Greg Abbott calling out the Texas State Guard to protect against President Barack Obama's "military takeover"! The federal government had planned a multistate military exercise, known as Jade Helm 15, which included Central Texas. And Abbott shamelessly pandered to hysterical people who thought martial law would be imposed, Texans taken prisoner, and former Walmart stores turned into detention centers. You just can't make this stuff up!

And then there's Dan Patrick's totally manufactured bathroom crisis. His absurd "bathroom bill" damaged Texas's business reputation, to say nothing of sowing hate and divisiveness. Truth be told, more politicians have been caught doing bad things in bathrooms than the entire transgender community. Patrick, however, whipped his base into a fearful frenzy despite the fact that there has never been a single incident of a transgender person doing anything wrong in a Texas bathroom.

False bravado and fearmongering can get you elected in a Republican primary in Texas. But they do nothing to solve our state's problems. And the problems are piling up fast. Tuition at our great universities has exploded and is now beyond the reach of most working- and middle-class families. Our public schools are starving, and the state's teacher retirement system is collapsing. Texas's roads, bridges, and dams are in bad shape. Millions can no longer afford health care. Maternal mortality rates are off the charts, teen pregnancy rates (and *repeat* teen pregnancy rates) are among the worst in the nation, Texas does precious little for the mentally ill (unless they're in county jails), and we are running out of water.

If that's not bad enough, look at what's happening with taxes! Local property taxes are skyrocketing, yet much of that money isn't helping communities. Instead, it's paying the state's bills, and Republicans don't do anything about it.

I could go on.

Here is what every Texas politician better figure out, and fast: Texas is a tremendous state today because, for years, we had effective, forward-looking leaders. Texas politicians were always fiscally responsible, and they had the wisdom to invest in world-class universities, which kept tuition affordable for working- and middle-class families. Our highways were the best in the nation. Texans carved a ship channel out of farmland, creating one of the world's busiest seaports. When a hurricane virtually destroyed Galveston, we raised the entire island! And when a terrible drought devasted Texas in the 1950s, we built thousands of dams.

Texas's leaders accomplished all of these things (and more) without overtaxing families or drowning our state in debt. They did it because of the enormous pride Texans have always had in our great state, and because of our desire to make Texas the best state in America. Our leaders had the the savvy to solve problems as they arose, and it's that kind of leadership Texans demand. Any politician who thinks he can win with false bravado and fearmongering, and nothing else of substance, is in for a big surprise. Just ask Dan Patrick, who performed worse in his reelection bid than any lieutenant governor in decades.

The problems we faced in 2014 were bad enough to drive me into the open arms of the Texas Democratic Party. By 2018, those problems had grown so severe that several statewide Democratic candidates nearly won. Four years from now (assuming our leaders don't change their ways), a Democrat will surely win a statewide race. And when that happens, all of the Lone Star State's politicians (including Republicans) will immediately grasp that Texans want problem-solvers, not political hacks—and they'll vote for Democrats just as surely as they'll vote for Republicans. When that day comes, we will have saved Texas politics!

....

Out of Comptrol is almost entirely the story of my 2013 decision to jump into the Texas comptroller race as a Democrat. It's meant to reveal the mysteries of politics and political campaigns just as they were revealed to me. I've added an epilogue chronicling the lieutenant governor race four years later, but to be honest, the two races—and all the issues I campaigned on—were the same.

The book is also meant to show what it was like to quit the Republican Party, join the Democrats, raise campaign money from Republicans, then use that money to promote a Democrat (me!). It was a wild, wonderful, eye-opening ride, and the experience restored my faith that Texans (and Americans) can actually work together again to solve problems. We just need to elect the right people (more CPAs would be a good start).

Finally, *Out of Comptrol* is meant to explain why Texas never seems to have enough money for schools, teacher retirement, roads—you name it—even though our taxes continue to skyrocket. The so-called conservatives running our state deliberately shift the tax burden from large corporate interests and slam it onto the backs of homeowners and small businesses. We pay more, yet we get so much less. Texans need to understand this.

When you finish reading *Out of Comptrol*, I expect you'll be amazed at how truly ineffective our top political leaders are. And I hope you'll join me in fighting for political competition in Texas, because that lack of competition is the root of all our difficulties. I expect you'll find the fight's worthwhile; when you look at the 2018 election results, saving Texas politics no longer seems so improbable!

Acknowledgments

When I was in my early thirties, I worked for Price Waterhouse's top global executive, Dominic Tarantino. In general, Dom knew more about business (and Price Waterhouse, in particular) than any person alive. I, on the other hand, knew next to nothing. Yet Dom made me feel valuable, not just in researching and speech writing but with running the business. Dom welcomed my ideas because, no matter how dumb some may have seemed, he knew a good one would come through.

When running for office, you hire a lot of young, energetic, enthusiastic people whose skills and experience are all over the map. But as I learned from Dom, if you listen carefully and make your staff feel valuable, some great ideas get generated. And it worked! My team and I came closer to beating the incumbent lieutenant governor—the most powerful political position in Texas—than any challenger in memory.

It's these truly wonderful young people, each of whom contributed mightily, I wish to acknowledge.

On my first campaign, for Texas comptroller, Emily Williams taught me how to raise money; Demi Smith ran the office; and Zach Brigham, who was invaluable in all aspects of the campaign, acted as my right-hand man. Four years later, Zach's help would allow me to convert defeat into the chance to run for lieutenant governor.

During my campaigns for comptroller and lieutenant governor, one young advisor, Chaille Jolink, worked on communications and even volunteered between races. Chaille has always been wonderful and very insightful.

When I ran for lieutenant governor, I asked a brilliant young political consultant, Courtney Grigsby, to launch and lead my effort. Early in the campaign, James Cardona and Elizabeth Connor joined to set up the fund-raising operation. Joe Bowen helped as a general consultant, and Scott Spiegel got me in front of TV cameras and into the newspapers. Rish Oberoi and Spencer Wise served as aides-de-camp

(I taught them both how to drive), Renee Hansen did a masterful job with finance, and Jen Ramos was outstanding in assisting with Hispanic outreach. And Rosalind Ceasar generously volunteered her time to help me get to know the Baptist ministers.

Then there were "the Gremlins"—UT students Ali Zaidi and Jared Hrebenar—who masterminded my digital program and were unbelievably effective in promoting my candidacy. I'll have more to say about the Gremlins in the epilogue; they are now celebrities in Democratic political circles thanks to the miracle they (almost) pulled off.

Working with these terrific people has been a wonderful experience!

The people I've acknowledged here are my friends. They worked very hard and loyally—not just for my election but for a bigger cause, one greater than our combined voices. Together, we worked to do some good for our state and this nation. And in the process, they made me feel young!

The Texas Oracle (who, like me, is not young) remains wise beyond description. I'm talking about Cameron Chandler, my old college buddy and closest advisor, who is featured prominently throughout this book and my life. Only the Texas Oracle can pick up the phone, chew me out thoroughly, hang up, and then call right back and act as if nothing happened. Except when I get yelled at by the Texas Oracle, something does happen: I come away much wiser (and much more likely to win). I can't thank Cameron enough!

I'm delighted to acknowledge the love and support of my wife, Suzanne; our sons, Michael and Christopher; and Michael's lovely wife, Jessica. If they hadn't been behind me all the way, I would never have considered entering politics.

The end of a campaign feels a lot like the day the children go off to college. For so long, and with such intensity and passion, your political family works together. All day and all night, that team effort builds to a crescendo. And then comes Election Day. The next morning, you wake up and that once inseparable family is coming apart, scattering, moving on to the next thing. As I write this, I'm still adjusting to my political campaign's empty nest. The good news? I'm not done, and we'll be together again.

Having my real and political families—such wonderful people—
share the ups and downs while, over the course of many years, striving
to make a difference in people's lives means the world to me! I proudly
acknowledge their contribution to my campaigns, my life, and the
important work that remains before us.

Introduction

"WHY AREN'T YOU A REPUBLICAN?"

I was stunned by the caller's demand. I tried to respond, but I could only manage to mumble. So he hit me again.

"Exxon. Price Waterhouse. Goldman Sachs. MBA. CPA. That's your background, Collier. So why aren't you a *Republican*?"

I cleared my throat, but I still couldn't speak. It wasn't the question that stunned me. I had been campaigning as a Democrat for weeks, and I had already answered that question a thousand times.

What I found stunning was the caller. I was getting yelled at by Mark White, the forty-third governor of Texas! Imagine being yelled at by a former governor of the greatest state in America.

Wow—had I come a long way. Only a few months earlier I was an accountant working in the oil patch. But since the start of my campaign, I had been sitting in a rented, cramped, run-down campaign office, calling business associates, explaining that I was running for Texas comptroller on the Democratic ticket, and asking for money. It's not an easy conversation when you've never run for office and all your friends are Republican. And suddenly I was on the phone with Texas's only living former Democratic governor, his razor-sharp mind and energetic baritone voice exactly as I remembered from the six o'clock news, back in the 1980s.

"You still haven't answered my question!" he barked. "Why aren't you a Republican?"

Reflexively, I mimicked former governor White's commanding style and shouted back: "Because they wouldn't HELP ME!"

Mark White kept charging: "You'll be good for the Democratic Party. People need to know that we're pro-business. With your resume, Collier, you need to go everywhere Wendy goes. Every time she takes the stage, you'd better be standing next to her!"

Gulp.

Standing next to Wendy Davis, the Texas state senator who would be the Democratic Party nominee for governor, would mean standing in front of big crowds, and TV cameras, and showing up on the evening news. What in the world had I gotten myself into?

"Where are you from? Pennsylvania? Don't let them hang that on you. You just tell 'em Sam Houston, Stephen F. Austin, lots of great Texans settled here. Now, here's who you need to call to figure out where you're gonna hit 'em! I like the fact that you're a CPA, but you gotta hit 'em, or else you'll put everyone to sleep!"

The call went on like that for a while. I listened, and I learned. I didn't remember many of the technical points. What I remembered most from our fifteen-minute conversation was Mark White's style. It was unlike anything I was used to in business. Simple. Powerful. Emotional. I knew I had a long way to go as a candidate, and despite his confidence in me, I had no idea how this was all going to turn out.

....

That call took place back in summer 2013, near the start of my big adventure in Texas politics.

In a fit of distemper over the firing of 11,500 public school teachers thanks to screwed-up revenue accounting, I'd decided at the age of fifty-three to campaign for Texas comptroller, the state's chief financial officer. I had never done anything in politics, and I knew only one politician: my local city councilman. If I had won the election, I would have been the first certified public accountant (CPA) to hold the state's top accounting position in Texas history, and I would have been one of the first Democrats in twenty years to win a statewide office. I figured I could make some big waves.

So I put in fifteen months of hard work raising money one phone call at a time, doing TV interviews, securing endorsements, running commercials, debating on live TV, making speeches, and advancing a reform agenda based on twenty-five years of professional experience. In the end, I lost to a rice famer who campaigned on guns and God and showed very little interest in (or understanding of) the office he was seeking. Welcome to Texas politics!

....

This book is about the 2014 Texas election cycle, the year that Governor Rick Perry abdicated the throne, triggering a cascade that left every statewide office up for grabs. It was the year that State Senator Wendy Davis became an overnight sensation thanks to pink tennis shoes and a pro-choice filibuster. It was the year that Battleground Texas, an army of political activists, were going to *turn Texas blue!* after being soundly defeated in every statewide election for the past twenty years.

This book is also about my decision to give up, once and for all, on the Republican Party and ask the Democrats to support my first-ever attempt to run for office.

There were plenty of surprises on the campaign trail, but by far the most pleasant surprise was how much I learned about politics and policy by listening to so many different points of view. I spoke to Democrats, Republicans, Independents, Libertarians, Greens, Christians, Jews, Muslims, atheists, gays, straights, young, old—you name it. I talked to people who love politics and to people who hate politics. I talked to people who think the future of Texas is bright, and I talked to people who think we are doomed. If you want to really understand the politics and the people in a place like Texas, take a year and a half and go talk to thousands of them!

In addition to retelling the tale of my excellent political adventure roughly as it unfolded, I have included a handful of essays so that I can share some of the insights I discovered by talking to so many wonderful Texans.

My preference for objectivity and analysis will no doubt come through. However, it's *just* possible that readers will find traces of disdain for Republican politicians in my writing. It's not because I don't like Republicans. I used to be one, and the vast majority of my friends and professional colleagues still are. No, my disdain is not for Republicans; it's for politicians who grab at power by bolting on to political machinery. These are the politicians who do whatever it takes to stay in power, even ignoring what's best for their constituents. If that isn't bad enough, you'll catch them using spin and deception to cover their tracks. That's where my disdain lies, and I'm not alone. Democrats and Republicans alike are with me on this.

But don't get the wrong idea. This book isn't sour grapes. I knew the odds were very long when I entered the race. Despite the outcome, I am as joyful as I've ever been. I am proud that I found the courage to participate, in a big way, in the democratic process. I am proud that I fought for things I believe in and for a state I love. And I'll do it again, if given the chance.

1

My Texas History

My connection to the great state of Texas began forty-two years ago.
I remember it vividly.

On a February day in 1975, my brother Tom and I were hors-
ing around in the basement of our home in southwestern Pennsylvania. My father came to the top of the stairs and called down that he
wanted to see each of us, one at a time, starting with Tom.

Dad is a commanding presence, more than six feet tall and more
than two hundred pounds, all muscle. He started his working life as
an apprentice to a tool and die maker before he decided to earn a
college degree, the first ever in his family. It took him twelve years of
very hard work, raising his family by day and taking college classes
at night. He earned a degree in mechanical engineering from Carne-
gie Mellon University, working his way into management at Westing-
house by being smart, tough, and fair. My brother and I have always
idolized him, and whenever he gave an order, we followed it and
didn't waste any time.

Tom started walking slowly up the stairs. Neither of us had any
idea what was coming, although I suspected that Dad was going to
brief us on the facts of life. From Dad, you'd expect a briefing, even on
this most delicate subject. And if you knew Dad, it wouldn't surprise
you that both of his sons got this briefing on the same evening, despite
the fact that Tom was a junior in high school and I was in the eighth
grade. It would be more efficient, he knew, to have the talk once.

While Tom was upstairs, I braced myself for what was sure to be
a terribly awkward experience, already knowing most of what I was
about to learn.

Tom came down the stairs looking pale. With neither of us saying a word, we passed each other, and I climbed the stairs.

Dad was standing in the bedroom that Tom and I shared. He looked plenty serious. I took my seat on the edge of the bed and tried to appear as nonchalant as possible. Dad began to speak.

"Mike, I've been asked to transfer to Texas."

What a relief, was my first thought.

"The move, if we go, will be this fall. You'll start the school year in Texas. Your younger brother and sister don't know yet, so we're not going to say anything for a little while. Do you have any questions?"

I looked out the window. It was one of those priceless Pennsylvania evenings when the snow covered everything lightly and the moon made it all so beautiful. We lived in the country, in a very hilly (some would say mountainous) part of Pennsylvania, about twenty miles from Pittsburgh and about forty miles from West Virginia. At age fourteen, I only had two deer hunting seasons under my belt after years of biding my time, wandering the woods and pretending with a BB gun, until I could hunt legally. What's more, I'd just raised enough paper route money to buy a Remington 30-06 deer rifle with a Leupold 4x scope. It was my pride and joy, and deer hunting—and our little mountains, and snow—were my passions. I couldn't believe we'd leave what I thought was a hunter's paradise.

I looked at Dad and asked, "When do you need my answer?"

He rolled his head back and laughed a great, warm, loving laugh. "I'm not asking, I'm telling."

The die was cast.

From that moment until August of that year when we moved out, I spent a lot of time looking at maps of Texas and reading whatever I could get my hands on about the state. I was relieved to read that Texas had deer hunting, as well as a place they called the Hill Country in the Austin area, where we were going to live. And although I knew it was hot in Texas in the summer, I learned that in the winter it snowed every once in a while.

What's more, deer hunting was done differently in Texas than it was in Pennsylvania. In Pennsylvania, you hunted wherever you wanted to, and so many hunters preferred to hunt in the same spots that it almost seemed crowded at times. In Texas, by contrast, hunters bought a deer lease and property owners, usually ranchers, controlled how many hunters had access to their property. I liked the idea, particularly because I thought I'd be less likely to get shot.

Okay, I thought, *I think I can make this work.*

....

We drove to Texas in August and by the time we arrived in Georgetown, a small town north of Austin (Austin at that time was just a small town north of San Antonio), I loved the place. Rural, beautiful, free, and friendly are words that came to mind.

We came to Texas during the later stages of the first technology wave that hit Texas in the 1970s. The state was attractive to industries that were looking for new places to set up shop. Land was plentiful, housing was inexpensive, and its beauty made it easy to persuade employees and their families to relocate there. It had some great universities, which meant that it was a talent magnet. And its leaders invested the state's oil wealth to support tuition, which meant that lots of people—including me and my siblings—could attend those universities. Texas seemed like paradise.

We settled in, and all the Collier kids did well. Tom was the first to go to college, dashing off to Texas A&M University to study engineering. I graduated next and went to the University of Texas at Austin to study music. My sister Patty went to UT as well, and my little brother Jim went to East Texas State University. Our middle-class parents didn't have to drown themselves in debt to pull this off. We felt like the luckiest people on earth.

At UT, I played trumpet in various orchestras and classical ensembles. I also marched in the Longhorn Band, and I loved it. LHB, as we called it, gave me opportunities that would never have been possible—meeting all kinds of people and traveling nationally. Having been raised first in rural Pennsylvania and then in rural Central Texas, I was a hayseed, as the saying goes. But thanks to LHB, I felt as if I had finally stepped out onto the world's stage.

LHB even marched in President Ronald Reagan's inaugural parade, thanks to an invitation from Texas's own Vice President George H. W. Bush. It was a very cold day, and the parade had been delayed due to the timing of the Iranian hostage release. When we finally got started, the sun was going down, and when we turned the corner on Pennsylvania Avenue and saw the reviewing stand in the distance, it was literally glowing under huge, Hollywood-style spotlights. I had never seen anything like it. President Reagan looked every bit the movie star, and I distinctly remember that it was the lighting that made all the difference in the world.

A few months later, I was headed into a rehearsal on the UT campus when a friend of mine rushed toward me and asked if I'd heard that the president had been shot only a few hours before. I hadn't heard, focused as I'd been on rehearsing my difficult trumpet part. Besides, I had no interest in politics. As far as I was concerned, Reagan was nothing more than a well-lit movie star acting as the president.

But later that night in the dorm I turned on the TV and was amazed by all that I saw. Secretary of State Alexander Haig made his famous "I am in control here" comment,[1] which got everyone talking about the presidential succession and the Constitution. Commentators were analyzing the stock market's reaction to the crisis. Defense analysts were bantering about the national security implications of a wounded president. There was all the drama of not knowing precisely where the vice president was, and whether we'd lost contact with him and for how long, and so forth. I found the whole thing mesmerizing. Overnight I become so fascinated by the inner workings of politics and commerce, and the way things actually worked in the real world, that suddenly I lost all interest in a career as a musician.

Problem was, I had no idea what I wanted to do instead.

A very close friend and fellow trumpet player, Cameron Chandler, had already switched his major to petroleum land management. The oil companies had designed the degree in order to help train new landmen, and UT had developed a specific degree plan around it. A landman's job is to handle the oil and gas leases that allow oil companies to drill and produce oil. I liked the degree plan because it combined law, business, and science; since I didn't know what I wanted to do with my life, I valued the variety. There had to be something in there that would appeal to me, I thought. So I followed Cameron's lead, changed majors, and began studying to become a petroleum landman.

With two years remaining at UT, I was walking across campus thinking about something I had just read in the newspaper related to some international crisis and how President Reagan was handling it. Prone to worrying as I am, I thought to myself that I sure hope our elected leaders know what they are doing. And suddenly, it hit me: Political leaders have to come from somewhere! If we want good political leaders, then good people need to make the decision to go into politics.

To say I felt a surge of ambition that instant is an understatement. It was a rush, probably the kind of feeling some people might describe as a calling.

I talked about my feeling around this time with a very close friend, Chuck Doty. Chuck had already graduated from UT and was flying fighter jets for the US Navy. We were sitting at the Driskill Hotel bar in Austin one day when I began to talk about running for office later in life. I went back and forth over whether I would run as a Republican or a Democrat when Chuck interrupted me. He said something that would stick with me the rest of my life.

"Every young man dreams of making a difference," he said, "but few actually do. You'll never run for office, Mike, because you'll end up with a mortgage and children and responsibilities. You'll never be in a position to actually do it."

Chuck was smarter than me, and I thought deeply about what he said. But my feelings about politics were stronger than he gave me credit for at the time. I still thought of it as a calling, although less like a religious calling and more like the awakening of what I knew would be a lifelong aspiration. It wasn't an aspiration to become famous or powerful like President Reagan, who by then I had come to respect. It was an aspiration to do some good in the world, to work on public policy matters with competence and integrity.

Overnight I developed an obsession with reading newspapers, reading history, and watching CNN (cable news had just burst on the scene, and I was addicted). It felt almost involuntary, as if I was drawn to prepare myself for the work ahead, whatever work that might be.

Along the way I heard political leaders say that everyone should, at some stage in their life, involve themselves in public policy. I always took that to mean ordinary citizens should learn something useful in the private sector, spend some time in government trying to make things better, and not stay too long. That idea always appealed to me.

Just before graduation I met Congressman Bill Archer at a reception in his honor. He was a powerful and popular congressman from the Houston area, and I was determined to meet him. The Longhorn Band was playing in the background, and during a short break I had no difficulty getting close, shaking his hand, introducing myself, and telling him that I had an interest in politics. I asked him for his advice. He gave it to me in no uncertain terms.

"Get a job," he said. "Launch a career, start a family, buy a house. Do all those things first, and then if you want to run for office, do it."

I thought his advice was excellent, and I decided to follow it.

....

Exxon hired me as a landman when I finished my degree. I was as proud as I could be, but I knew that a career as a landman wasn't for me. Being a landman is a great job, and you can make great money. I have a number of friends who are landmen, and I respect the role they play in the energy industry. But I found the job to be one-dimensional, and I couldn't see it as a means of developing my resume, the know-how, and the contacts I needed to make the kind of contribution I wanted to make in public life.

So after two years and one promotion, I went back to UT to earn an MBA and take my career in a new direction. I had considered trying to get into Harvard, but with the state of Texas underwriting the cost of the degree, it made much more sense for me to stay in Texas. Besides, I loved UT from my undergraduate days, and I could hardly wait to get back on campus.

In the MBA program, I concentrated on finance and accounting, and I knew very quickly that I'd made the right decision. I found that I loved financial and statistical analysis and that, for me, the process of digging through data and understanding what it all meant was joyful and important. I loved cutting through statements like "everyone knows this" or "everyone knows that" and forming my own opinion based on the facts. I loved it so much that I briefly considered a career in academia, one where I could specialize in some area of financial analysis and spend my time researching and writing.

But instead, I met Suzanne Laskowski, a history major at UT. We were introduced on a blind date, and I fell in love the minute I saw her. It took her a little time to decide she liked me too. But soon we became serious, and after graduation, I knew that I wanted to make money so that we could get married and start a family. I decided that rather than toying with the idea of a PhD, I'd better start my career.

I stumbled onto Price Waterhouse (now known as PwC) by pure happenstance: A friend from the MBA program took a job there and told me about it. He worked as an auditor, a job that involves researching and confirming client companies' financial statements. I loved the sound of it, and I managed to convince the PwC partners in Austin to hire me as an entry-level auditor. While other MBA grads were pulling down almost six figures in their first jobs after graduation, I took the PwC job at a fraction of that. It just seemed like the right thing to do; I saw it as a way to continue investing in my career.

Auditing a company involves reporting to the company's board of directors about whether the management team is accounting and reporting its finances properly and completely. In practice, it means going into the client company, analyzing data, asking tough questions, and reporting on what is really happening. I learned to love the job, and I was good at it. Little did I know at the time that I was building the very skill set I would need to work on the most vexing public policy issue we would face in my lifetime: public finance.

PwC required all accounting professionals to become certified public accountants before they could be promoted to manager, and I didn't have an accounting degree. I did, however, have enough college credit hours in accounting to satisfy the Texas State Board of Public Accountancy's requirement, and I persuaded the partners that I could pass the CPA exam if I had enough time to prepare. On that basis they hired me, and within three years, I had studied for and passed the exam. I can't say I passed it on the first try, but I finally got there.

After my first promotion at PwC, one of the firm's audit clients, a small high-tech company in Austin that made industrial-scale CT scanners, called and asked me whether I would be interested in leaving PwC and working as their chief financial officer. Ever the risk taker, I took the job just before we ran smack into a global recession. The company barely survived, and our first son, Michael, had just been born. I lost my nerve and sheepishly called PwC, asking if they would take me back. I was more than a little relieved when they said yes.

I wasn't the only young professional in PwC's history to wander away and then come running back, and I knew that when people strayed, there was penance to pay. So I put every ounce of effort I had into making amends and rehabilitating my standing in the firm. Before long, I was being given good assignments again, a signal that if I stayed long enough, I might be considered for partner.

By now I had bounced from Exxon to graduate school to PwC to a high-tech company and then back to PwC. I became painfully aware that the business world might start to see me as a "hopper," someone who does something new every two years. That's not how I wanted my career to unfold. So I made a strategic decision to stay at PwC for at least a decade, regardless of whether I liked it or not, and regardless of what other opportunities were available. I decided to put everything I had into the firm, never looking back, and to see how far I could go.

That decision worked very well for me: I thrived as an auditor, and I was ultimately promoted to audit manager. Within three years, I was selected to serve as the executive assistant to PwC's world chairman. This meant a move to New York for Suzanne and me and our two young sons, Michael and Christopher.

While we lived in New York, I traveled extensively in the United States, Europe, and Asia with Dom Tarantino, PwC's top executive, whose job was to shape PwC's strategy by working with and guiding each of the national accounting firms in the global network. I traveled to London, Paris, Beijing, Shanghai, Hong Kong, Tokyo, Taipei, Singapore, Kuala Lumpur, Bangkok, Melbourne, Sydney, and Adelaide. I also traveled extensively throughout the United States and Canada. It's impossible to describe how much I learned about the world, business, leadership, and politics during that time, traveling the world and working under the tutelage of one of PwC's most venerated leaders.

In 1997, with our two sons in elementary school, we were sent back to Texas, this time to Houston, where I was placed on the partner track in the mergers and acquisitions (M&A) practice. In the accounting profession, M&A work is a first cousin of the audit: One company intends to buy another company, and they send a team of accountants in to do a thorough financial analysis. This helps the executives of the buyer put a good deal together. I loved that job even more than I loved auditing. I was good at it, and I became a partner.

During the ten years that I worked on energy-related acquisitions, I learned more about the dynamics of the energy business than I would ever have learned as a landman, and I filled my rolodex with business contacts from around the state. I also traveled to London, Paris, Lisbon, Toronto, Calgary, Amsterdam, Rotterdam, The Hague, Zurich, Milan, Azerbaijan, Istanbul, and Trinidad, as well as what seemed like just about every major city in the United States. I learned how to walk into a complex, high-stakes game of poker and call the situation just as I saw it. I also felt very lucky to have found a good-paying career, one that I enjoyed and that perfectly suited my temperament as an honest broker and an analytical geek.

PwC has an early retirement program, and as I approached age fifty, I felt increasingly drawn to it. I was visiting my parents one weekend, and I floated the idea of retiring early by my mother, who always has good judgment. I told Mom that on the one hand, it was long before I could afford to actually retire. But on the other hand, I knew that I wouldn't be doing anything new at PwC if I stayed. I also told her I had always thought about doing something in public policy and, if I took early retirement, I could create a sense of urgency for myself.

Her eyes immediately gave her away. "Oh, Michael, you really should do it!"

....

Partners in big accounting firms like PwC are very well compensated. I was making more money than I needed, and I was saving and investing aggressively. But as the final decision to retire approached, I realized that my income had become a part of my identity, and I knew that having one's identity wrapped up in money wouldn't lead to long-term fulfillment—at least not for me. So after some soul-searching, I mustered the courage, and I "walked" my big paycheck, trading it for a very small early retirement check. It was only a fraction of what Suzanne and I needed to live on and to put our two sons through college. I created a sense of urgency all right. I also felt profoundly liberated. Nervous, but liberated.

It wasn't long before a job offer landed in my lap. The job was chief financial officer of Layline Petroleum, a company that Goldman Sachs Investment Partners had backed with my help while I was at PwC. Layline was founded by two of the smartest men I had ever met, and together they made a powerhouse team. Goldman needed a chief financial officer who could work well with the Layline guys, and yet who could still represent the investors' interests.

I started at Layline in August 2011, and I loved it. We drilled some good wells, made some acquisitions, and built up the company. In a short time, we were talking to another company that wanted to buy Layline and completely take over. That's what Goldman had in mind when they hired me, and they ultimately made a nice return on their investment.

Unfortunately, I hadn't lifted a finger to find a role in public life. It's just too hard to be the chief financial officer of a small company and do much else. We were just a few months away from selling Layline, and I was about to retire for a second time. And yet I still had no idea how I might get involved in public policy and begin to pursue my lifelong dream.

2

....

Republican or Democrat?

A few months before the sale of Layline closed, a good friend and neighbor had just won a special election to serve on the Houston City Council. David Martin had been on the local school board, and he'd just taken a big stride in the political arena. I figured he'd have some contacts and some ideas to help me get started in the public arena.

David agreed to meet for lunch. As we talked, I let David assume that I was a Republican. This was a natural assumption, given my business background and the fact that I lived in Kingwood, Texas, a suburb in far North Houston known in political circles as Ted Cruz country.

Fact is, though, I had become ambivalent about the Republican Party in Texas. I frankly did not like or trust our long-running governor, Rick Perry. Everyone knew he was a bantamweight intellectually, but he was becoming a heavyweight politically. And that is never a good combination.

Perry was the lieutenant governor when then-governor George W. Bush resigned to become president. That automatically made Perry the governor, and from there he won election after election until he became the longest-serving governor in Texas history. Perry rode the crest of an oil boom, and he had the best hair and the coolest Texas swagger of any modern Texas politician.

Ordinarily, a Texas governor doesn't have much power within the state. But the governor is responsible for making government appointments: in all, some two thousand agency heads and commissioners. After more than a decade in office, Perry had the chance to appoint people of his choice to each and every one of those positions, and he demanded absolute loyalty.

As it turns out, if a Texas governor stays in office too long, he ends up with immense power. The result in Texas was a closed political system: one where nobody dared to challenge their dear leader.

You could just feel that things were changing fast in Texas politics, and not for the better. Arrogance was beginning to overwhelm judgment, removing our capacity to deal honestly with complex issues. I had seen this kind of hubris overwhelm companies before, like Enron. I knew it couldn't possibly be good for Texas.

At the same time, there was another Texas politician making a name for himself, although unlike Perry, he was doing excellent work and serving his constituents with sincerity and humility. Bill White, a Houston business leader who had served in the Department of Energy during the Clinton years, had become the mayor of Houston. Bill was an excellent leader, and he was very popular. His executive skills and empathy were on vivid display when Hurricane Katrina hit the Gulf Coast and Houston took in New Orleans refugees by the thousands. A few years later, he did a masterful job leading recovery efforts when Hurricane Ike hit Houston. He was brilliant, hardworking, and honest. He was the exact opposite of Rick Perry, I thought. I saw in Bill White everything I was looking for in a political leader.

Bill White was a Texas Democrat. So I began to wonder whether I might be one, too.

In 2010, White challenged Perry for governor, and I enthusiastically voted for him. I was disappointed when Perry won, and when I saw Bill on a sidewalk in downtown Houston one day, I introduced myself so I could tell him so. We had a short conversation, one that left me fired up about the prospect of making friends in the Democratic Party.

I went back to my computer that day and discovered the Kingwood Democrats. I'd lived in Kingwood for years, yet I'd had no idea that there were *any* Democrats in Kingwood. I decided right then to attend one of their meetings.

I reached out to the president of the Kingwood Democrats, Egberto Willies. Egberto responded very warmly and said he would be delighted to introduce me at the next meeting.

I'd never attended a political meeting before, and it was quite an experience. True to his word, Egberto introduced me, and I stood up in front of the twenty or so attendees. I told them who I was, I thanked them for letting me attend their meeting, and I sat down.

Egberto laughed, gestured to me to stand back up, and said: "Mike comes from the dark side—he'd better explain himself!"

So I did. I told everyone that I had reached that point in my life that I wanted to get involved in politics and policy. Having watched Bill White work as mayor, and being upset by how insular the Republican Party had become over the past decade, I told everyone that I wanted to know more about the Democrats.

I found the meeting to be very interesting and not at all what I'd expected. Somehow I had the idea that political gatherings were venom-infused hate sessions. I guess I'd been watching too much Fox News. Instead, the Democrats talked about issues. A generous helping of human empathy and a real passion for individual liberty underpinned their point of view. But there was no vitriol. The speakers offered their ideas on technical matters, and attendees raised their hands and asked probing questions. I was pleasantly surprised.

When the meeting ended, a few club members came straight at me with a hearty handshake to say, "Welcome to the Kingwood Democrats!" My new friends proudly told me that there was room for many viewpoints on issues in the Democratic Party as long as everyone had the common desire to work honestly, and intelligently, to improve society.

I thought to myself: *The Democratic Party is exactly where I belong!*

....

I planned to attend as many Democrat meetings as I could and to get involved as a volunteer wherever possible. Unfortunately, the Layline job was across town in the Energy Corridor, a strip of highway in the far west suburbs where many of the big energy companies are located. A seventy-five-minute commute, morning and night, wiped out any hope of my attending more Democrat meetings in Kingwood.

Nevertheless, I began to think of myself as a Texas Democrat. But I also decided, early on, to keep quiet about it. Divulging even the slightest sympathy for Democrats, I thought at the time, might damage me in the business world. Bill White might be able to get away with it, but he was Houston's own Bill White. An average Joe like me had to be careful, or so I thought. So I kept my mouth shut.

....

Shortly after my exploratory lunch with my neighbor David Martin—during which I said not one word about my new affiliation with the Democratic Party—he came up with an intriguing idea. "You're a CPA with a strong resume," David said. "Why not run for Houston city controller? It makes sense: The incumbent is term limited, the city's headed for financial trouble thanks to a large pension overhang, and we need as much financial expertise as we can get." If I was interested, David could make some introductions and help me get the ball rolling.

I immediately liked the idea. I had lived and worked in Houston for a long time, and I knew a lot of people, particularly people in the business community. So even though I didn't know anything about electoral politics, I suspected it was a good place to start.

I also liked the fact that by Texas state law, municipal races are nonpartisan. In practice, I'd need the support of one of the parties to pitch in by putting up yard signs and doing the things you have to do to get elected, but there would be no official reference anywhere to a political party. In other words, I could run as a Republican and a Democrat at the same time, which is the same as being neither. That suited me just fine.

I told David I really liked the idea—and thus I began my political odyssey.

3

....

"Your Party Is Doomed!"

After telling David that I intended to run for city controller, he called to tell me that I should hire a political consultant. He also offered to introduce me to one, a big player he knew in Houston. I figured his consultant friend would be a Republican, whereas by then I considered myself a Texas Democrat. But since the race would be nonpartisan, I decided to just go with the flow.

Within a few days, I found myself having breakfast with the political consultant, whom I'll call Jim. David warned me that Jim was hard-boiled, but that didn't bother me. I'd worked in mergers and acquisitions for a decade; I'd become immune to hard-boiled people.

Jim and I met in a very Republican neighborhood. He didn't waste any time with polite conversation.

"Go make a list of everyone who'll give you money," he said. I wasn't to leave anyone out: friends, relatives, business associates, all of them. Jim told me to sort them by the maximum amount each would give and to indicate whether they would make phone calls and raise money on my behalf. "Once you've done that, we'll meet again. Goodbye." I figured he was just testing me. There was no way I was going to make a bunch of phone calls asking my friends and family for money! That was something a politician would do, not this accountant.

Before we parted company, Jim wrote down the phone number of a fellow named Bob Lemer. He didn't tell me why or even who Bob was. He just said, "Call him. And don't mention my name."

I called Bob that day. He turned out to be a retired partner with one of the big accounting firms, which gave us something in common. His son and I had even worked together for a few years at PwC. As soon as I'd introduced myself and told him that I was considering running for city controller, he said he wanted to meet me right away. "I should tell you that I'm supporting another CPA in town for the position," he said, "a fellow named Bill Frazer. The three of us ought to get together."

Bob, Bill, and I had an enjoyable meeting a few days later over coffee. Bob was clearly passionate about public policy. I liked him instantly, and I liked Bill and thought he would make a great city controller. Unfortunately for Bill, I was planning to run for the position anyway, which wasn't what Bill and Bob were hoping to hear.

Then they had an idea. Why didn't I let Bill run for city controller, and I run for state comptroller?

I was flattered, but I thought the idea was patently absurd. The state comptroller was one of the most powerful positions in all of Texas. Surely they didn't think I was dumb enough to try *that* my first time out of the gate! Most people regard the office of Texas comptroller as a stepping-stone to lieutenant governor or even governor. The job goes to a Republican political operative, not a nonpolitical CPA outsider! It was all I could do not to laugh out loud at the suggestion.

So I declined. I told them I was going to run for city controller and either Bill would do good work in the position or I would. They were perfect gentlemen about it, but when I said good-bye and left Bob and Bill at the restaurant, I could tell they weren't all that happy with me.

....

Having met with Bob Lemer as instructed, I turned my attention to drawing up my list of potential contributors. I didn't spend too much time on it, because I still thought it was a make-work exercise, more of a test of my seriousness than anything I'd actually need. I figured only a chump would call hundreds of friends and ask for campaign money.

Jim and I arranged to meet again at the same restaurant. He scanned the list, sniffing at it and me. I got the distinct impression that he was looking for Republican heavy hitters and was disappointed that I didn't know any. He abruptly changed the subject and started lecturing me on Municipal Finance 101, with a heavy emphasis on debt.

"I understand debt," I told him. "In fact, I suspect that it's actually the Tea Partiers that are driving us into debt, whether they know it or not."

Jim's face froze. His expression was perfectly blank. It appeared I had struck a nerve. So I leaned in and said, "You guys better marginalize the Tea Party, or the Tea Party is going to marginalize the Republican Party!"

Jim didn't utter a sound or move a muscle. He just glared back at me. The silence was deafening. I could tell I was toast.

When we walked together to our cars a few moments later, he was suddenly friendly to me, friendly in the way you treat someone in business when you're about to give them the brush-off. I would never see or speak to Jim again. I left him several voice mails, but he never returned my calls.

....

A few weeks later I was at a Houston Astros baseball game, where I ran into an old friend, Neal Carlson, who like most everyone I know is a staunch Republican. Neal and I knew each other from PwC days, and he had moved on to Goldman Sachs, where he was working his way up the ladder in the financial services industry. He was a West Point grad with a West Point bearing, as honest and dependable as they come, and very civic minded.

We caught up, and I told him about my impulse to run for Houston city controller. Neal immediately latched on to the possibilities. I told him about Jim, and Jim's refusal to return my calls. Neal said he knew Jim and figured he was just too busy to work with me. But there was another Republican consultant—I'll call him Henry—that Neal suggested I meet. Henry was trying to build up his consulting business and would almost certainly take the meeting.

Neal followed through, and within a few days Neal, Henry, and I were meeting over coffee at a restaurant near my office. I remember it well, because at this meeting I gave up on the Republican Party for good.

I don't mean to be disparaging of Henry. He actually seemed like a sincere, polished, good person, and he seemed very enthusiastic about taking me on as a potential new client. I liked his style as well: He was impeccably dressed, and he was obviously very intelligent and articulate. I could easily imagine being in the trenches with Henry, fighting to become one of the few Republicans to hold citywide office in Houston.

But very early in our conversation, completely out of nowhere, he looked at me and asked, "You're pro-life, right?"

I pretended I didn't hear the question; we had just met, and I didn't want to get into the abortion issue. After all, we were there to talk about the city controller job. So I let the conversation drift back to city finance without acknowledging the question, and soon we were having a productive session again.

After about twenty minutes, I came back to Henry's earlier question by saying, "Henry, as to your question about whether I'm pro-life: in fact, I'm pro-choice."

The look on Henry's face—and Neal's—was one of astonishment. We sat there for a moment in silence, until Neal broke the spell.

"Mike, I'm very sorry," he said. "I never would have guessed that—"

I cut Neal off and quipped to Henry, "What does abortion have to do with the finances of the city of Houston?"

"Well, nothing," Henry said. "But the Republican Party won't support you unless you're pro-life."

"Are you telling me," I said after a moment, "that the Republicans would rather have an incompetent crook as city controller than an honest, skilled CFO, simply because he wouldn't campaign on an issue that has nothing to do with the office in the first place?"

"That's right," Henry said. "If you want the Republican precinct chairmen to get behind you, knock on doors, and put up yard signs, you've got to fill out a questionnaire. And the first question is whether you're pro-life."

I was stunned. I had heard of litmus tests, but this was ridiculous.

"What else is on that questionnaire?" I asked.

"Are you pro-family?" Henry asked sternly. "Are you Christian?"

I felt a surge of adrenaline, and I leaned forward a little, to get in Henry's face.

"As to the pro-family question, I support gay rights."

Henry stared back.

"And as to the Christian question . . . I'm a Catholic. I don't know whether that makes me a Christian or not in your world."

I did nothing to conceal my pique, and Henry's face told the story: He wasn't going to pick up a new client that day.

There was a long stretch of silence, during which I sat there thinking about how easy it would be just to tell Henry what he wanted to hear, to tell Republican voters what they wanted to hear. After all, I didn't have to take truth serum. I could just lie about my real position on the social issues and focus on the financial issues. That way I could skate into office with the help of the Republican juggernaut.

But politics is full of phonies. What good is one more?

After a long silence, I spoke up—and what came out surprised even me.

"Well, Henry, if what you're telling me is true, your party is doomed."

Polite handshakes followed, and we parted company.

....

It was a very long drive home that afternoon. For a moment I forgot about Bill White, and the Kingwood Democrats who had welcomed me so warmly. Instead, I was saddened by the feeling of alienation from a party I had felt attached to for twenty-five years. The hard Right of the Republican Party had grown so rigid and uncompromising that ordinary people, like me, were just going to have to walk out.

As much as I appreciated the Kingwood Democrats, and Bill White, I mostly felt confused and disappointed. I needed time to think. The Houston city controller job was off the table.

4

....

Okay, Maybe I Am
Crazy (Angry?) Enough

Some time later I was reading the newspaper one morning as we were preparing to finalize the sale of Layline. I stumbled onto an article about a press conference at the start of the 2013 Texas legislative session[1]— an article that, as it turned out, would knock my hat into the ring.

A reporter at the press conference had asked Governor Rick Perry about public education spending. The state had made massive cuts the previous session, blaming them on a looming deficit that never materialized. The cuts were painful, and deep: About 11,500 teachers were fired or pushed into early retirement.[2]

I knew just how painful those cuts in funding had been. My wife Suzanne had been a volunteer, and an active one at that, at all the schools our sons attended. She'd worked in the copy room at Kingwood High for several years, and she had many friends among the teachers in Kingwood. So she saw the devastating effects of the cuts through the teachers' eyes. Layoffs and early retirements forced some of the best teachers out. There was no money for materials or books or computers or band instruments. Tears flowed like a river.

The schools had endured the cuts, believing that the budget deficit made them necessary. As it turned out, however, the comptroller who predicted the deficits, Susan Combs, had gotten it all wrong. The state didn't have a massive deficit. The state had a massive *surplus*.[3] How was it possible to make a mistake like that, I wondered? Everyone suspected that something fishy had happened.

In response to the reporter's question about his role in the controversy over the education cuts, Perry just pounded his chest and denied that there was any real problem. He bragged that since he'd become governor, overall spending on public education was up seventy percent, despite the cuts.[4] In other words, Perry was implying that despite the massive cuts that had just happened, he'd led the way to improving education funding in Texas.

I did some sniffing around the Internet, and it took less than three minutes for me to conclude that Perry was deliberately deceiving Texans,[5] the very people who trusted him to lead. It was disgraceful.

In saying that he'd increased education funding by seventy percent, Perry was ignoring inflation, and he was ignoring all the ins and outs of school funding. When you factored all these things in, Texas investment in public education on a per student basis had actually gone *down* ten percent since he had become governor.[6] He'd cherry-picked one very misleading statistic and put it over as fact. It was an obvious deception. Worse, not a single politician stood up to call him out on it.

Public education is one of the single most important services any government provides its citizens. The fact that Perry would be so glib and self-serving on a matter of such profound importance had me seeing red. Suddenly my reticence to publicly declare that I was a Democrat gave way to a very strong desire to do just that. I'm a PwC man, a CPA, and someone whose entire career is based on upholding the public trust. Becoming a Democrat and speaking out against a political monopoly that deliberately misleads voters wasn't something I felt I might do. It started to feel like something I *must* do.

....

My interest in public education runs very deep. I trace it to a weekend-long seminar I attended in 2006. The retreat had been sponsored by an organization called the Center for Houston's Future. The partner in charge of the PwC office asked me to attend the event. I was trying to make a name for myself in mergers and acquisitions (M&A) then, so I agreed, despite the fact that at the time, I hated weekend retreats. As an M&A consultant, I was on the road all the time, and if I was lucky enough to have a quiet weekend at home, I wanted to spend that time with Suzanne, Michael, and Christopher, or on my sailboat on Galveston Bay. Attending a retreat at The Woodlands Conference Center to discuss Houston's future seemed like a particularly awful disruption to my relaxation plans.

When Friday afternoon came, I left my office and made the forty-five-minute drive to The Woodlands with my ever-present suitcase by my side. My mood was absolutely rotten as I pulled into the resort parking lot. I was distracted for a moment by the sight of a man walking from the parking lot to the conference center wearing a distinctly out-of-place white sweater. It was the kind you see in the movies at ski resorts, nothing like the jeans, boots, and dark sport coat of the Houston business-casual uniform. *Strange*, I thought.

I checked into my room and braced myself for the mix-and-mingle small talk to come (I didn't know a single participant), and I was just as nervous as I always get before any social event. As soon as I found the reception, I bumped into the man with the white sweater. Why not start there? So I introduced myself, and he in turn introduced himself, and we started to chat. He seemed like a good guy. He said his name was Dan, and I could hear a Pittsburgh accent in his voice.

"Are you from Pittsburgh?" I asked.

"Yes, indeed I am!" We struck up a long and enjoyable conversation about the place, and when we regrouped the next morning for the actual seminar, I naturally sat next to Dan.

The moderator opened the discussion by asking everyone to introduce themselves. When it was my turn, I reeled off my usual summary. "My name is Mike Collier. I'm a partner at PwC, and my line of work is merger-and-acquisition consulting. I've lived in Houston since 1997 with my wife and two sons, and I am delighted to be here and to get to know everyone."

It was Dan's turn. "Hi, I'm Dan DiNardo. I'm the bishop of the Archdiocese of Houston–Galveston, and I am delighted to be here also."

Dang! I thought to myself. I've been chatting up the new bishop. Is this cool or what?

We then got under way, hearing from a few dozen experts on such things as transportation, education, crime, economics, and so forth. We then broke into teams, each team diving deeply into one topic. The whole idea was simple: Get community leaders in a room and then get them thinking and talking about the issues that confront our community. Don't worry too much about what the output looks like. If you get the right folks talking, something good is bound to happen.

Dan and I and a few others landed on the public education team. Dan's insight was far superior to the rest of ours because as bishop, he was actually responsible for running a large Catholic school with thousands of students. He was very impressive, and we all enjoyed our time together and wrapping our minds around the challenge we face in educating our young people.

I don't recall the specifics of what we came up with. But I do recall that it completely changed my outlook on the importance of public education. I began to see public education the way an oil refinery manager sees his refinery. The refinery manager has a big challenge: He's got to get the "kit" to operate just right in order to convert crude oil, which isn't particularly useful when it comes out of the ground, into products that he can sell. What's more, he has to do it on the fly: That crude oil is coming at him, and he's got to get the job done.

In the same way, those kids are coming at us, and we've got to get the job done.

And as I thought about it, I realized that our job in public education is even harder than refining. If the refining manager botches the process, he can always mix the products back together and take another run at it. But if we botch public education, we can't just take another run at it. When you get education wrong, you can't get those years back for those kids. If our children come through the system and they haven't learned anything, if they aren't self-sufficient, then they begin to cost us all dearly.

Now, many years later, I was reading about what I considered to be an assault on public education, at the hands of a Republican governor who had the audacity to try to cover his tracks.

Education

In 1836 the Delegates of the People of Texas unanimously approved the Texas Declaration of Independence and sent it to Santa Anna, the president of Mexico. They had a lot to say about his government, including this:

> It has failed to establish any public system of education, although possessed of almost boundless resources . . . it is an axiom in political science, that unless a people are educated and enlightened, it is idle to expect the continuance of civil liberty, or the capacity for self-government.[9]

I happen to agree with the delegates of old. In fact, I would go one step further and say that unless people are educated, they aren't going to find good jobs. Most Texans, I believe, agree with me.

But a lot has changed in our state since its founding.

In 2001–02, Texas was eighteenth out of fifty states in terms of state and local government expenditures as a percent of personal income.[10] By 2011–12, we had sunk to twenty-seventh.[11] In absolute dollars, Texas ranked thirty-sixth in 2003–04 in current expenditures for public K–12 schools per student.[12] By 2013–14 we came in forty-fifth.[13]

This financial squeeze is hurting academic achievement in Texas, and parents, teachers, students, and employers know it. SAT scores in Texas are among the worst in the country. We ranked forty-seventh out of fifty states in a recent College Board report.[14]

Defenders of our education system tell everyone that this reflects the high percentage of Texas students who sit for the test. In states where fewer students take the test, the theory goes, the average SAT scores are higher. But if you look at any subgrouping of states with high participation rates, you'll find that Texas is consistently near the very bottom.

Defenders of our system also brag that Texas has a higher graduation rate than other states. This, of course, is nonsense. Few statistics are as easy to manipulate as the graduation rate, and even the right-leaning Texas Association of Business tells us that data on high school graduation rates can be very misleading.[15]

Public education in Texas is failing, and our future is at risk. Yet unbelievably, this is what the official Republican Party of Texas platform had to say about knowledge-based education in 2012 (about the time the state was firing 11,500 teachers):

> We oppose the teaching of Higher Order Thinking Skills
> (HOTS) (values clarification), critical thinking skills and
> similar programs that . . . focus on behavior modification
> and have the purpose of challenging the student's fixed
> beliefs and undermining parental authority.[16]

It's almost comical to think that politicians can rev up their base to the point that something like this gets written into a platform statement. It was yanked from the platform in 2014 amid all the laughter and heckling directed at Texas by civilized society. The Texas Republican Party communications director actually said—and you can't make this up—that the platform was all a mistake, but he couldn't change it because it had been approved by a vote. Sounds like the exact opposite of a mistake, if you ask me.

In 2012 and in 2014, the Republican Party of Texas platform had this to say under the category of "Educational Spending":

> Since data is clear that additional money does not trans-
> late into educational achievement, and higher education
> costs are out of control, we support reducing taxpayer
> funding to all levels of education institutions.[17]

I'd love to get my hands on their "clear data," because frankly, I don't think it exists. When a state is in the bottom twenty percent of the nation in terms of funding, and when a state is in the bottom twenty percent of the nation in terms of SAT scores, I suspect there is a correlation.

I'm not suggesting that we simply throw money at the problem indiscriminately. I am fiscally conservative, which means I hate wasting money. If Republicans had said, "Wasted money does not translate into educational achievement," instead of "Additional money does not translate into educational achievement," they might have said something useful. But merely

(Continued . . .)

dialing investment up when voters demand it, or dialing investment down (and firing tens of thousands of teachers) when voters are asleep, without having the conviction to attack head-on how the money is spent, is never going to translate into educational achievement in Texas.

Sadly, many politicians waste precious time and voter attention (falsely) claiming that school choice and charter schools and vouchers for private schools are the only things that can save us. That's just not the case. Texas has 5.2 million[18] students spread out across 260,000 square miles. Of those 5.2 million, there are only 228,000 students enrolled in charter schools in Texas.[19] There are only 309,000 students in private schools.[20] Only 82 of Texas's 254 counties have more than one private school in them.[21] Half of the counties in Texas have no private schools at all.[22]

The simple fact is that choice might work in some parts of the state, but it will not work in ALL parts of the state. That's why, year after year, voters shoot down schemes to radically expand charters, choice, and vouchers. For the four-million-plus students who have no choice but to attend traditional public school, we must do a better job. And when you consider projections that by 2020, some sixty percent of all jobs in Texas will require college-level training,[23] it's clear that our prosperity as a state hangs in the balance.

....

I happen to believe that the business world offers some terrific insight into how we might shake things up and achieve public education excellence in Texas. Just like a major corporation, the Texas public school system is a large, decentralized operation. And like a corporation, it seeks to drive operating decisions as close to the customer as possible while achieving superior overall results. Why not do what world-class corporations do?

First, executives of successful corporations know their businesses inside and out. Executive decision-makers, before they rise to the senior ranks, spend years working in lower levels of the company, learning its products, markets, technologies, and people. When they become executives, they make great decisions. In contrast, the key decision-makers presiding over Texas's public education system are lawyers, bureaucrats, politicians, and lobbyists. Few have ever set foot in a classroom, and many are openly hostile to professional educators. As a result, they do really stupid things, like forcing excessive testing down everyone's throats. Texas could learn from world-class companies and allow professional educators to play a much more meaningful role in key policy decisions.

Second, world-class corporations give local managers wide latitude to make market-based decisions, but at the same time they impose strict financial controls on each and every operating unit. They don't just let local management do whatever it pleases with the company's money. Texas could learn from this and impose strict financial controls on school districts. If my money is going to be sent to someone else's school system, I want that money going into the classroom (in the form of excellent teachers who are paid well, smaller class sizes, and use of specialists for special-needs students). I don't want that money going to bloated administration and unsavory contractors.

Third, world-class corporations are committed to success. An executive who openly and consistently disparages his own company will be shown the door in a hurry. It takes deep, sustained, emotional commitment on the part of executive leadership to achieve superior results. Commitment to excellence in traditional public education is badly needed in Texas, with the tone set at the very top, as opposed to a mistaken belief that charter, choice, and voucher schemes hold the answer for Texas. Hostility toward traditional public schools such as we find today produces an unacceptable outcome.

Finally, successful corporations are innovative. They constantly scan the horizon for technologies that increase productivity and profitability. Web-enabled learning technologies utilizing artificial intelligence, distributed through the traditional public school system, must surely hold the answer to our education challenge in Texas. Corporate executives who hunt for performance improvement at lower cost always turn to enabling technology. Texas politicians could learn from this mind-set and seek new technologies that supercharge traditional public school performance without increasing (or perhaps even reducing) the cost.

(Continued . . .)

....

The Delegates of the People of Texas, meeting at Washington on the Brazos in 1836, might not have anticipated the complexities we face today in educating and enlightening our people. But I doubt that would have diminished their enthusiasm. The great Sam Houston, himself a delegate, once said, "Knowledge is the food of genius, and my son, let no opportunity escape you to treasure up knowledge."[24]

I have little doubt as to what Mr. Houston would expect us to do.

....

At the office that morning, feeling all wound up over the Perry article, I sat down to have coffee with a close friend, Terry Lanier. We talked about the news, and he could see that I was fuming. Terry said he agreed that Perry was getting too big for his britches.

Right then and there I decided to come out of the closet.

"Terry, I've about had it with these Republicans and the way they treat us with such disrespect. I can't stand the fact that they can lie about something as important as education and get away with it. I have half a mind to run for Texas comptroller when we get Layline sold off, and if I do, I'm going to run as a Democrat so I can hold their feet to the fire!"

Terry is a big ol' boy, played football in high school, is Texan through and through, and a die-hard Republican. He started to laugh and squeal like a little boy. I sat there laughing too, waiting for Terry to compose himself. Finally, he managed to choke out the words "Good luck with that!"

I walked down the hall, hearing his laughter grow fainter as I got to the other side of the building. But I could hear him still laughing. It seemed to last for ten minutes.

He finally calmed down, and I wandered back down the hall a second time. This time, in all seriousness, Terry said it was probably just a matter of time before Democrats started winning statewide. "And," he said, "if we're going to have a Democrat in office, I'd feel a lot better if it was you."

....

Well, I had one Republican ready to get behind me if I was dumb enough to run for state comptroller. I thought I would see if I could go two for two.

So, a few days later, when my old friend Cameron from UT was visiting Houston, we went to an Astros game and talked about everything under the sun, including (as Cameron and I always did) politics. I told him about my investigating the Houston city controller role and the conversations I'd had with the consultants. And then I told him that I had met with the Kingwood Democrats, and that I was thinking about making the switch.

Cameron was and is a staunch Republican. He wasn't at all surprised that I was interested in running for office—but as a Democrat? When I told him that, he was stunned.

"Think about it," I told him. "Think about this debacle over school funding. Do you realize that we fired 11,500 teachers thanks to Republicans? That wouldn't have happened if we had a truly competitive political environment in Texas. And if someone with my resume is afraid to run as a Democrat, how on earth will we ever have two competing political parties in a pro-business, conservative state like Texas?"

My comment about firing teachers landed on Cameron like a ton of bricks; he'd thought that the state had simply cut overhead, not fired 11,500 teachers. He thought over what I'd said to him carefully.

"I knew all the way back to our college days that you were a dad-gum Democrat," he concluded.

....

A few days later, lightning struck. It was one of those days when you know your life is never going to be the same.

By sheer coincidence, a story broke: Comptroller Susan Combs had decided to step down at the end of her term. Cameron heard it first, over the radio as he drove to work, and called my cell phone to tell me.

I immediately dug into the newspapers, and there was the article on Combs. I was stunned at the serendipity. About midway through the article the reporter started writing about likely candidates—Tommy Williams, Republican; Harvey Hilderbran, Republican; Glenn Hegar, Republican; and Raul Torres, Republican.[7]

Where are the Democrats? I thought to myself.

I went online and did some more digging, and I discovered a political consultant in Austin by the name of Jason Stanford who was quoted as saying there weren't any Democrats ready to announce they would run for the post.[8]

My jaw hit the floor. I called Cameron right back. "Well, that does it. I'm going to get out ahead of this and run for Texas comptroller on the Democratic ticket."

Staunch Republican notwithstanding, Cameron offered me his unequivocal support. "I don't know how I'm going to explain this to my buddies up here in Dallas, but as far as I'm concerned, it's Collier the Democrat all the way!"

Two for two, I thought. *Two down, and five million to go.*

5

....

Jason Stanford

The name Jason Stanford—the consultant quoted as saying that no Democrats were planning (yet) to run for Texas comptroller after Susan Combs stepped down—had stuck with me. I'd looked at his website and decided he was probably a good guy, and I'd jotted down his number to call once I was ready.

The date was June 5, 2013, and we had just closed on the sale of Layline's assets. I was racing to get everyone paid. There are mountains of calculations to be done in wrapping up a company and paying everyone their final check, bonus, equity, and severance. I was running a mile a minute.

Around 3 p.m., I found the scrap of paper with Jason's telephone number on it. For a moment, I couldn't decide whether I was ready to call or not. But my adrenaline was flowing as I tried to wrap up the company, and that meant I would be "on" when I called. What good would come from waiting? And there was something apropos about calling right then, not letting one day go by between Layline and my next great adventure. It was the moment of truth.

So I dialed the number, and the receptionist put me on hold while she tracked down Jason. As I waited, I couldn't help but wonder whether I would get the same brush-off that I'd received from the Republican consultants.

"Jason Stanford speaking."

He sounded very friendly, almost humble, and I knew instantly that he was nothing like hard-boiled Jim, the Republican consultant from a few weeks ago.

"Hello, Jason. My name is Mike Collier, and I'm the CFO of Layline Petroleum in Houston. We're selling the company today, and I'd like to speak to you about running for Texas comptroller."

I explained my reasoning to him with as much simplicity, clarity, and strength as I knew how. I told him about the Republican consultants I'd met with, my wish to run as a Democrat, my feelings about the Combs vacancy and the lack of Democrats running for the position, my strong belief that people with business credentials should be involved in public life. I delivered the pitch as though I was presenting to the board of directors on a merger.

When Jason spoke again, he sounded like he suspected someone was playing a practical joke.

"Have you ever run for office before?" he asked slowly.

"No," I said, wary of where this might be heading. "I've been in business all my life."

"Well, let me tell you a little bit about politics, Mike."

Yep. Here comes the brush-off.

"People think politics is about making speeches and riding in parades and kissing babies," Jason said. "But it's really about getting on the phone and making a pitch for money. You've got to be crisp, compelling. You sound good on the phone, so next time I'm in Houston, maybe we should meet."

Not the brush-off I thought was coming!

....

I'd finally found a political consultant with a spark of interest in me; suddenly Jason Stanford became the most important person in my professional life. That "maybe we should meet" comment was my first real victory on the road to becoming involved in politics. The challenge now was to parlay it into a campaign that could earn three million votes in just seventeen months.

I didn't buy Jason's "next time I'm in Houston" line. Who knows when that would be? I, on the other hand, felt a real sense of urgency. If I was going to run a statewide campaign in Texas, without knowing anything or anyone, I knew I'd better get cracking.

I waited about two days and called Jason again. I said I was coming to Austin and that I'd have time to meet. Jason was pleased to hear from me, and I began to suspect his "next time I'm in Houston" shtick was really a small test to see how serious I was. We decided to have coffee at the Driskill Hotel in downtown Austin, the same place where my friend Chuck said I would never actually run for office.

The Driskill is an old hotel near the Capitol. It was very busy that morning because the legislature was in session, and well-dressed men and women, lobbyists and politicians, no doubt, were everywhere. The hotel building itself is ancient, harking back to an earlier era in Texas history, and it reminded me of the old county courthouses where I would run title records as a landman. It's cool being able to actually see bits of old Texas. But as I sat in the lobby waiting for Jason, there was something about the people that morning that left me feeling very cold. I didn't know them. I didn't know their game. Was I really prepared to leave my business comfort zone and jump into a high-stakes political contest that I knew nothing about? It was a real gut check.

Then Jason spotted me, came over to introduce himself, and sat down. Thankfully he looked very businesslike. He could pass for a PwC partner. Having done merger and acquisition work for more than a decade, I'm good at picking out the scoundrels, and Jason wasn't one of them. His "good guy" vibe settled my nerves as I sat there surrounded by the lobbyists and politicians, on their turf.

Jason and I had a short, pleasant conversation. There is nothing more valuable than an honest collaboration and nothing more threatening than a dishonest one. I found myself hoping that Jason would turn out to be as honest as he seemed. Ultimately, he passed with flying colors.

He made it very clear that no matter how hard I worked, or how talented I turned out to be, I could not win this election. "If you run," he said, "it should be to learn how it's done, to build relationships, to earn some name recognition, and to lay the groundwork for 2018." (His expectation was that one of the very popular Castro brothers, Democrats from San Antonio, would run for governor then, and their run would support my second attempt at running for comptroller.) I told Jason that I had the same instinct and that I wanted to do this.

Of course, telling me that I couldn't win was like waving a red cape in front of a bull.

....

To keep things moving, Jason said he would try to get a meeting with Will Hailer, the new executive director of the Texas Democratic Party. The next day, Jason sent a text and said we would meet with Will the following Tuesday.

The night before I was scheduled to drive to Austin for the meeting, I got an email from Jason. YOU'LL BE MEETING CHAIRMAN HINOJOSA AS WELL. EVERYONE'S IN TOWN FOR A BIG EVENT TOMORROW. BE SURE TO WEAR A TIE.

A big event, and one that involved Gilberto Hinojosa, chairman of the Texas Democratic Party? I liked the sound of it. Like the investment bankers say: Whatever happens this week, don't get thrown off the deal. This old expression from my professional days would be my guide for some time.

Early the next morning I got a text from Jason. WEAR AN ORANGE TIE. I hadn't the slightest idea why I should wear an orange tie, and I didn't have one. The stores wouldn't be open that early in the morning, and I couldn't imagine why the color of my tie would be important. So I headed to Austin with a blue tie.

As I made the three-hour drive from my home in Kingwood to the state capital, I listened to the news on National Public Radio (I'm an NPR devotee). The Texas Senate was scheduled to meet over an anti-abortion bill, and supposedly one of the Democratic senators was planning to stage a filibuster. It was the last day of the session, so this would force the governor to call another special session if he wanted to pass the bill.

NPR might have mentioned the senator's name, but I didn't catch it. They might have mentioned the specifics of the legislation, but I was oblivious. Beyond what I'd researched about the comptroller's office, I knew almost nothing about Texas politics. I was on a mission to attract attention to my qualifications to be our state's CFO and to shake up the financial games being played in Austin. Beyond that, I was a complete outsider.

Jason met me at the parking garage. He was wearing an orange tie, which he took off and handed to me. I hurriedly put it on, using my reflection in the car door window. I got it right the first time, which was good, because Jason had us rushing to get to our meetings. That's when I learned we were meeting with Chairman Hinojosa and Will Hailer in the Capitol building itself, known to insiders as "the Pink Dome." I had never set foot in it before.

As Jason and I walked the two blocks to the Capitol, I was surprised to see TV trucks and a long line of people waiting to get in. They looked like UT students: They were wearing burnt orange T-shirts, and they seemed very excited. Once inside the Capitol, I could see more TV crews, more orange-clad youth, and the occasional well-dressed grown-up. Jason, of course, was at my side.

After passing through security, we found ourselves in the midst of all the people and excitement. Clearly, something was about to happen. There were TV crews and cameras swarming around inside the Capitol, which made Jason nervous. "Mike, stay away from the cameras for now," he said. I took his advice: I'm not shy, and I'd done corporate video shoots in my professional life, but I knew that the level of media involvement in politics would be far different. I was quite happy to wait to be on TV until after I'd figured out whether I was going to run—and hopefully had some idea what I was doing.

Avoiding the cameras, Jason reached out to shake the hand of a kind-looking man with a wonderful smile, a bushy mustache, and a backpack slung over his shoulder. He turned out to be Chairman Hinojosa. Next we bumped into Senator Kirk Watson, whose name I recognized because he had been mayor of Austin. Jason introduced me, saying, "Mike is considering a run for comptroller." Watson didn't hesitate for one second before shooting back, "You should, man!" It was surprising; he knew nothing about me.

Next came Glen Maxey, a former state representative, whose face and name were familiar because he was my representative when I lived in Austin. He was also famous for being Texas's first openly gay legislator. Glen had the same reaction when Jason introduced me. Immediately, he blurted out, "You should run!"

I pulled Jason away from the crowd. "Okay, Jason, these guys don't know me from Adam, and they want me to run for comptroller. What's going on here?"

"You're dressed like a grown-up," Jason explained. "Nobody wants a clown running down ballot."

After looking around awhile, Jason and I walked up a few flights to reach a hideaway office. Will Hailer was waiting for us, along with Chairman Hinojosa and Glen Maxey. As we walked in, everyone stood to shake hands and was very polite. Will Hailer is a mountain of a man, standing about six feet eight inches. He appeared to be a very pleasant, quiet person. We all sat down, and they wrapped up their conversation before turning their attention to me. I was surprised at how relaxed and even lighthearted they were.

Their conversation revolved around a woman named Wendy and the filibuster that was about to happen in that very building. They didn't mention her last name, and at the time I wouldn't have known it. But in retrospect, it was the first time I'd heard the name Wendy (as in Wendy Davis).

To start the ball rolling, Jason repeated who I was and why I was there. I ran through my elevator pitch, which took all of fifteen seconds. Chairman Hinojosa spoke for a few minutes, thanking me for wanting to do this and talking about what it's like to run for office in Texas.

Jason had reassured me before the meeting that my having been a Republican was not a bad thing, but I could still sense some tension from the others. Glen Maxey asked which primary I'd previously voted in. "Republican," I told him, suddenly realizing that this might disqualify me from running as a Democrat. But to my surprise, it didn't: Glen offered that you can sign an affidavit saying you've changed parties and that would solve the problem.

"Do you have any pets?" he suddenly asked me.

"Yes," I said, "my wife and I have six cats."

"Cats!" Glen shrieked. He then turned to Chairman Hinojosa. "It's okay, he's got cats. He's a Democrat!"

Through the whole brief conversation, Will never said a word. When we got up to leave, he simply said, "We'll be in touch."

I couldn't have known then how hard Will would work to help me, or that we would become good friends.

After the meeting, Jason and I fought our way past all the people wearing burnt orange T-shirts who were trying to squeeze into the Senate gallery for Wendy Davis's famous filibuster against abortion legislation. I would learn later that the emergency demand for T-shirts—the people who'd come to protest wanted to wear the same color, as a sign of solidarity—could only be met by the T-shirt shops that stocked burnt orange, the school color of the University of Texas, which was just a few blocks from the Capitol. So orange became the color you wore to support Wendy, which is why Jason had me wear his orange tie. As unbelievable as it may seem, in politics, these things matter.

We managed to squirm our way out of the Capitol, past the hordes of people and TV cameras, and we were finally in the open and headed to the parking garage.

"Any feedback?" I asked him. I was wondering whether he thought Will and Chairman Hinojosa would support me.

Instead, Jason answered, "Don't ever acknowledge your consultant in a meeting."

Evidently I had turned to Jason a couple of times for guidance and reassurance. In business, it's pretty standard to show that you listen to your advisors. But in politics, I guess you have to project a very different image. Still, I took Jason's comment to be a good sign; he'd sailed past the question of whether the party leaders would support me and jumped right into advising me on candidate style points.

When we got to the car, Jason said, "I'll speak to Will, and I'll be in touch."

6

....

Well, Chuck,
I Proved You Wrong

The next morning, Jason sent me an email with a questionnaire that he'd developed for prospective clients to help him size up their political potential. This was the beginning of an extensive inspection of my life, career, and point of view on vital issues. I answered each question as completely and as honestly as I could. I didn't want to start raising and spending money to be comptroller only to find out that my point of view was incompatible with the Texas Democratic Party's positions.

In retrospect, this was the first and only time during the campaign that I felt free to fully express myself. As a lay student of politics, I knew that a candidate doesn't freewheel: A good candidate will hone a winning message and stay on it with as much discipline as he can muster. But for now, knowing that a miscalculation by either me or the party could end in embarrassment and lots of money sent down the tubes, I was happy to answer every question as completely and comprehensively as I could.

The first question was a simple one: Why was I running?

I suspect lots of candidates run because they are vain, ambitious, or bored. But this question was easy for me to answer from the heart. I was (and still am) thoroughly dissatisfied with politics and politicians. Like many Americans, I felt that our political system wasn't attracting the best people. It was attracting far too many people who'd say or do absolutely anything to get elected and then reelected. Many don't seem to care about leaving things better than they found them. And many make an art form out of being dishonest, masterfully spinning the truth to suit themselves. Taking credit when things go well, and blaming everyone under the sun when things go wrong, seems to be the modus operandi for many modern politicians.

In Texas, our problem is particularly acute, since for some twenty years we've had limited, if any, political competition. In the business world, I'd seen strong leaders who surrounded themselves with "yes" men, were never challenged, and as a result started making really awful decisions. But business has a natural correcting mechanism in the form of an unforgiving stock market. Bad decisions can't be papered over forever; investors can spot trends, and they'll see that the enterprise is making dumb decisions and declining in value. The stock price falls, and the board of directors dumps the bad leader.

In politics, there is no equivalent of a stock price to help voters see that bad leaders are running the operation into the ground. Thus, it's up to rival politicians to get people's attention in order to make the necessary changes before it's too late. Competition from a strong Texas Democratic Party, I argued, would force Republican politicians to protect the interests of the people who live and work here, not just their personal ambitions or the machinery of the Republican Party.

This, I wrote Jason, was the fundamental reason I wanted to run for office. It's not to ride in parades or kiss babies or make speeches or see my name in lights. I'd tolerate all of that in exchange for a chance to influence, for the better, our political lives in Texas.

Jason and I went back and forth and covered every conceivable topic. I wrote to Jason about abortion, guns, immigration, gay rights, you name it. But he also wanted to know about my education, my work experience, my family, my health, my hobbies, and my taste in music. I told him that Tom Petty rules, and he agreed. Throughout the entire exercise, I put as much emphasis on integrity as I could. I was raised to value integrity, my career as a CPA is founded on integrity, and the thing that disturbs me the most about politicians is their lack of it.

....

I had an inkling that Jason was keeping Will Hailer posted about our dialogue. Shortly after I completed the questionnaire, Will called and suggested that we meet for dinner in Houston. *A dinner meeting is a very good sign*, I thought.

We agreed to meet at Damian's, one of my favorite restaurants in Houston. I chose it because of the significance to me on a personal level. Many years ago, when I worked as a landman for Exxon, I found myself at lunch at Damian's feeling almost overwhelmed by how much I hated my job. (Exxon is a company that I greatly admire, but working there as a twenty-five-year-old landman, ambitious and marking time, I was miserable.) Sitting at lunch at Damian's twenty-eight years ago, I remembered what my buddy Chuck had said to me about political life: *You'll never be in a position to actually do it.* I remembered thinking that Chuck might actually have been right. And I remembered thinking how determined I was to prove him wrong despite what seemed at the time like very, very long odds.

But here I was: back at Damian's, about to hear from Will that the Texas Democratic Party was going to green-light my campaign for statewide office, three spots down the ballot from governor! I felt an unbelievable sense of accomplishment.

We kept it simple and wrapped up our dinner early because Will had to push on to Beaumont, about ninety miles from Houston, for meetings in the morning. He told me that although the Democratic Party would support my candidacy for comptroller, I wouldn't necessarily be spared a primary opponent. And then he explained to me what came next.

"You've got to spend the next month or so calling everyone you know and asking for money," he said. "That usually amounts to two or three hundred people."

My jaw hit the floor. Hard-boiled Jim had already broken this news to me, but I'd refused to believe him. I honestly (foolishly?) thought that when a political party got behind a candidate, an armored truck showed up and dropped off the money for the campaign. Now I was seeing the hard reality: I was going to have to call hundreds of people out of the blue, ask them for money, and raise a campaign war chest one conversation at a time. And they might very well think I'd gone crazy.

"Can we announce my campaign first?" I asked. "It will seem

more real to people when I call them if they've already read about me in the newspaper."

"No, Mike, that's not how it's done," Will said. "You make the calls first, you see if you have support, and then you consider whether or not to make the announcement."

I thought about it. "Well, you guys know what you are doing and I don't. So I'll do just as you suggest, and we'll talk again in a month's time."

Will smiled broadly at that. I would later learn that first-time candidates often go down in flames because they can't bring themselves to beg for money. I'm sure Will knew how much I loathed what I was hearing, but he could see that I was willing to try.

We said our good-byes, and I headed home, pleased that I was still "in the deal" but nauseated at the idea of calling friends, family, and colleagues and begging them for money.

....

When I awoke the next morning, I tracked down the list I'd made when I was considering a run for Houston city controller. I added every acquaintance and professional colleague I could think of. I searched through my contact list, business card rolodex, professional directories, everything. I came up with 367 names of people I would call. But contrary to hard-boiled Jim's advice, I excluded family members, immediate neighbors, and close friends. I had committed to putting $250,000 of my own money into the campaign, and that would be plenty to cover for the people I was closest to. I didn't want to take their money and then come back and cry on their shoulders if I blew it.

I sent the list to Jason. Unlike the Republican consultant who'd sniffed at me and my list, Jason was actually quite positive. None of my contacts were typical Democratic donors, and he viewed that as a good thing. It was my first hint that Democratic candidates in Texas are, in essence, competing for limited resources from a finite number of donors, so my bringing new donors to the election cycle would be good for every Democrat in the race.

The accountant in me quickly concluded that if every person on my list gave me $1,000—something I didn't think was even remotely possible—I would still only raise $367,000. Add my $250,000, and I would have just over $600,000 to spend. That wouldn't be nearly enough. Mail pieces, TV commercials in major Texas media markets, candidate travel, paid staff to help with coordination and communication, campaign office rent, consultants to organize volunteers to knock on doors and drive people to the polls: This was expensive stuff. Newspapers were saying that the governor's race would cost $25 million, and the last serious Democrat to run for comptroller had spent $6 million, I was told.

I was going to have to raise money from people and donor organizations I didn't know and who didn't know me. I didn't have the slightest idea how that was done. But, thanks to Jason and Will, I knew where I had to start.

7

....

Bracing for Launch

I was pleased with the first month of my political odyssey: I'd gotten the Democratic Party to give me the green light to run, and I had a consultant who was willing to help me. I also knew that I had a very long campaign ahead of me, starting with hundreds of phone calls to acquaintances and professional contacts. But with Election Day still sixteen months away I decided that this could wait until August. Right now, it was still July, and I thought I should enjoy some vacation time with family and friends. I figured there wouldn't be much time for vacation once the statewide campaign was under way.

My first little escape that month was to fly to Las Vegas with Suzanne and our close friends Anne and Mike Bratcher for the Fourth of July. For twenty years, we've gone together to Las Vegas to celebrate our respective anniversaries, usually marking the occasion with dinner on Independence Day itself.

I have an odd way of enjoying Las Vegas. I wake up very early and read two newspapers before I go for a long walk. Then, during the day, I read (or work, if I have to take care of anything), and I spend some time lifting weights. In the evenings we have dinner and see a show, and then I go to bed so I can get up early and hit the newspapers. Such is the life of a workaholic.

On this particular trip, I brought study materials so that I could use my vacation time to analyze our state's finances. I didn't want to start making phone calls and asking for money until I had a better idea of what I was talking about. Since it was the education cut in the eighty-second Texas legislature that spurred me to action, and since I already knew I was going to campaign very hard on education, I figured I'd better look very carefully at what had actually happened with the budget cuts. Our Vegas vacation was the perfect time to squirrel myself away and study the issue.

And the more I read, the angrier I got.

The comptroller is required by law to issue a Biennial Revenue Estimate (BRE) at the start of each legislative session. The BRE is an estimate of tax revenues that will come into the state's coffers during the upcoming budget period, and lawmakers are required to fit their spending into that estimate. It's a great way to avoid accidentally over-spending state revenues. But as it turns out, it's also a great way to manipulate the legislative process (and to do horrific things like fire 11,500 teachers unnecessarily).

In January 2011, the BRE triggered massive cuts in education in the 2012–2013 budget. Comptroller Combs predicted that Texas would start the 2012–2013 budget cycle $4.3 billion "in the hole," meaning that the first $4.3 billion in revenues that came in would have to go to repay the previous budget cycle.[1] With $4.3 billion taken away at the start, and with Combs predicting that revenue growth would be relatively flat in 2012–2013, Combs had created the appearance that the Texas legislature would have to make deep cuts in everything, including education. The teachers got fired as a result.

Turns out, we'd never had a $4.3 billion hole that we had to fill at the start of the budget cycle: We had a $1.1 billion surplus.[2] Combs was flat wrong, to the tune of $5.4 billion. I found this simply hard to believe.

But it got much, much worse as I studied further. The whole time Combs was estimating that future revenues would be flat, she was bragging that the Texas economy was growing like gangbusters. When our state's economy grows, our revenues grow. Anyone with any financial sense knows this. Yet Combs had sent a two-page letter to the legislature stating that although our economy would grow in the coming years, our revenues wouldn't.[3] I couldn't believe my eyes, and the legislature had completely missed it.

Ultimately, the state would enjoy an $8.8 billion surplus.[4] The education cuts that cost all those teachers their jobs were completely unnecessary. It should have been obvious to everyone at the time the cuts were voted on. Had anyone simply looked at the ledgers, they would have seen that cash was pouring into the Texas Treasury.

As I studied the debacle, I wondered what permanent solution I might propose as comptroller so that this would never happen again. Just promising to do a better job would be lame. I wanted to protect Texans from political chicanery that might come long after I was gone. That's when I decided that the comptroller should update the revenue forecast each and every quarter, rather than every other year. Quarterly reporting works in business, and it will work in government. Here's why: When you have to defend your work every three months, you don't dare play games with the numbers. You also get very good at it, because your credibility is on the line almost continuously. And most importantly, quarterly revisions would give decision-makers much more timely information.

I called Jason from Las Vegas and ran the idea by him. He liked it, and I started to get excited about campaigning on the issue. I'd have at least one very powerful reform that I knew Texans would appreciate. It was an Independence Day well spent.

....

Just after Las Vegas, I made a quick trip to Georgetown to see my parents and to say hello to Mr. Buie, an oilman who'd hired me one summer while I was in college. He is retired now and living on a ranch that sits just a few miles from my parents' much more modest home. For more than twenty-five years, I'd driven by Mr. Buie's house on the way to my parents', yet I'd never once stopped to say hello. As I drove by, I would feel ashamed that I hadn't stayed in touch.

Well, now I had a great reason to pay him a visit. So I dialed his telephone number, and I was delighted to hear Mr. Buie's voice and to find out that he remembered me. He invited me over, and we talked for about an hour. He asked a thousand great questions about me, my sons, my parents, my career, my health, and my campaign. I remembered vividly how much I'd valued working for him many years ago, and he very graciously waved me off when I tried to apologize for not having called on him before.

Quarterly Forecasting[1] *

Our current Texas comptroller cut his tax revenue forecast for 2016–2017 by $4.6 billion. As required by law, his revision was part of the Certification Revenue Estimate issued at the beginning of each two-year budget cycle.

Thus, my greatest fear while running for the comptroller job came to pass. Texas was hit by a surprise decline in oil prices, resulting in a decline in tax revenues to the state. Our new comptroller had no choice but to reduce his revenue forecast.

Having spent the majority of my professional life in and around the oil industry, and having lived through more than one "out of the blue" oil price decline, I had this terrible fear that an oil price collapse on my watch (had I won in 2014) would undo everything that Democrats (including me) were campaigning on. We wanted to improve our investment in roads, schools, and water infrastructure without raising taxes. The oil business was booming at the time, and we knew that with prudent fiscal management we could achieve these goals.

I worried that an oil recession would make this very difficult. As a first-time candidate, I did not want to fall into the trap of making false promises to win an election.

That's why I campaigned on updating the state's revenue forecast every three months.

That's how we do it in business, and it would be a real game-changer for a modern Texas. If we had a downturn, we could manage our way through it in a dynamic way without making clumsy mistakes. It would be a tremendous improvement over the ancient method of predicting revenues at the start of each legislative session, baking a two-year budget around the numbers, and then not revising the forecast until after the governor has signed the budget and lawmakers have gone home.

I looked back over the budget debacle of 2011, when lawmakers eliminated thousands of teacher jobs thanks to a bad revenue forecast. I saw

---

1 *Originally published in a slightly different version as Mike Collier, "Quarterly Revenue Forecasts Make Sense for Texas," *The Texas Tribune, TribTalk,* November 3, 2015, https://www.tribtalk.org/2015/11/03/quarterly-revenue-forecasts-make-sense-for-texas.

that the cuts would not have been necessary had the revenue forecast been updated during the legislative session. I reached the conclusion that quarterly revenue forecasts would have saved Texas from the 2011 bloodbath, to say nothing of the deep education deficit that today poses a very real threat to our prosperity as a state.

Imagine if our new comptroller had adopted quarterly revenue forecasting when he entered office in January 2015. A revised forecast would have been published in the middle of the eighty-fourth legislative session. Another forecast would have been published near the end. And it would have been clear by then that state tax revenues would be impacted by low oil prices.

In response to such a warning, the Texas legislature could have agreed to finalize the budget only after the fall forecast became available. That would have required a special session, but Texans would have been happy to see their legislature working hard to do the job right. By the fall it would have been obvious that revenues were not going to be as strong as the outdated, rosy forecasts had suggested. And it would have been obvious that massive cuts in the business margins tax, in the face of softening revenues, might result in insufficient funds for public education and transportation in the days ahead.

Old ways of running Texas's finances simply won't work as we become the largest economic engine in America. Our population is exploding, and with it the challenges we face in providing education, transportation, water, and basic services that the citizens of a truly great state deserve. If we want to be both conservative and effective, we must embrace change.

Quarterly revenue forecasting is a great example of the kind of change that can improve people's lives at almost no cost to the state. What are we waiting for?

Times were tough in the oil patch back in 1982 when Mr. Buie hired me to work as an intern. I was only three years out of high school, and I bragged all over town that I was going to be working in the oil business. My high school friends, all home for the summer, were envious and angry.

And then Mr. Buie called the night before my first day.

"Mike, this is Glynn Buie," he said.

"Hello, Mr. Buie."

"Mike, things are a little slow in the oil business right now—"

Uh-oh, I thought. *Is he going to yank my job?* I was mortified, thinking of having to explain that to everyone.

"So when you come to work tomorrow, wear work clothes," he concluded. "There are some projects for you around the ranch."

What a relief.

The next day, I turned up in work clothes, and Mr. Buie turned me over to Mrs. Buie, who set me to work in the flower garden near the road. I kept my head down as every car went buy. The last thing I needed was everyone around town buzzing that Mike, the big oilman, was pulling weeds in Mrs. Buie's garden. Thankfully, nobody saw me.

I spent about half the summer doing oil and gas work and half of it doing work around the ranch, only some of which involved the flower garden. Not a bad deal, and it helped me land my landman job at Exxon. To this day, I am very grateful to Mr. and Mrs. Buie for helping me launch my career and for teaching me a few things about ranching and gardening to boot.

Now, more than two decades later, Mr. Buie and I were talking politics. He enjoyed telling me about his childhood in East Texas and about the day when he and his father were driving somewhere and his father said, "Look over there, son, that man's a Republican!" Mr. Buie was young at the time, and he remembered taking a good, long look at the man to see what a Republican actually looked like.

Texas was every bit as Democratic then as it is Republican now. To understand the history of the two parties, you've got to go all the way back to Reconstruction. Back then, Texans hated the Republican Party because it was the party of the North and the Civil War. (Mr. Buie even mentioned that he'd lost a great-uncle in one of the few Civil

War clashes that took place in Texas.) As we all know, the two parties reversed their polarity in the South back in the 1980s, so it was fascinating to listen to Mr. Buie talk about the old days, when he and his dad would gawk at a Republican.

Mr. Buie, who has very keen insight into all things Texas, advised me to minimize the fact that I was running as a Democrat and to emphasize the fact that I have an MBA and a business career. He later mailed me a campaign donation, which I greatly appreciated, despite the fact that suddenly *I* was the one being gawked at.

The Civil War and Reconstruction came up more than once while I was talking to people on the campaign trail. Texans are deeply emotional about their state's history, and many families had members who'd been killed fighting for the South. Mr. Buie's deep Southern drawl is rich with Texas history, and I worried while I was listening to him that I might have two strikes against me: I was a Democrat and I was born in Pennsylvania. But then I remembered that some of the defenders of the Alamo—among the truest of Texas heroes—were of Scotch-Irish descent from the Blue Ridge and Appalachian regions. Judging from my sainted mother's Scotch-Irish temperament, they must have been a headstrong lot. When I considered that, plus the fact that I had lived in Texas longer than the average Texan had been alive, I felt I could hold my head high.

....

After a quick visit with my parents, and the wonderful conversation with Mr. Buie, we headed out on our other big July event: our annual Port Aransas beach weekend with Suzanne's extended family.

It's hard to say why I love Port Aransas as much as I do. I saw it for the first time in high school when some friends of the family invited me to camp on the beach in a big air-conditioned RV. Twice our high school band chartered buses and drove to Corpus Christi to perform in a band festival, and we visited the Port Aransas beach both times. With each visit, the place grew on me.

The beaches at Port Aransas are very wide, and the sand is terrifically soft. The air is always wonderfully warm, balmy, and breezy.

The water sometimes has some Mississippi mud still in suspension, giving it a slightly brownish color, but that doesn't bother me one bit. The town itself is not the least bit fancy: It's a tiny fishing community that swells in the summer with a combination of rednecks, families, and Come-And-Take-It! beer drinkers. Everyone is in a fabulous, Texas-style, laid-back mood. I just love it.

Later in life, I'd always been too busy to join Suzanne, our young sons, and her family for the decades-old tradition of sitting on the Port Aransas beach for a week (which we affectionately refer to as the Laskowski Beach Week). But in 2006, after I had worked my way into the partnership and had earned a few stripes at PwC, I decided to join them. And something came over me that week spent reading and walking alongside the warm waters of the Gulf of Mexico. It did me in, and to this day, I can't get enough of the place.

When we all go, there are more than twenty of us, and we range in age from nine to eighty years old. We rent two beach houses for a week, and we spend most of that time sitting under big tents and reading. It's the only time of the year that I don't try to work. Instead, I set goals as to how many books I will read, and I work very hard to achieve my objective. The books are always history or biography, or sometimes a treatise on fiscal or economic policy. Once a geek, always a geek.

I hadn't said anything about my political plans except to Suzanne and the boys before Laskowski Beach Week. But I'm a big talker, and that's nearly all I talked about all week. Good thing I've got a tolerant family.

There are Democrats as well as Republicans in my wife's extended family, and they all thought I was stark raving mad, but they were enthusiastic. And I could sense they were looking forward to the spectacle. Since we had an entire week together, and since we all trust one another, the conversation was very free flowing and honest. I found that my message of creating competition in Texas politics, as well as taking politics out of the comptroller role, resonated with everyone, even the Republicans. Staying on message during the campaign would not be difficult, I thought.

When we were interacting as a family, I was as relaxed and happy as always. But when I found myself alone from time to time, walking along the beach, the whole idea of running for comptroller was nerve-racking. Yet it was about to happen, and I figured I'd get used to the sick feeling I got just thinking about it. As soon as we returned from Port Aransas, I'd have to get on the phone and start asking colleagues and business associates for money.

I will always blush when I think about the morning when, after setting up the tents and settling in for a nice long relaxing day of reading on the beach, I looked over my shoulder and saw a TV news truck driving toward me. For a split second, I thought the news crew had been dispatched to interview me about the campaign. I even worried about how I looked: As someone who upholds the old 1970s tradition of wearing ratty shorts and a T-shirt at the beach or on my sailboat, I knew this could be a problem.

The TV truck drove slowly toward our little tent city, and then kept right on going. It wasn't me they were looking for. Little did I know at this early stage in the campaign that TV crews driving around in trucks don't ever, ever stop to interview down-ballot candidates like me. Later in the campaign I overheard a statewide candidate from a few years earlier say that he didn't think lighting himself on fire would make it to the evening news.

If any of my wife's family saw me react (cower, really) at the sight of a TV truck, I'm sure they thought I looked ridiculous.

By the end of the week in Port Aransas, I felt like the bridegroom whose hand still hovers over the mailbox after letting the wedding invitations go: A marriage proposal is nothing compared to the moment when the invitations get dropped in the mail. That makes it public. At that point, there's no turning back. After a week on the beach with the Laskowski clan, with me talking nonstop about my plan to run for comptroller, I knew there would be no turning back without eating a lot of crow. And I was not about to eat crow.

8

....

Call Time

We returned from the beach on July 29, and I started making fund-raising phone calls on July 30. By now I had hired Emily Williams, whom Jason had introduced to me, to teach me the basics of political fund-raising. She had sent me a spreadsheet to keep up with what's known in the trade as "call time"—when a candidate sits somewhere making fund-raising phone calls. Later in the process, Emily would help me develop a list of people who had contributed to Democratic candidates in the past. But we decided to start with my list.

Using my cell phone, and parked at my desk at home, I started making phone calls. I would start making calls at 9:00 a.m., I would call until noon, I would take a break until 1:00 p.m., and I would finish at 5:00 p.m. This was a pattern I generally followed from August 2013 until Election Day fifteen months later, whether I was at home, working out of a low-rent campaign office, or driving between campaign stops. I'd guess I made more than 25,000 phone calls.

I had the very clear perception that nobody in the Democratic Party was going to lift one finger to help me (other than my consultants) until I demonstrated that I could raise money for a political campaign. I had asked Jason several times about creating a website, taking campaign photos, ordering yard signs and buttons and stickers, but in each case Jason simply said, "Raise money!" I realized pretty quickly that without cash, you aren't real, and nobody wants to be associated with a candidate who isn't real.

Thus, as I started making phone calls, I had a feeling that my political aspirations, which had been a big part of my life for as long as I could remember, hung in the immediate balance. It was also extraordinarily awkward, embarrassing, and even frightening to make fund-raising calls to my list of business contacts. I had cultivated these relationships over twenty years through hard work and dedication to excellence—and my colleagues were mostly Republicans.

The phone calls went something like this:

"Hey, Bob, Mike Collier here, how you doing?"

"Great, Mike, good to hear from you! What are you working on these days?"

"Well, I don't recall the last time we spoke, but I took early retirement from PwC a few months ago, and Goldman Sachs picked me up and put me to work as CFO of Layline Petroleum, which we just sold."

This would inevitably lead to a long conversation about Goldman and Layline, how the deal had gone down, and such business talk. I enjoyed that part of the conversation very much, but I knew in the back of my mind that it was temporary. Soon, I was going to drop a bomb.

When the moment was right, I would say, "What I'm working on now may surprise you. I've decided to run for Texas comptroller."

This always hit them like a ton of bricks. We in the business world tend to have a very low opinion of politicians. But as the conversation unfolded, I found that I was good at easing my colleagues into agreeing that if we want good people in office, then good people need to run. In the vast majority of cases, the conversation turned around and became positive.

Until, of course, I mentioned that I was running as a Democrat.

I knew early on that I'd have to get used to feeling the tone shift from "Hey, great to hear from you" to something more akin to "You and I aren't supposed to be speaking to each other, because we are not on the same team." The conversations were pretty hard, and I was certainly not going to go for the gold and ask for money on that first call. Instead, I made my case that Texas would be better off if we had a truly independent, financially savvy comptroller to hold the politicians accountable.

Most of my Republican colleagues liked what I had to say about policy, but they nevertheless were struggling with the idea that their acquaintance and business associate was a Democrat. They needed time to process what they had just heard. I had no idea whether they would support me or cast me off.

The thought that I might be turning off my business network was terrifying, and to be honest, I almost called off the campaign after the first day of phone calls. I had called perhaps fifteen people, I had strained the relationship with all but one or two of them, and I had no money to show for it. I had to face the very real possibility that I would call everyone I knew, poison every well I could, receive no support, abort the mission, and look like a damn fool.

At the end of that first day, I went for a long walk, feeling miserable. Somewhere out on a Kingwood greenbelt trail, I got a text from Jason. *How did your first day go?*

I've been on the phone all day, I texted back.

How many pledges?

None yet.

No more texts; the phone rang almost immediately.

"I know you really want to do this, Mike," Jason said, "but we have to decide if this is going to work."

The prospect of Jason and the Democrats losing faith in me after only one day of fund-raising made my heart sink. Had I known at the outset that I would have to "qualify" as a Democratic candidate by raising money from Republicans—Republicans who don't usually give money to politicians in the first place—I might have considered the whole thing impossible before getting started.

But something told me to keep going. The work was important, and surely my colleagues would come to see that. I had no way to predict how their thinking might evolve, but I had this gut feeling that some of them might come to see the Texas Democratic Party in the same light that I did. They would see that a pro-business, no-nonsense, corruption-fighting Democrat could be a counterbalance to the Republican political machine that was closing its grip on Texas. I just needed to give folks time, I thought, and I managed to convince Jason as well. We pressed on.

It took almost all of August to make the first 367 calls on my list. I called only to explain myself and to ask my colleagues to consider supporting me, and I said I would call back in a month or so, once they'd had some time to think about it. Jason and Emily were delighted that I was working so hard, but I wasn't asking for money yet, so no money was coming in. I could tell they had their doubts. I confess that I became frustrated and unhappy that Emily wouldn't let me start calling Democratic donors until I had some fund-raising success with Republicans. According to her, donors wouldn't support a first-time candidate whom they didn't know if the candidate's friends wouldn't even support him. I, on the other hand, worried about asking my Republican contacts to write me a check before I knew whether the Democratic donors were going to support me. It was a real chicken or egg dilemma, and it frustrated me: I must be the only person in history, I thought, who had to prove his viability as a candidate by raising money from members of the opposing party.

At one point, Jason felt compelled to voice his doubts about me. He said that all failed candidates have a reason for not asking for money. My reason—or, as he seemed to suggest, my *excuse*—was that my colleagues were all Republicans. Jason's comment didn't sit well with me, and I decided to drive to Austin and do a call-time session from Jason's office. I wanted Jason and Emily to hear what it was like for me.

A funny thing happened as I walked up to Jason's office that morning. I was carrying several three-ring binders of printed materials in a large briefcase. Jason looked at the briefcase, the large, square kind that holds an enormous amount of paper. "What could possibly be in that?" he asked. I told him that these were my homework materials: printouts of the state's financial statements, budgets, reports on key financial issues, and so forth. I was going to put myself out there in a very public way as a financial expert who ought to be the chief financial officer of a large and complex state; I was going to approach the job in the same way I approached a large client assignment as a PwC partner. I didn't want to find myself being asked a question I couldn't answer.

As I explained to Jason, I'd made a list of the areas of state finance that I would study. These ranged from topics as basic as understanding our state's balance sheet and income statement to such technical areas as Medicaid expansion, highway funding, education funding, water funding, health and human services expenditures, the various enterprise funds, public–private partnerships, pension liabilities, and so forth. I then devoted one full day of study to each area as a first step in understanding our state. I spent every Saturday and Sunday doing homework, excepting only those days when I was traveling to campaign events. It took me three months to get the groundwork laid and another month to synthesize everything into a fact book that I carried with me everywhere I went.

Jason rolled his head back, laughed, and asked, "Why would you care about any of that? We're trying to get you elected!"

After a good laugh (a PwC man could not possibly take a comment like that seriously), I rolled up my sleeves and started call time.

I picked five people from my call list and said to Jason and Emily, "Okay, I'm going to hit these folks for money right after I tell them I'm running, just like you guys want me to." Predictably, the calls were a disaster. Not only did I not get any money, but my colleagues almost hung up on me. Jason and Emily could only hear my side of the conversation, but it became pretty obvious to them that asking for money right off the bat, under the circumstances, would fail miserably.

Then I picked a few people and showed Emily and Jason how I was easing folks into this. I made the call, had a good chat, but I didn't ask for money. I simply said that I wanted them to give this some thought, and that I would call back later in the fall. Jason and Emily seemed impressed with how I conducted myself, and I guessed they were finally on board with my tactics.

We agreed to wait until after Labor Day, when I'd circle back to everyone I'd talked to and ask for money. If the money didn't start flowing in September, we would call the whole thing off. But if it did, then we would go to the next level: We'd finally start calling Democratic donors.

In other words, my September fund-raising performance would determine my future, and I was feeling the heat.

9

....

Hazing the Rookie

Near the end of August, Jason called and said we needed to shoot an introductory TV commercial. We'd put it on my website, and if money allowed, we'd push it out via paid e-media advertising when (or *if*) we announced my campaign.

On the one hand, I was happy to have a distraction from making phone calls. On the other hand, video shoots were very new to me, and like everything else so far in this campaign, I had no idea of what to expect.

I hired a TV communications team from Florida that Jason knew and whom I thought, based on a conversation and proposal, would do good work. I chose them in part because they had a track record of helping Democrats win in big elections. I wasn't surprised that Jason would recommend a team from out of state, considering that Democrats in Texas hadn't won statewide in two decades. I told Jason I wanted to work with consultants who were accustomed to winning, not losing. I also hired an e-media team from Oregon, also introduced to me by Jason, who had cut their teeth on President Obama's campaign, which told me they would bring state-of-the art e-media know-how. I had no idea at the outset how important these two teams would be to my campaign. Jason and the media teams he brought to me really knew what they were doing.

Everyone got to work, and by mid-August, our team had developed a script for a two-minute video. It read as follows:

Here in Texas, our economy is booming.

But no matter how successful we are, our politicians just can't seem to get it right.

They cut school funding by 25 percent.

Our property taxes keep going up.

And they can't even maintain our roads.

I'm Mike Collier and I know something about finance, managing money, and holding people accountable.

From there it offered a brief recitation of my resume, and it closed with this:

And unlike our current comptroller, whose revenue estimates were off by $12 billion,

I know how to forecast revenues accurately.

If you want the government you deserve, instead of the government you've been getting,

And a comptroller with the courage to tell you the truth, and the know-how to hold the politicians accountable,

Then I hope you'll join me.

I'm Mike Collier. The Watchdog. Together, we'll not only shake up Austin, we'll fix the way our state does business.

I was okay with most of it, but I didn't like the idea of making a frontal assault against the incumbent comptroller. I just didn't want to be unpleasant. I also didn't like calling myself the Watchdog, which was clearly beneath my dignity. And I wanted to change the word "government" to the word "circus" at the end because that's my style.

I made these edits, and I sent the script back to Jason. After a few minutes, Jason wrote back: *Thanks for the edits, now let the professionals do their work.*

I didn't pick up on the subtlety: The professionals weren't going to change a thing.

Along with the script came a list of scenes, props, and extras I had to assemble. I had to find a Hispanic family for a picnic scene;

another family for a breakfast-at-someone's-home scene; veterans and a memorial; an elementary school playground; some senior citizens in a park; a business conference room with a dozen professionals as extras; an executive office with American and Texas flags; an oil drilling rig with roughnecks; a construction site with engineering drawings and workers; and a pick-up truck driving down a dusty road. In each case I had to find the location (and secure permission to use it), the extras, and the props, and I had about five days to do it all.

I stared at the list for a long, long time, asking myself whether this was even possible. I couldn't believe I'd have to pull all this together myself. Somehow I felt like the new guy who was being hazed by the experienced hands.

Good thing I had Jon Labate to help me out.

Jon was a terrific military veteran whom I had met while I was at Layline. My CEO came to me one day, handed me Jon's resume, and said we should help a veteran by hiring Jon. I read the resume and noticed that he was born near Pittsburgh. I called Jon, and we agreed to meet.

I liked Jon from the start. He carried himself with a military bearing, he was smart and humble, and although he didn't have any experience in accounting or finance, I could tell that he could learn. I told him that I wanted to hire him to work at Layline.

Soon after Jon and I met, however, we decided to sell the company, and it no longer made sense to hire him to work there. I started calling people I knew in the energy business to help him find a job. He landed a job at Halliburton with my help, but the fit wasn't a good one, and he had a hard time bringing himself to ask for my help a second time. I trusted him, though, so I hired him as my assistant right after the Layline sale ended.

His first assignment was to do some research and help me analyze some performance metrics for Texas. What Jon found surprised me:

- Texas was one of the worst states in terms of public education investment per student, despite the fact that we have a very high proportion of poor children and children whose native language is not English (these students cost more money to educate);[1]

- Our public schools were turning out some of the worst students in the country (Texas students' SAT scores are forty-sixth out of fifty states);[2]

- Our transportation infrastructure was in decline (we had dropped from the nineteenth [in 2001] to the twenty-third state [in 2012] in lane-miles per person);[3]

- We had used debt extensively to build roads and we are running out of credit capacity;[4]

- Texas state and local debt combined had grown so large that we are one of the most indebted states in America;[5]

- We had the highest rate of uninsured people in Texas, which means that Texas taxpayers are paying far more for indigent care than taxpayers in other states;[6]

- We had the fourth highest rate of teen pregnancy, and the very highest rate of repeat teen pregnancy in the country;[7]

- And we were in a real water crisis thanks to a terrible drought after years of kicking the can down the road.[8]

What Jon brought me was a picture of a state in financial decline, not the economic miracle our Republican leaders were bragging about. It was like a flashback to the Enron era, when the executives had everyone believing the company was an economic and financial powerhouse, when in fact they were digging a hole so deep they couldn't crawl out of it.

Jon was proving to be a very capable assistant, as I knew he would be. Although we never discussed his party leanings directly, I had the distinct impression that he was a Republican and that he was skeptical the Democrats would let me either run my own campaign or run the comptroller's office my way. But I was able to convince Jon that I chose the party—the party didn't choose me—and soon Jon became committed to my success.

I was delighted that Jon was on my side, especially now that I needed help pulling everything together for the video shoot.

....

Jon Labate and I worked very hard, and very quickly, to line up props and extras and sites to shoot the video. It was hard work with lots of awkward phone calls and multiple attempts, but in the end, we pulled it off—or rather, I should say we got close. In only one respect did we completely fail, and that was in finding veterans to participate in the shoot. As a veteran, Jon did everything he could think of. But he got nowhere: His boss was running as a Democrat, and all the veterans he could find were Republicans.

I jumped in and made phone calls myself, but I got nowhere. Even though I was the client, which meant I could easily just call up the TV guys and tell them I wasn't having any luck, I had a very powerful instinct that I needed to "deliver." I needed my consultants to see that I was a refuse-to-lose kind of guy. It would set the tone for the campaign, and I knew that since I was not yet raising money, and everyone was wondering whether they were wasting their time on me, I couldn't afford to miss any opportunity to show how determined I was. I told Jon we really needed veterans. We had to keep looking.

Jon discovered an assisted living center in Kingwood just for veterans where the local VFW meets each month, and it turns out they were meeting two days before the shoot. Surely we could talk a couple of veterans into helping a fellow Kingwood man. I called the VFW commander, told him my story, and asked if I could address the meeting. He said he'd think about it, and then he didn't call me back.

So Jon and I drove to the assisted living center and found the VFW meeting room. We hung out until the commander arrived to set up, and we introduced ourselves. He was polite but clearly irritated that we would just turn up at his meeting. He said he would talk to his members and see whether there would be any volunteers, but Jon and I were not welcome to speak to the members directly.

While Jon and I were waiting outside the meeting, I decided to try something. I stopped the on-site manager (who happened to walk by as the VFW commander was dismissing us) and asked if he could recommend one of the veterans who lived in the center to round up a few

Are Texas Politicians Truly Conservative?[1*]

Is any politician truly conservative? Or are they all playing the same shell game? When it comes to fighting government debt, Texans believe their Republican heroes are truly conservative. But the numbers suggest they might be mistaken.

In 2002, when Rick Perry was first elected governor, Texas owed $14.8 billion to bondholders, and we owed $2.3 billion to pensioners (this is the unfunded pension liability that we owe to retired state workers and teachers). By the end of 2014 our bonded indebtedness had grown to $40.8 billion and our unfunded pension liability had grown to $38.9 billion. This represents average annual growth in debt and pension liability of 13.5 percent per year, which is much faster than average annual growth in our economy of 6.5 percent and average annual growth in our population of less than three percent.

In February the state issued its financial statements, and during 2015 our bonded indebtedness grew another 7.8 percent to $44 billion.

These figures represent debt at the state level. School district and local bond indebtedness in Texas amounted to over $200 billion in 2014. And the research group State Budget Solutions estimated in 2014 that total unfunded state and local pension obligation exceeded $250 billion.

At roughly $500 billion, total state and local debt and pension liability was more than thirty percent of Texas's total economic output of $1.6 trillion in 2014. And just like our national debt, our state debt is growing faster than our economy. My Republican friends would like to blame Democrats, but Republicans have been in charge for two decades.

Some Texas politicians will have us believe that we balance our books, as required by our constitution. While it's true that we balance our general fund, we are not required to balance every fund in government. We are not required to balance our highway funds; we are not required to balance our pension funds; and we are not required to balance our school district and

---

1 *Originally published as: Mike Collier, "Mike Collier: Are Texas Politicians Truly Fiscal Conservatives?" *Dallas Morning News*, April 7, 2016, http://www.dallasnews.com/opinion/latest-columns/20160407-mike-collier-are-texas-politicians-truly-fiscal-conservatives.ece.

local funds. Indeed, the state is starving school districts and local governments of the financial resources they need to run their operations, forcing them to take on debt.

Some Texas politicians also brag that we are a very low-tax state. It helps that they ignore the taxes our children will be paying on our behalf, which is really what government debt represents. And we'll even force young Texans to pay interest along the way for the privilege of carrying our weight. Public debt is not like corporate debt, where the shareholders who incur the obligation are the ones who pay it back. Public debt is a transfer of wealth from our children to our pockets, pure and simple.

A truly conservative politician would use debt very, very sparingly. And he darn sure would never lie about it or try to conceal it. Yet while Texas Republicans are racking up debt by the billions, many have the audacity to claim (falsely) that they are keeping the books balanced.

Texans are a conservative people, and when we have reliable information we make excellent decisions. We should take the lead in ending the debt crisis that plagues politics in America. We should demand straight talk, as a condition of public service, when it comes to our state's finances. We should tell our politicians (at the ballot box) that we will not tolerate spin, misleading statements, or shell games that keep voters off balance while smothering our children in debt.

If any state can do it, Texas can do it. By casting our votes for politicians who shoot straight—and withholding our votes from politicians who spin—we will change our political culture and begin to solve our growing debt problem. Straight talk in politics will solve a lot of problems, frankly. The rest of the country will surely take note, and they might even follow our lead. When they do, the words "Texas miracle" will take on new, lasting, and national significance.

friends for our video shoot the next day. I told him that we would do the shoot in Kingwood, and that we would supply the transportation. He was friendly, didn't mind the idea at all, and said, "Come with me." Finally, I thought, we were going to make some headway.

The manager walked me down a hallway and into a very large dining room, where the residents had just been seated and were waiting for their meal. There must have been one hundred residents, the majority of them women, and all were quite elderly. The manager found a microphone and asked everyone for their attention. "We have a visitor who would like to say a few words."

People turned, looked, and went dead silent to hear what I had to say.

Now, I'm not bashful. Ask my wife and my neighbors about what it's like to go with me to karaoke bars. But this was awkward beyond all description. I couldn't help but think that this was some way to make my first stump speech!

But the journey of a thousand miles starts with the first step, so I launched into it.

"Hello, my name is Mike, I'm running for office; the job is comptroller. I'm running as a Democrat, we have a video shoot in two days, and I'm looking for volunteers to help for a few hours."

All I got was silence. Silence and stares. Some of the women were smiling at me the way elderly women smile at a younger man who looks lighthearted. It's a look I'm very familiar with. But the men just stared, and everyone was silent for a long time.

There being no volunteers (and no movement, to be honest), I thanked everyone and told them if anyone would like to help me, please just tell your server. With a hundred people staring at me silently, I waved awkwardly and slowly started walking toward the door. I smiled back at the elderly women who were still smiling very sweetly at me. The men were absolutely stone-faced.

As I was walking out, I heard a man ask in a gruff, almost angry voice, "Did he say he was a Democrat?"

I never heard the response. But I knew what it meant: They were gawking at the Democrat the way Mr. Buie and his father had gawked at the Republican.

Jon and I waited for a long time for the VFW meeting to break up, but ultimately we called it a night and went home. The next day, I called the commander and asked if he'd had any luck. He stunned me by saying, "Mike, we talked about you for a long time. But Mike— we're just not going to help a Democrat. I'm sorry, but nobody is going to help you."

I knew that running as a Democrat in Texas was going to be challenging, but I had no idea that veterans, whom I revere, would completely dismiss me based on how they felt about my party, not having the slightest idea who I was or what I stood for. I was beginning to see what I was up against.

The TV people understood. There would be no veterans in our video.

10

....

A Star Is Born

The day of the shoot was one of the longest, hottest, and at first one of the most nerve-racking days of my life. From the moment I awoke, I was a complete bundle of nerves. Not only was I inexperienced as an actor in front of a camera, but I had pulled in a number of friends and former PwC coworkers to serve as extras, and they had to be properly dressed and on time. I had locations scouted without fully knowing whether they would work. I had to get an entire production company moving in a motorcade from location to location with little time to spare, and I would have friends and neighbors buzzing over the spectacle. I had no idea what working with a bunch of film people would be like, and I had not seen the rewritten script. Perhaps the most stressful part was knowing that after a very long day of shooting, the entire entourage would move into lovely offices in downtown Houston owned by a good friend, George Pilko, and I was terrified we were going to tear up the place.

I got up very early and started loading changes of clothes into the back of my car. We had a dozen shots, which meant a dozen changes of clothes.

The first shot was to take place in a nearby park. Jon Labate had all the props, and he was at the park setting up a picnic table with a fruit basket when I arrived around 7:15 a.m. Our extras were good friends Oscar and Kathy Velasco, whose daughter had to be at school by 8:00 a.m., so we had to start early. When I arrived, I was amazed to see two large vans full of video equipment, and several cars for the technical people. I counted ten people in all, from camera operator to sound engineer to the helpers they call "grips." Add to that the TV consultants, Bob Doyle and Dave Heller, Jason, who had driven in for the day, plus Jon Labate, and I could see that it was going to be a nightmare getting everyone from location to location.

It was a pleasure seeing Oscar and Kathy and their daughter for our first early morning shoot. As anxious as I was, seeing them soothed my nerves almost completely. We took our seats at the picnic table, the camera equipment and lights were ready to go, and we got some last-minute instructions from Dave on how to have a make-believe conversation for TV. There wouldn't be sound, so the commercial would just show me appearing to speak, with the Velasco family listening and pretending to enjoy the conversation.

In the end, we did actually enjoy it! I have always been a stand-up comedian at heart, and I turned it on. I babbled and said the most ridiculous things to get everyone laughing, and they in turn said and did ridiculous things back, and we gave Dave and company lots of footage. I began to relax and realize that as long as the logistics came together, this could actually be fun.

It was a scorcher of a day. Mid-July in Houston—when the temperature and humidity are up—is a real thrill. There's even a tunnel system in downtown Houston that connects most of the major skyscrapers, allowing people to go days at a time without ever stepping into the humidity.

But this day was going to be different. More than half the shots were outdoors. Each shot called for me to change clothes, sometimes behind my car door in a parking lot, and the clothes I was to change into had been in the car warming up for me. There is nothing worse, when you are hot and sweaty, than putting on a shirt that has been warmed to 150 degrees.

One story during the day's shoot stands out. Since we didn't have veterans, Dave suggested I find a hardware store and get some "B roll" taping done there. There is a local hardware store where I shop all the time, so I popped in to see if we could do some filming. Luckily, the owner was there, although I could see that he was a little concerned because no business owner wants to be seen supporting a Democrat in deep red territory. I promised him that I would make sure the name of his store was concealed, and on that basis, he agreed.

By the time we were ready for the shot, the owner had left and his daytime manager was in charge. He cringed when I told him the owner had okayed our doing a video shoot, but he welcomed us in. When I'd spoken to the owner that morning, I hadn't realized just how involved a video shoot is. The team members came in and took over several aisles, ran cables and cords to set up lights and cameras, and made a huge spectacle of themselves. This hardware store is not a massive building like the national brands, and our crew shut down at least a quarter of the store. Workers were confused, shoppers annoyed, and the owner's mother, who is one of the sweetest ladies I've ever seen, was horrified. So was I, and I hid in the back where they cut keys, hoping none of my neighbors would see me.

Finally they were ready to shoot, and they picked one of the employees to stand with me and have a pretend conversation. Ed was his name, and he was a Republican through and through. With tape rolling but without sound, I explained why we were there and, when the time was right, that I was a Democrat. We caught his expression on camera, and we caught my reaction to his reaction. Too bad you couldn't hear what we were saying, because it was the same conversation I ended up having with literally thousands of Republicans. In the end, Ed said he would vote for me but I would be the only Democrat he would consider voting for.

We pressed on with the rest of the shots, and finally, after ten hours of mostly outdoor shooting and about eight clothing changes, we arrived at George's office to do the business scenes, including my monologue. To say that we were hot, sweaty, and smelly is an understatement.

We arrived at George's office just as he was releasing his people so that we'd have the run of the place. The film crew started bringing in lights and cameras and tracks and dollies and cables, and I braced myself for a real miserable evening. I found a spare office and changed into a suit and tie. By the time I emerged, looking good but smelling awful, my extras, mostly PwC folks who'd walked down the street from their office, had assembled, excited about the evening's work that lay ahead.

Shooting B roll for a TV commercial is the most tedious thing

I've ever done. It took twenty minutes for the crew to set up the camera, lighting, and background for a simple shot of me walking down the hallway and speaking to a colleague about some project, and then when it was finally time to roll, we walked down that hallway at least a dozen times. That effort produced about three seconds of TV commercial.

I pride myself on endurance, but by the end of the day I was finding myself running low on energy, and I was very concerned that the last shot of the day, me speaking into the camera reading the script that we had worked up, would be flat and tired. To make matters worse, it took almost an hour to get the office set up to Dave's satisfaction, with me sitting motionless behind a desk while they made sure the lighting and the props were just right.

But while I was sitting at that desk waiting for the crew to finish, I couldn't help but reflect on how amazing all of this was. And I went back, yet again, to the conversation I'd had with Chuck Doty back in our twenties and thought about all the years since then.

Over the three decades since our last conversation, I'd kept Chuck's prediction—*you'll never run for office*—in mind. Every major education or career decision made since then was done to accomplish my goal and to prove Chuck wrong. Well, I did it. I was running for a very big office, and I had the feeling that if I did well I could craft a role for myself in public policy and achieve my lifelong goal. It was a very satisfying feeling.

Chuck had pursued his dreams as well: He had become one of the navy's best fighter pilots, and he'd almost made it into TOPGUN—the US Navy Strike Fighter Tactics Instructor program. But sadly, he was killed while flying a training mission during the first Gulf War. He was my closest friend, and his death was an awful blow.

Thinking about it, as I sat behind that desk, I wished that Chuck were alive to see that I'd pulled it off.

After what seemed like an hour, the crew was ready. Bob, Dave, and Jason confirmed on their monitors that the shot looked good. In other words, I looked good on TV, which we knew was essential to winning an election in modern politics. Bob then stood beside the camera, balancing a laptop in one hand and dialing up the script with the other. He would read one line of the script to me, I'd practice it, and we'd film just that one line (over and over), and then we'd go on to the next line and repeat the process.

Before we got under way, I asked Bob to read the whole script so that I could confirm that he'd made the changes I wanted. As he read the script, I realized the only change he made was to let me call Texas government a circus. The two most important changes—not referring to myself as the Watchdog, and removing the unkind reference to the incumbent comptroller—had been ignored. I'd suspected this might happen, and now I had to make a quick decision: Would I fight the team and do it my way, or would I yield to the team and do it their way?

I remembered something Paul Hobby told me just before I started the campaign. Paul is a well-known Houston businessman, son of a former Texas lieutenant governor and grandson of a former Texas governor. He'd run for comptroller many years earlier as a Democrat and had come within a few thousand votes of winning. I didn't know Paul before calling to introduce myself at the start of the campaign, and I was delighted that he took the call and was willing to offer me his advice. At one point he admonished me to remember this: "When it's time to walk onstage, so to speak, it's you alone in front of voters. The consultants won't be onstage with you. They'll be behind the curtain." I took that to mean that a candidate should get the most out of his consultants, but he should never forget that it's his campaign and career on the line. As I reflected on Paul's advice, I thought I should put my foot down and do it my way.

But at the same time, I was a consultant myself, and on many occasions I'd worked with senior executives who had less experience than I had in the specialized world of mergers and acquisitions. I had learned the fine art of helping clients adjust their thinking in increments and over time. Some clients could be led in this regard, other clients couldn't. Those who were willing to let the consultants lead them tended to make much better decisions.

Now I was the client and my consultants were trying to lead me. They had years of experience in the specialized world of political communication, and I had no idea what I was doing. So I decided to follow their lead, and I made no complaint about their refusal to change the script.

But they did let me call our Texas government a circus, and later I would find out that one of my PwC friends saw the video and blurted, "Yep, that's our Mike!"

We began to film the speech, line by line. Now, I had been a trumpet player in high school and in college, and I had played every manner of trumpet solo, from a stand-up solo with an orchestra, to a wedding march in a big church, taps at a funeral, and a fifty-yard-line solo at a UT–Baylor football game. When you play trumpet, everyone in the audience can hear everything you do. There is no such thing as a slight error. It's one of the hardest instruments to play, and the trumpet player can make or break a musical passage for the whole orchestra.

One thing every good trumpet player knows is that if you are going to miss a note, you need to miss it in a big way. You can shy away from a hard note, or you can hammer it. So you learn to hammer the hardest notes: It makes you less likely to miss, and if you do miss, at least the audience knows you've got guts.

When the cameras started rolling, I was reliving my trumpet days. I spoke loud, I spoke with energy, I spoke with commitment, I looked at the camera as if I was spoiling for a fistfight, and I nailed it.

Everyone's reaction was terrific, and I knew I had passed a very important test. When I hear people say that I'm not the typical accountant, and I often hear that, I chuckle to myself in agreement. In reality, I'm the typical trumpet player.

It took another hour or so to record the whole script and to wrap up for the day. It would be a couple of weeks before I saw the finished product, but I drove home that night feeling very satisfied with our effort and very glad the day of the shoot was behind me.

Over the course of the campaign, Dave and Bob would collaborate on several videos, with Bob weighing in on overall communication strategy and Dave doing the creative work. It was their video work that attracted the attention of the Democratic Party faithful to my campaign.

11

....

Discovering Texas,
One Phone Call at a Time

Early the next morning, Suzanne and I flew to Chicago for a wedding. We would be there over the weekend, flying home on Sunday night so that I could start calling back through my "primed" list and finally asking for money. The weather in Chicago was beautiful, and the parties were fabulous. But all weekend long, I had a sick feeling. Another couple was visiting from Texas, and I didn't say one word about the campaign. I had no idea whether I would emerge as a real candidate, and I wasn't quite ready to put myself out there with people from Texas I didn't know well. All I kept thinking was that when we returned home it would be my moment of truth.

Monday morning finally came, and I braced myself for what I thought would be the most important day of my life. I knew that my viability as a candidate hinged on whether I could raise money that day. And I had no idea what to expect. It was an absolutely terrible feeling.

But when I dialed up a PwC partner who was a mentor to me before I retired, he pledged $5,000. I was surprised and as happy as I could be. I called another colleague, someone I had worked with many years ago at PwC but who had moved to another firm, and he asked if anyone from PwC had contributed. I told him that one of the partners had contributed $5,000, and he said he would match it, but on one condition: If anyone from PwC made a larger contribution, I had to let him know.

Within thirty minutes, I had raised $10,000. I was as excited as a schoolboy, and I kept after it. By the end of the day, the total pledges amounted to $17,200. I told Emily and Jason, and their response was

understandably very enthusiastic. Since I'd turned the corner by raising good money from my list of mostly Republican friends and colleagues, Emily said that she would get me set up in a database with
all the Democratic donors in the state and that we would start raising money in earnest. It was a thrilling feeling, after three months of
patiently working to position myself to be a real candidate, to know
that now we were giving the race a real try.

As far as I was concerned, my campaign for statewide office started
that day.

....

That early success was particularly gratifying because I knew my
approach had helped my Republican colleagues get over their ambiva-
lence about helping a Democrat. Of the 367 people I knew well enough
to call and ask for money, all but two confirmed that they were Republicans. (Twice my colleague on the phone said he was a Democrat, and
both times I reflexively said, "Really?") Of the Republicans, eighty
percent said they would vote for me, and sixty percent agreed to contribute to my campaign. Their average contribution was about $500.
I began to believe that if I could only have a one-on-one conversation
with every Republican in the state, I could win. Of course, in a state as
large as Texas, you can't have a one-on-one conversation with enough
people to make even the slightest dent on voter math.

I didn't know it at this early stage, but I came to learn that my
"pitch" to supporters, whether it came during a fund-raising call, a
stump speech, a TV interview, or a TV commercial, appealed to Republicans and Democrats alike. Members of both parties, it seemed, were
equally enthusiastic about me. When the subject was finance, specifically my aspiration to take politics out of the office and fight corruption,
the Democrat versus Republican distinction melted completely away.

But I could also tell that distinction was not going to melt away so
easily when it came to social issues. Despite the fact that I refused to
campaign on abortion and gay rights, some ten percent of my Republican friends said they couldn't help me because of my party's various social positions. I always tried to keep things friendly by saying,

"I may try to convince you otherwise, but I'm not going to try very hard."

....

Texas has five major media markets, and it costs millions of dollars to get your name out in the public. To raise that kind of money, I was going to have to call thousands of people, almost none of whom would have any idea who I was.

There are perhaps as many as twenty-five thousand people in Texas who have a history of contributing to Democratic politicians. Political contributions are reported to the Texas Ethics Commission, so this information is publicly available. Identifying donors is easy. Reaching them—and persuading them to contribute—is difficult. First, I had no campaign experience, so potential donors had no idea whether they were wasting their money on me or not. Second, I was running for comptroller, and few people knew what the comptroller actually does. It's hard to get people excited to help you win an election when the post they're seeking is a mystery. And finally, everyone who has a history of donating to political candidates is bombarded by requests for money from every other candidate from around the state (sometimes from other states as well).

In short, I was beginning to see why some people considered running for statewide office without any political experience or connections to be a really stupid idea. Still, with the primary election in six months, and the general election in fourteen months, I was determined to work as hard as I possibly could. That meant I was going to have to work every minute of every day.

About this time Emily suggested I meet with Zach Brigham, a UT grad who was doing fund-raising work for the Harris Country Democratic Party and who was interested in working for one of the statewide candidates. I met him and liked him, and soon he was aboard as my call-time manager. Emily had taken a full-time position as the publisher of an online political newspaper, but she agreed to stay with the campaign another month or so while Zach got up to speed. To round out the campaign team, I hired a young woman and friend of the family, Demi Smith. We rented a very small office in Humble, a small town within easy reach of the three of us. As statewide campaign teams go, we were lean and mean.

Zach, Demi, and I would meet at the campaign office at 9:00 a.m., we would have lunch in one of a handful of restaurants near the office (we paid for our own lunches and didn't pass the cost on to the campaign), and we would work together until roughly 5:00 p.m. In the evening, I would do homework, write email, complete questionnaires, and so on. From time to time I would travel to a campaign event, but for the first few months of the campaign, all we did was spend months working together in that office, raising money. Zach and Demi would pull lists of donors together, I would make the calls, and they would track the pledges, mail the thank-you notes, and otherwise allow me to focus on phone calls and nothing else.

On a typical day I could make one hundred phone calls, more or less. I suppose I left over twenty thousand phone messages, of which perhaps only twenty-five people (!) returned my call. It didn't bother me one bit; they were only doing what I would have done. If a candidate really wants my money, he'll keep calling me.

There were some days when I left ninety-nine voice mails and only spoke to one person, who would tell me that all their money was going to Wendy Davis for governor. I would always say thank you and end the conversation politely. The feeling was sincere, but nevertheless I would go days at a time without any money coming into my coffers.

Believe it or not, it wasn't that hard to keep calling, all day long, day after day. The only thing I could control was how hard I worked, and I decided that if people said nothing more about me when this was done, they would say that I worked my tail off. It worked for me in business, and it would work for me in politics. We simply never let up.

As the weeks wore on, I began to get word that Democrats around the state were starting to ask who this Collier guy was. Nobody knew me, but everybody was hearing from me. Leaving one hundred identical voice mails a day is very, very hard work, but it seemed that it was getting my name out there.

In late September, I asked Jason when we were going to publicly announce my candidacy. There were folks on my list who were still trying to decide whether to support me, and I thought announcing would help me seem more "real" to them and to other potential donors. Jason said we should wait and make an announcement in October, after Wendy Davis announced that she was running for governor. According to Jason, a down-ballot candidate with no political experience would be a fool to run except on a ticket with a strong candidate at the top. If I announced before Wendy, it would tell everyone that I either didn't know this or didn't care, which would make me look like a goofball. So I accepted Jason's advice and kept making phone calls.

....

Trying to raise money from Republicans could be a headache sometimes, but for the most part we were amicable, and the give-and-take was very honest. And as I continued the hundreds of conversations, certain key themes emerged.

My Republican colleagues would almost invariably want to talk about President Obama's performance. I found it remarkable just how much Texas Republicans (perhaps all Republicans) dislike him. It's beyond dislike, really. Many think that he is ruining our country, and some believe he's doing it intentionally. I would challenge my colleagues, politely. Wasn't unemployment coming down? Didn't President Obama take out Osama Bin Laden? Hasn't the number of American soldiers killed on foreign soil declined? Some of my Republican friends would fly into a rage when exposed to these facts. Not one of them was able to give me a solid reason to believe that Obama was actually trying to ruin the country.

I learned quickly, however, that even the mildest attempt to defend our president resulted in severe blowback. So I decided, when speaking with Republicans, that I was better off simply sidestepping the whole topic by saying, "Obama is not running for comptroller, so he has nothing to do with my campaign."

Another issue that came up often was the idea that all Democrats are socialists. It was easy to argue that *I* wasn't a socialist, given my business background. I am a committed capitalist, and I prefer to let

the free market allocate labor and capital resources, with as little inter-
ference as possible. When government does interfere with markets, it
should do so with great caution, and only for the purpose of making
sure markets produce a better overall result than if left untouched.
Most of my Republican colleagues are committed capitalists, too.
But sometimes I would hear people tell me that the Democratic Party
would force me to do this, or that, if elected. I would remind my
Republican colleagues that the whole reason I'd given up on their
party, despite the fact that Democrats haven't won in Texas for a long
time, was precisely because—unlike the Republican Party, which was
going to cram its ideology down my throat—the Democrats were willing to let me be me.

Sometimes I would hear that only a crazy person would vote
against Republicans because Republicans are the ones who create jobs.
I would counter that Texas is in the middle of the pack, relative to
other states, in terms of unemployment. In July 2008, before the Great
Recession, nineteen states enjoyed lower unemployment than Texas
(based on civilian labor force data, seasonally adjusted).[1] Despite all
the hype and noise about Texas job growth thanks to the shale boom,
Texas still lagged behind seventeen other states in percent unemployment in July 2013.[2] I'd argue that Republicans were okay at keeping
up the status quo, but that's it. A state as prosperous and proud as
Texas ought to do much better. I would argue that we'd have much
lower unemployment, and Texans would be making more money, if
we didn't have such a train wreck of an education system after twenty
years of Republican incompetence. Not many of my Republican colleagues disagreed with me.

And I had a terrific time countering the assertion that thanks to
Republicans, companies were leaving California and coming to Texas
to enjoy our fabulous business climate. I would point out that of all
the companies that left California from 2008 through 2014, only fifteen percent came to Texas. Eighty-five percent moved to other states.[3]
Said another way, the overwhelming majority of companies that left
California chose *not* to move to Texas.

Having seen the data, I simply refused to take the "Republicans are
the job creators" comment lying down. Democrats, not Republicans,

were the ones willing to invest in education, transportation, and water infrastructure to ensure that we brought good-paying jobs into Texas. Republicans, in contrast, were refusing to educate our children, or invest in our transportation infrastructure, which together would surely choke off our economic expansion in the years ahead.

We talked at length about using tax incentives to lure companies, and jobs, to Texas. My point of view was that if done properly, incentives could benefit the state. But I was very suspicious that some politicians were wasting millions of dollars on tax incentives not to lure companies to Texas, but to take credit for companies who already planned to come here. I would argue that tax incentives are analogous to a strategic investment a company might make in a new plant. In that case, the chief financial officer's job is to make sure the math is done properly so that the company gets a return on its investment. I had visions of politicians begging companies to take our money before moving here; otherwise, the politicians don't make headlines. I said as comptroller, I'd overhaul the approval and monitoring mechanisms to make absolutely sure we would get value for our money. My Republican colleagues were all over it.

One topic that I never tired of discussing was wiping out corruption and waste in Texas government. It won't surprise anyone that Republicans are all over this issue. What might come as a surprise is that Democrats are just as passionate about not wasting money as Republicans. I never met a Democrat on the campaign trail who wanted to waste money! Solve problems, yes. But waste money, no.

And everyone I spoke to was in favor of returning the Texas Performance Review to the comptroller's office. There was a legendary comptroller many years ago by the name of Bob Bullock. He was the first to notice that in a state as decentralized as Texas (our state government is really the amalgamation of more than one hundred autonomous state agencies), there was no systematic way to hunt down waste. So he created the Texas Performance Review, to be conducted by the comptroller, with broad authority to dive into any agency and look for ways to improve its financial operation. His successor, John Sharp, also legendary, transformed the performance reviews into an art form, allowing the state to identify $10 billion in savings over ten years in the 1990s by some estimates.[4] He was so effective in running the reviews that he was later asked to see whether the same could be done at the federal level.

Both Bullock and Sharp were Democrats.

Sharp's successor was Carol Keeton Strayhorn, who at one point made the legislature angry enough to strip the function away from her. I tried to learn what she had done wrong, and I heard everything from being too aggressive to simply being a woman. Regardless of the specific reason, it's easy to see how a comptroller could upset the apple cart, given that some politicians and their henchmen make fortunes from fraud, waste, and abuse.

That, I argued to the people I was calling, was exactly why I wanted to bring the performance review function back to the Texas comptroller's office. I would be fiercely independent of the politicians who had been running things for a long time, which meant that the reviews would do Texas some good. My Republican colleagues all appreciated knowing more about the history of performance reviews, and they agreed with me that we ought to bring them back.

Although I wasn't attracting much press attention at this early stage of the campaign, one of the Republican comptroller candidates, Harvey Hilderbran, spotted my website and decided to campaign on the issue as well. He lost the Republican primary, however, to Glenn Hegar, whom I'll discuss in detail later. Hegar didn't want to have anything to do with performance reviews. I just assumed that Hegar didn't want to agitate the higher-ups in the Republican Party; after all, his political career would be toast if he did.

Sometimes I would selfishly point out to the people I was calling that none of the Republican statewide candidates had any business experience to speak of, except perhaps for Senator Dan Patrick (candidate for lieutenant governor), who was in business but who'd run his business into the ground. Most of the Republican candidates were lawyers or career politicians.

And when I would suggest that we needed more accountants in office—because the one area where many politicians have proven themselves to be inadequate was finance—the reaction from my Republican colleagues was overwhelmingly positive.

It was also obvious to everyone I called that we weren't keeping up with transportation or water infrastructure in Texas. Same for education: I heard consistently, from Republicans and Democrats alike, that we were doing an abysmal job with public education and that we were risking our future in the process. Not once in thousands of calls did I hear a single comment suggesting that Texas was doing an acceptable job with public education. Not once.

On the negative side of the ledger, I heard over and over from my Republican colleagues: "I'm sick of paying half my earnings in taxes!" It was as if I, as a Texas Democrat, would somehow make the situation worse. Well, I hate paying taxes too. And I would have fun with my Republican colleagues by asking where they thought all the waste was. "The problem is Washington!" I would hear over and over. My response would routinely be: "Don't you think it's crazy to gut Texas's infrastructure and mortgage our state's future because we don't trust the politicians in Washington?"

A spirited debate rarely followed.

....

In all, I had thousands of conversations with Democrats, Republicans, Independents, Libertarians, and anyone else I could think of. As they went on, I became more and more convinced that when it comes to financial matters, Texans are more alike than not alike. So I began to develop a simple summary of our financial aspirations in Texas that I used over and over on the campaign trail: "We must invest in roads, schools, and water; we must not become addicted to debt; and we must not raise taxes." Over the course of the campaign, I said this almost every time I made a speech, spoke to a voter, or did an interview. I never once heard an objection to it from any Texan, regardless of political persuasion.

Medicaid

Medicaid expansion is one of the largest financial decisions the state will ever make, amounting to something like $100 billion over ten years. Our state's chief financial officer has a duty to weigh in. Sadly, none of the Republican candidates for the job had the courage to mention a word about it.

When Governor Perry was in office, he didn't hold his tongue. He told us that expanding Medicaid could bankrupt Texas.[5] Problem is, he didn't tell us why.

I hunted down a handful of independent studies on the subject, and I wasn't surprised to learn that Perry was dead wrong. Expanding Medicaid will cost Texas $15 billion over ten years, or $1.5 billion per year.[6] That's about the size of the tax cuts Perry demanded shortly after he declared Medicaid expansion would bankrupt the state.[7] If Perry's tax cuts for big corporations wouldn't bankrupt Texas, then neither would Medicaid expansion.

It doesn't stop there. Offsetting the $1.5 billion per year average outlay to expand Medicaid will be savings against the $3 billion per year that Texas Health and Human Services said was the net unreimbursed, uncompensated care costs incurred by hospitals in a recent report.[8] Our insurance premiums, health-care costs, and the percentage of property taxes that fund charity hospitals would all decrease if we expanded Medicaid. And the state's outlay would be offset even more by new tax revenues resulting from the $100 billion of federal money that would come to Texas to fund its share of expansion over a ten-year period.[9]

Expanding Medicaid will clearly not bankrupt Texas, in contrast to Perry's false claim. In fact, if the studies are correct, it would be a very good financial deal for Texas. When you consider that expansion would also result in a much healthier and more productive workforce, expansion seems like a no-brainer.

Maybe that's why the Texas Association of Business called on the legislature to stop hiding behind Perry's remarks and expand Medicaid.[10]

I wasn't surprised that the Republican legislature and Rick Perry would skate past all these facts in their haste to slam Washington. That's what political hacks do. What surprised me the most about the Medicaid expansion issue was that Republicans were deliberately ignoring the business

(Continued . . .)

community. Aren't Republicans supposed to be pro-business all the way?

As far as I am concerned, Republican politicians are not necessarily pro-business. They ignore businesses' demand for better schools; they ignore businesses' call for transportation infrastructure that works; they ignore businesses' demand for a functioning water system; they ignore businesses' demand that we stop drowning in debt. And they ignore businesses' call to expand Medicaid.

Being pro-business means facing policy decisions with skill and integrity. It does not mean chasing vote-getting headlines at the expense of sound policy and covering your tracks with sound bites and false assertions.

A friend of mine who is the chief financial officer of a small company asked me a very astute question: If Texas is currently paying $3 billion per year to fund health care for those who are currently uninsured, and if expanding Medicaid means the federal government will spend $10 billion per year to insure these people (on top of Texas's share of $1.5 billion), doesn't that mean expansion of Medicaid will constitute a dramatic increase in the level of service (and the overall cost) of caring for the working poor?

The answer to that question was clearly yes: Expanding Medicaid under the Affordable Care Act would increase the range of services available to the working poor by a wide margin. Whether or not that's good public policy is a judgment call the legislature must make. Ignoring the issue entirely is simply unacceptable.

And that was exactly where I took the Medicaid issue on the campaign trail: I simply wanted the legislature to do its job. I wanted the legislature to study the pros and cons of Medicaid expansion, vote up or down, and then go home and face their constituents. Refusing to even consider expanding Medicaid, and pretending that Rick Perry wasn't being his usual misleading self, struck me as completely unacceptable.

A different CFO friend had this to say about expanding Medicaid: "Mike, you Democrats are so naive. All we'll be doing if we expand Medicaid is sending our tax money to Washington, where they'll just send it back, round-trip, with strings attached."

I fired back, "Look who's being naive. Since other states have expanded Medicaid and Texas hasn't, our money is not on a round-trip. It's on a one-way ticket to California, New York, Ohio, and the rest of the thirty-two states that have expanded Medicaid." In contrast, if Texas chose to expand Medicaid, our money would stay right here. In fact, the other states would start sending money our way, because we have the highest number of uninsured in the United States.[11]

Many of my Republican colleagues also complained that expanding Medicaid would create dependence on government, something Republicans always rail against. But that argument made no sense. Medicaid expansion would only affect people who went out and found a job. Doesn't that suggest, I would ask, that expanding Medicaid is the opposite of creating dependence?

Republicans also fear expansion of the federal government's role in our state. When Washington injects billions of dollars into a state, as would be the case with Medicaid expansion, that state loses a piece of its sovereignty. Relying on Washington and the collective judgment of Washington politicians can be risky. What if Washington pulls the plug on their $10 billion per year? Will Texas have to pick up that tab? Or will we have to drop millions of people from Medicaid overnight to save our neck financially?

These are valid concerns, but they don't justify ignoring the problem completely. Medicaid expansion is a complex decision, and we have a moral obligation to deal with the complexities head-on and with sincerity.

And if we really want to do this right, we'll consider Medicaid expansion in the context of a larger crisis in Texas: The working poor simply cannot afford health care anymore. And it's not their fault. Health care has become expensive because people with high-paying jobs want breakthrough treatments, new drugs, improved medical protocols, and better results. And the fact that they're willing to pay for these things drives the cost of health care beyond the reach of the working poor.

So politicians face a choice. They can find a cost-effective means of helping the working poor gain access to health care without creating dependence on government. Or, alternatively, they can just ignore the unfolding crisis. The Texas legislature has chosen the latter, hiding behind unsupported assertions of bankruptcy and dependency, and in so doing they have chosen a path that's very bad for Texas and its people.

12

....

Does the Dark Side Tempt You?

Jason, who has been working with Democratic candidates for a long time in Texas, didn't think there was any way Democrats would win in the 2014 election cycle. So near the middle of September, I suppose with his conscience bothering him, he called with a proposition. After seeing my success at raising money from Republicans, he said that if I were willing to switch to the Republican Party, I might be able to win the nomination and the election. He said he would introduce me to Brint Ryan who, unbeknownst to me at the time, was known to make huge campaign contributions to comptroller candidates that he liked. Jason said he knew Brint and could arrange the meeting. Since I hadn't filed any official papers binding me to the Democratic Party, I could make the change and off we would go.

Brint Ryan, it turns out, founded a CPA firm that helps clients with their Texas tax bills. No wonder he would want to install a friend in the comptroller's office. By outward appearance, he's one of the wealthiest people in Texas. Whether he earned his wealth by helping companies reduce their Texas taxes, I don't know. But whatever he does and however he does it, it appears to me he's awfully good at it.

I wasn't particularly surprised that Jason, a loyal Democrat, would suggest that I become a Republican in order to win the election. After all, I'd hired him to help me become comptroller, and he's an honest broker. The fact that he would suggest improving my chances of winning by switching to the Republican Party was just Jason doing his job. He, like so many other people, didn't see me as a partisan politician. I was going to "take politics out and put competence in" to the office, and that's what Jason was trying to help me do. It didn't matter which party, or even if no party, got behind me in order to do it.

All the same, I told Jason no.

I've met a fair number of CPAs and attorneys who represent clients before the comptroller. Several of them mentioned Brint Ryan as having made such large contributions to Texas politicians that it created the appearance of a conflict of interest. One Big 4 partner was adamant that any person who represents clients before the comptroller—for example, to advise them on how to reduce their state taxes—should be prohibited from contributing anything to a prospective comptroller's election campaign.

If this was the game, I had no interest in playing it. I told Jason that I had found a home among Texas Democrats, and that was that.

....

One night, just before Suzanne and I sat down to dinner (as empty nesters, we thoroughly enjoy our dinners together, often sitting in front of the TV watching the network evening news or the *PBS News Hour*), I received an email from my TV team with the two-minute introductory video attached for my review. I grabbed Suzanne's hand and insisted she sit next to me on the sofa and watch the video with me on my iPad. Neither of us knew what to expect. But we launched the video, and it was just hysterical. There I was, looking and sounding every bit the politician! My TV team had done a great job, and I was delighted at how good they made me look. I couldn't be happier, and I knew that when we finally announced the campaign, pushed the video via e-media, and posted it to my website, my friends and family would think it was a real hoot.

Jason called a day or so later to say that the Democratic candidates had worked out a timeline for campaign announcements. Wendy would go first, then Leticia Van de Putte for lieutenant governor, then Sam Houston for attorney general, and then me for comptroller. We would make our announcements on consecutive days. Jason would send out a press release about me, and then I'd drive to Austin and

Is It Time to End Tax Incentives?

Few spectacles are as unsettling to a fiscally conservative Texan as the sight of a politician racing across the country to bribe a company into moving here. Yet it happens constantly, and it's a race to the bottom.

Businesses, for their part, have highly paid managers who have mastered the art of poker's bluff. They know precisely how to pit two states against each other and get a huge tax break for their shareholders. One thing they've got going for them is that politicians don't drive a hard bargain. In fact, many do just the opposite. They can't wait to throw money at big companies because that produces a "Toyota Moves to Dallas Thanks to Rick Perry!" headline.

I come from the business world, and I know how the game is played. First of all, very few companies would put themselves, their employees, their employees' families, their suppliers, and their customers through the trauma of a big move just to capture a temporary tax break. They move because there is a strategic reason to do so: proximity to markets, access to skilled workers, lower cost of living, and so forth. When they start considering a move for strategic reasons such as these, they pick two or more candidate states and start negotiating. They tell each state that they'd better come up with a bigger tax break or the other state will become the company's new home.

And it works like a charm. Politicians fall all over themselves to cough up the money (our money!), while the men, women, and businesses that are already here keep paying their taxes.

It's time we bring this to a complete, permanent halt. The leaders of the fifty states should enter into a gentlemen's agreement that they will stop, once and for all, the practice of giving tax incentives to companies, for any purpose. Let companies pick the state where they are best able to make a profit. It will work wonderfully, for everyone.

Imagine what life would be like if incentives were a thing of the past. States would still compete for businesses, but they would do so by offering the best schools, the best transportation infrastructure, an attractive regulatory environment, the smartest workforce, low crime rates, parks, and amenities. In other words, politicians would do their jobs and make their states great places to live, do business, and raise a family. They wouldn't get away with providing lousy roads and terrible schools, letting crime go through the roof, or turning parks into apartments, if they couldn't use bribe money to get companies to move here.

And the loyal people and businesses already here won't suffer the indignity of getting passed over for tax breaks in favor of newcomers.

This idea would fail miserably if some states eliminated tax incentives while others still used them. Only if every state agreed would it work. But it would work so wonderfully, and taxpayers would be so grateful for it, that they would wonder why they hadn't eliminated tax incentives years ago.

I can hear the big companies and politicians now. "This will kill jobs in America!" Fact is, they would be dead wrong. Eliminating tax incentives would have zero impact on job creation, and it would be a small but important step toward getting our financial houses in order. And it would eliminate one of the many reasons voters don't trust politicians, which in and of itself would be a very good thing. We're going to need all the trust we can get when it's finally time to deal with the financial crisis that's coming as America careens toward financial insolvency.

do some TV interviews that he was setting up around town. My heart skipped a beat.

The first interview was with Paul Brown at YNN, a cable news channel owned by Time Warner. We'd start at 10:00 a.m., and Paul would interview me in the studio for four minutes. I was as nervous as I could be that morning as I suited up and headed out the door. I drove from my home in Kingwood, and during the three-hour drive to Austin, I called my old UT friend Cameron Chandler to compare notes. This was the first time I'd called Cameron to coach me on what to say; as the campaign unfolded, I came to rely on him so much that we would start and end each day with a twenty-minute conversation, and I would call as many times in between as necessary to make sure I was saying things just right.

Cameron is a staunch Republican and I'm a Democrat, yet we didn't disagree on financial matters. That was just one more powerful indication to me that Texans are far more alike than we tend to think. He and I rarely disagreed on any policy, for that matter, and he never made a suggestion that seemed to me to be out of line with my own thinking. Nobody understands me politically as well as Cameron, and as a lifelong Republican, I knew he could help me get my point across in a way that would be acceptable to a true cross section of voters in Texas. As time went on, I began to call Cameron the Texas Oracle.

After the three-hour drive to Austin, and after reflecting on Cameron's wise counsel and with his help practicing my lines, I turned up at the studio for my first on-camera interview. I was shaking like a leaf. Even though it was taped and not live, I knew that it would be aired in its entirety and preserved forever. I had no idea what questions were coming my way or what it would be like trying to think on my feet in front of the cameras. Make a blunder, and my opponent would have material to cram into a TV commercial. And there were no do overs if I failed to hammer home an important point.

Jason, who does a lot of TV interviews, told me to relax. He said it was easy. I couldn't imagine, however, that I would ever become nonchalant about being on TV. I made a quick phone call to Dave Heller, my TV consultant, and he said, "Mike, relax! We're talking TV here.

The only thing that matters is how you look!" Dave's comment did wonders for my nerves.

Soon I was in the studio, mic'd up and ready. Countdown from six, five, four . . . cue the music. Then Paul introduced me and the topic, looking into the camera while I looked at Paul, and off we went.

As soon as I started answering his first question, I stopped being nervous. I've been in the hot seat many times as a merger and acquisition consultant, presenting to senior executives and board members, and I discovered that morning that TV isn't any more difficult.

The one thing I found difficult was remembering what the question had been after I launched into my answer. I was afraid that when I saw the tape, it would look as if I was being evasive. But I wasn't evading; I was simply struggling to perform, considering how new everything was.

My finest moment (or so I naively thought) came when Paul asked me to tell the viewers why I was running. Smooth as silk, and honest to a fault, without a hint of Texas twang or swagger (PwC had worked hard to wring both out of me), I explained myself: "I think we need a competitive political environment, and I think, from my perspective—the reason why I'm running—is that I think we need a watchdog. Someone who can hold the legislature accountable. Someone who knows how to do the analysis. Someone who's got the courage. We haven't had that, and I think I could be very useful to Texas."

A triumph, I thought as I finished my remarks. So suave, even when speaking off the cuff to rolling cameras. Dang, I'm good . . .

We wrapped, and Paul turned to me and said something along the lines of "Great job, you've done this before?" I thanked him and assured him that I hadn't.

But Jason was not happy at all. I was not getting even close to answering the "What's in it for me?" question. Jason explained that until you can answer that question, powerfully and right off the bat, voters aren't going to pay any attention to you. There wasn't a thing in what I'd said to motivate a soul to action, nothing that might get a tired factory worker, drinking a cold beer at the end of a long week while half watching the news and half daydreaming about deer season, to jump off the sofa and say, "Marge! Listen to this guy Collier!"

What was I expecting that worker to say? "He's a-gonna bring political competition! Why, he knows how to do the analysis! We've got to vote for him!"

Jason called my TV appearance that day "a teachable moment," and he walked me through a hypothetical interview.

"Let's say the interviewer says, 'So, as comptroller your job is to collect the taxes, right?' Then Collier, being Collier, says, 'Right. The comptroller collects the taxes, which takes the skill and experience of an accountant.' Which is just an awful answer. Instead, Collier the high-impact candidate should say, 'You're darn right, and if the comptroller is on the payroll of the special interest, you can bet he or she is going to look the other way, which means hardworking Texans are going to get screwed!'"

I have years of experience presenting in a business setting. There, your audience is listening very carefully for the "What's in it for me?" part, and they are well versed in the subject. Politics is completely different, and in a way that took me a long time to grasp. People watching the evening news don't have any idea who you are or what you're talking about. They have a million things on their mind, and you're just background noise. So rather than pick through your comments in order to spot the "What's in it for me?" part, they're far more likely to tune you out or go to the kitchen and grab a beer. You not only have to grab their attention, you also have to convince them in about three seconds that what's in it for them is so compelling that they'll go out and vote for you. In fact, to win an election, your message has to be so compelling that they go out and get their friends to vote for you too.

In other words, a technically correct answer does nothing. A statement that is crisp, compelling, and all about the listener is what matters. I could merely promise to manage the state's tax collection process with skill and efficiency—or I could promise to hunt down the tax cheaters so that hardworking families don't get penalized for being honest.

The challenge for me was going to be engaging an audience without being glib or misleading. Glibness is the lazy route politicians often take, and it's why we dislike politicians. It would take almost the entire campaign for me to fully grasp Jason's advice and to begin to find a new voice, one that retained substance and yet was instantly compelling to the listener.

Later that day Jason and I drove over to another local TV station to do an interview, and I turned up on the local evening news in Austin. My parents were watching, and they called to say they were thrilled to see me on TV. They said I did good. Not great, but good. I watched the segment on the local station's website, and sure enough I was smooth but, frankly, useless.

I also learned something vital about politics that day. The reporter opened the segment by saying something like "Wendy Davis's announcement that she is running for governor has already sent ripples through the political world as other candidates decide to jump into the race." *Wait a minute*, I thought to myself. I decided to run a long time ago, and it had nothing to do with Wendy. Why is this guy making my campaign about Wendy when my campaign is about me?

I knew right then that I was going to have to work doubly hard to get folks to pay attention to my campaign and not my negligible impact on Wendy's campaign. It was my first taste of what life would be like as a down-ballot candidate.

13

....

Signs of Life

Right after the TV announcement, Emily called me to say that a potential donor wanted to meet me for coffee. I arrived early at the W Hotel in Austin for the 8:00 a.m. meeting, bought some coffee and a newspaper, and found a place to sit and wait for the appointed hour. A few minutes before 8:00, I saw a man about my age, with an executive bearing (the donor was a retired CEO), looking around the hotel lobby, and I suspected it was him. I introduced myself, and we were seated a few minutes before Emily arrived.

This potential donor and I hit it off almost immediately. He was born in Midland, he is an economist by training, and he was the cofounder and CEO of a company that he took public a few years earlier. He seemed interested in politics for all the right reasons. He is a concerned citizen, and he had resources to back candidates that would improve our society. He was intrigued by my resume and campaign thesis. I was delighted to meet someone with his intellect, and we spent as much time talking about business as we did about politics.

He had been living in Virginia and had recently moved back to Texas, and he told me that he'd decided to get involved in Texas politics because the Republican Party's iron grip on the state was becoming a barrier to rational thinking and behavior in national politics. He had no dealings with the Texas comptroller and no ambition for himself. He's just a concerned citizen from Midland, and I welcomed his interest in my campaign.

In retirement, he had become an angel investor, a special breed of investor who helps start-up companies get on their feet. They provide seed money, expertise, introductions, and management advice.

It's something I hope to do when I'm finally retired. At the end of our breakfast meeting, he said he viewed his role in my campaign as an angel investor and that he would send some money before the end of the year. Needless to say, I was delighted.

It was the beginning of a very productive collaboration. This particular donor would become one of my top media advisors: He knew a lot about TV ads, having run a company that placed a lot of ads, and he was always good for some advice when I needed a second opinion on the things my TV team was telling me.

A good CFO knows that selecting good investors is one key to success. You don't just take money from anyone. You look for investors who bring strategic value, and I could tell he would be that kind of investor in my campaign. When his check arrived, it was a big one. But more importantly, as the campaign unfolded, he would prove to be an excellent sounding board and coach. He played the angel investor role to perfection.

....

My first post-announcement campaign event was a gala dinner in October in Galveston (with Election Day just over a year away) where all the Democratic Party county chairpersons and their teams were attending a conference. Zach and I drove from Houston and walked into the beautiful Moody Gardens banquet hall. I braced myself. Here I was, an official Democrat candidate for one of the state's top offices, yet I knew hardly anyone, I knew almost nothing about campaigning, and for years I had been a Republican businessman.

I had just entered the reception area, where hundreds of old friends were enjoying seeing one another. Before I was able to introduce myself to anyone, I heard a woman's voice booming over the crowd: "There he is! There's my fellow Longhorn Bandsman!" Charging toward me—and obviously willing to knock people over if they didn't get out of her way—was Donna Beth McCormick. She and I had spoken by telephone once, but we had never met in person. Donna Beth is a very active Democrat who at the time was president of the Texas Democratic Women's association. She was also a member of the Longhorn

Band (LHB) about ten years before I was, and we were both in the Longhorn Alumni Band. She's the kind of person who would walk through fire for anyone connected to LHB.

Donna Beth threw her arms around me and gave me a big hug, and then she forcefully spun me around and started introducing me to anyone and everyone. She never left my side, and by the time dinner was served, I'd met at least fifty people. Everyone was very polite, and many thanked me for running.

I got a sense, for the first time, of the surprising social-club aspect of being involved in a political party. I was also struck by how different a crowd of Democrats looked compared to a crowd of Republicans, of which I was more familiar. The Democrats were by far more jovial, and there were fewer indications of egos clashing. No gaudy displays of wealth or one-upmanship. Just good-natured, friendly, humble people. I also noticed that there were relatively very few middle-aged white men who looked as if they might be from the professional or executive ranks. That surprised me, but it didn't bother me at all.

As we entered the main ballroom to be seated for dinner, I saw former governor Mark White shaking hands and getting ready to take his seat near the front of the hall.

You can't miss Mark White. He's taller than six feet, and he has a shock of white hair, a beaming smile, and a booming voice. And he has more energy and packs more punch than most people I have ever known. We'd already spoken once by telephone (a conversation recounted in the introduction to this book), but I had never met him in person, and I was looking forward to it.

Donna Beth pulled my arm in the direction of the governor, and by the time I got to his table, with most of the three hundred or so guests starting to take their seats behind us, I stuck my hand out and said hello. When he realized it was me, he made a real show out of shaking my hand and slapping me on the shoulder. He grabbed my arm and didn't let go as he walked me around his table introducing me to folks. I had the distinct impression that he wanted everyone in the banquet hall to see that he, the most senior and most accomplished politician in the Texas Democratic Party, was behind this unknown, upstart comptroller candidate.

I soon found an empty seat, and I introduced myself to everyone at the table. I was surprised to discover that very few people knew who I was or that I was running for comptroller, despite the fact that we had announced my candidacy to several news outlets and had pushed my introductory video out to tens of thousands of Democrats via e-media.

While I was waiting in the buffet line, a small commotion erupted. A gregarious and energetic woman, accompanied by an assistant, came weaving through the crowd toward me. Everyone knew her: It was Texas Senator Leticia Van de Putte from San Antonio, a leader of the Hispanic caucus, and now the candidate for lieutenant governor. She knew who I was, and she spun me around to pose for a picture that her assistant took on her iPhone. Then she took back the phone and said, "I'm tweeting this out: Mike Collier for Comptroller!"

My jaw dropped to the floor. Here was one of the highest-profile leaders of the Democratic Party endorsing me, and we had just met. This will go a long way, I thought, to discourage other Democrats from running against me in the primary.

I grabbed a plate of food and found my way to my seat. The program for the evening was something I would grow very accustomed to over the course of a long campaign. A moderator would introduce a series of elected officials or candidates, and each would speak for five or ten minutes and do his or her best to leave an impression and inspire the audience. Then the star of the program would show up and try to deliver a stem-winder to get people genuinely enthused about the election and ready to work for months to turn people out at the polls.

As the program started, I thought this would be an important test. I had studied the issues carefully and was very comfortable running as a Democrat. I had been making calls all summer to potential donors, and I wasn't running into resistance from any Democrats who knew that I had just joined the party. But I didn't know what to expect from a good old-fashioned political rally. Were the speakers going to rail against the business community? Would I still feel at home in the Democratic Party after tonight? I remember being happy that I didn't have a speaking role: I could sit, listen, and then decide what to do if things didn't feel right to me.

What came next, though, was terrific. The speakers were passionate, but they were sensible through and through. I found their rhetoric to be very conversational, almost as though two friends were talking over politics while in line at the grocery store. There was no hateful speech, and none of the over-the-top histrionics that comes with Republican speechmaking, where the implication is always that if you aren't a Republican, you must be bent on ruining everything we hold dear. There was far more substance in what the Democratic speakers had to say than I had heard from any Republican politician in years. The speakers were upbeat and genuinely enthusiastic about the possibilities of fulfillment from work in the political arena. It was very uplifting.

Not every speaker that evening was skilled, but everyone seemed to see the world the way I did. It felt like a continuation of the same conversation I'd had many months ago with the Kingwood Democrats when they told me there was room in the Democratic Party for many points of view, as long as everyone was working honestly and thoughtfully toward solving society's problems. I felt a real kinship with the Democrats that evening, one that went beyond just the support they were giving to my campaign.

Finally, the star of the evening was introduced. About twenty minutes before she was to speak, Wendy Davis arrived in the hall and took her seat. The rest of us were eating, but we put down our silverware and stood to applaud her entry.

This was the first time I had ever seen Wendy in person. She was very attractive, and I thought she seemed very genuine and kind. Later the press would attack her for being less than genuine, but my instincts are fairly reliable, and over the course of a very long campaign, she never gave me any reason to doubt her. I would pick up the newspaper or go online and read what people were saying about Wendy, and I would think to myself: I've met Wendy and she's not the least bit like any of these things they are saying. I thought from the beginning—and still believe to this day—that Wendy would have made a thoughtful, sincere, and effective governor.

Wendy took the podium and delivered a good speech. The writing was good, and she looked and sounded very poised. I could see her as a highly effective business executive delivering a presentation to a corporate board of directors. And when she finished, upbeat music was piped in ("Girl on Fire") to whip up the crowd.

The volume on the music was turned down, however, making it almost inaudible. And the lighting was terrible: It was the usual hotel ballroom medium-to-poor lighting, not the brilliant lighting that I knew instinctively would give Wendy a rock star presence. This was the first indication I had that Democrats aren't as good as the Republicans at stagecraft. That's because Republicans in Texas rely solely on stagecraft and fluff, which lets them stay away from discussing the issues in a substantive way. Just think how effective we Democrats might be if we mastered stagecraft and were substantive to boot!

Despite the lame music and dreadful lighting, an enormous crowd gathered to take pictures and see how close they could get to Wendy. She was clearly a magnet, and I was looking forward to getting to know her as the campaign went on—and with any luck, we'd serve together in Austin.

As I drove home, I realized how much progress I had made. I had a former governor coaching me, a serious donor backing me, and the tacit endorsement of one of the highest-profile Democratic politicians in the state. I knew I had a very long way to go, and I still had very little idea of what to expect, but I felt a sense of momentum. The whole thing began to feel real. It was a good feeling.

14

....

Any Stump Will Do

Around this time, late October (and roughly one year before Election Day), a few invitations to speak started coming in from Democratic club presidents who knew Zach. Otherwise, there really wasn't much to do except make phone calls.

Whenever I did venture out to meet with a club, I enjoyed the experience without exception. The Democratic clubs are social clubs, and they typically meet once a month in the evenings at a local restaurant. It was sometimes a little awkward at first, speaking to people who were eating at a restaurant, sometimes with other diners within earshot. But like everything else about campaigning, I got used to it.

These early appearances allowed me to begin learning the finer art of stump speaking. I always started my talk by explaining why I was running and providing an overview of the financial issues I was concerned about. I felt very much at home, although when we opened up for questions, I invariably found myself getting asked about matters I had never heard of. I was new to politics, and my audiences were political activists who knew a whole lot more than me. But if I didn't know the answer, I simply said that I didn't know the answer. It's what we do in business (although in business you hope this doesn't happen too often).

I was encouraged to see that Democrats liked me, and I heard over and over that my stump speech was "refreshing." In fact, it was uncanny how often I heard that word on the campaign trail—at least once a day, and I'm not exaggerating. I wasn't sure what was so refreshing about what I was saying, but I began to suspect that folks enjoyed hearing about the issues in a substantive way and that they were delighted when I didn't bluff my way through an answer. I really felt like I was on to something.

From late October until late January, I made about ten appearances at club meetings, mostly in Houston, although I made a couple of trips to Dallas and Austin. Otherwise I called donors, as many as I could each day. There were very few other activities, and I was beginning to marvel at how tedious it all was. Painfully tedious, to be frank. I asked Demi to keep an updated "Countdown to Election Day" on the white board in our office. My stated reason was to keep everyone focused on using every minute of every day to win the election. My real reason was that I didn't think I could possibly stand the tedium, and I found it soothing to remind myself that I had only a few hundred days of it left.

....

January marked the beginning of primary season, and I started to receive invitations to attend candidate forums and other speaking engagements around the state. I had done enough Democratic club meetings to become comfortable on the stump, but the invitations now were more serious, and once again I felt as if I was wandering into the unknown.

My first such speech was to a group of Democratic lawyers in Austin. Jason and Emily, who had not yet heard me do any stump speaking, came to the event. I spoke for about ten minutes, talking about the need to "take politics out and put competence in" to the comptroller's office. I talked about how our state had made huge cuts to education on the basis of a bad forecast and how quarterly forecasts would ensure that it never happened again. I talked about Texas Performance Reviews. And I talked about the fact that we as a state were taking on debt and why that wasn't good.

The crowd was friendly, receptive, and engaged. I heard the word "refreshing" a few times. I thought I had done well.

But Jason's response was muted, to say the least. All he would say was that I had a long way to go. He didn't elaborate, and we didn't have time to go off alone and really talk about what he meant and what I ought to do differently. I figured it was the same problem that Jason had signaled back when I did the TV interviews to make my initial announcement. My stump speech was a technical presentation: refreshing, substantive, interesting, but nothing to get excited about. There was no "What's in it for me?" It would be months before I grasped that concept. Darn good thing I didn't have a primary opponent, because I would surely have lost to someone with more experience.

Candidate forums were plentiful, and for the most part they were put together by local Democratic organizations. The purpose of these forums was to let candidates who had a primary competitor make their case to the voters. Those of us without primary competitors were nevertheless invited, and it was a great opportunity for me to start moving around, meeting people, and improving my stump speech.

The atmosphere of the candidate forums was a bit like a school pep rally. Held in a community hall or gymnasium, people would mill around ahead of time and candidates would work the crowd, shaking hands and handing out "push cards": little flyers with the candidate's name and picture and a few words about what they stood for. Most candidates had custom name tags with their logos on them so that they could be walking advertisements. I had neither a name tag nor a push card. I simply didn't think I needed either as the putative nominee for the fourth most powerful position in the state. With hindsight, I realize this was a mistake. People who come to candidate forums expect their candidates to have name tags and push cards, and you don't want to disappoint the people you hope will go out there and work very hard for you.

I got the impression that the activists who turn up at candidate forums really enjoy their role in politics. These people know one another and have worked together, sometimes for many election cycles, to help candidates get elected. Of course, none of them knew who I was yet, but when we did meet, they seemed genuinely happy that I was there, and I heard "Thank you for running" so many times I could hardly believe it.

I often wondered whether Republicans heard "Thank you for running" on the campaign trail. After all, they are deeply entrenched and getting their way on most things. As a Democrat in Texas, you know it's going to be hard to win, but you also know that you're trying to dislodge a Republican political machine that puts power ahead of sound policy. And you know that someone's got to challenge them—and the activists who work with you know it as well. When they thanked me, it was always heartfelt.

I am often asked whether, if I had it all to do over again, I would switch back and run as a Republican. My answer is always "Why on earth would I do that?"

....

I could sense that Wendy and Leticia were the real stars of the election cycle, and I was simply a supporting actor at best. I didn't mind it one bit. I was a rookie, all I ever talked about were financial issues, and I really didn't think anyone would find me or my topic all that exciting even if I tried to be a star.

I enjoyed getting to know the rest of my supporting cast around this time: Sam Houston (no relation to Texas's founding father), who was running for attorney general; Steve Brown, who was running for Texas railroad commissioner (which regulates the oil and gas industry); and John Cook, who was running for land commissioner. Sam and Steve were terrific candidates, very conventional in their approach, and a pleasure to hang out with. John Cook was fun, too, but a lot less conventional. He was much taller than the rest of us, he always wore a western outfit, and he carried a guitar everywhere he went. After his stump speech, he would whip out his guitar and sing a customized version of Tom Petty's "I Won't Back Down." It was a real spectacle.

I learned from John Cook, and listening to his singing, that stump speaking is all about repetition. John said the exact same thing every time, and he sang the exact same song every time. Hundreds of times. I learned that candidates must never fear being repetitive. In fact, repetition is the *sine qua non* of electoral politics. The chances of people hearing a candidate more than once are slim. And if they do, they are probably political junkies, and they'll understand. The alternative to repetition is to treat each stump speech as something new, as if you're engaged in an ongoing dialogue with the audience. The problem is that the audience changes with every speech. The candidate might enjoy the dialogue, but no two voters will hear the same message. And in politics that's a disaster. John and his western outfit and his guitar and his crazy Tom Petty adaptation drove the point home more forcefully than any consultant's advice ever could.

....

There was another down-ballot candidate running for agriculture commissioner named Jim Hogan. None of us had ever met him, and he never came out on the campaign trail. He filed for office and stayed home. We all resented the fact that we were breaking our backs to try to win the election, and if we managed to do it, Hogan would cruise in with us. He would have been an awfully lonely fellow in government had we won.

Excluding Jim Hogan, we began referring to ourselves as "The Down-Ballot Boys," as if we were the backup band to the lead singers Wendy and Leticia. I always enjoyed the heck out of that.

There were other candidates as well. Not every candidate who spoke at the candidate forums had poise, or made good speeches, or gave the impression they were strong leaders. But all the candidates, good or bad, seemed to me to be in the game because they cared about their state and because they wanted to be part of an important and worthwhile process. Many would have been much stronger if they'd had the money to hire professionals, yet money becomes very hard to raise the farther down ballot you go. But we all cherished one another, and I can honestly say that I never once saw egos clash among the Democratic candidates on the campaign trail.

....

About this time I was invited to fly to a West Texas town, where I'd meet with the Democratic Party county chairwoman and attend a fund-raiser in my honor. The flight, hotel, and meals would cost about

$300, and I figured I would easily make up this amount in donations from the event. I happily agreed.

The chairwoman, a senior citizen whom I'll call Ms. Green, met me at the airport, and she was as sweet as she could be. She gave me a driving tour of the town, and she mentioned that she had lost her husband some time back. We talked up a storm, and finally we made our way to a nearby law office where a conference room had been set up for the event. Two of her lady friends were arranging homemade cookies, fruit, cheese, and lemonade. Because we were early, we chatted about politics, then weather, and then aches and pains. I spend as much time as I can with my parents, and I did the same with my grandparents while they were living, and I don't mind the fact that old age is creeping up on me too. I was enjoying the conversation thoroughly.

The event was scheduled to start at 5:00 p.m. Folks seemed to be running late, so the four of us kept chatting. By 6:00 p.m., two guests had arrived. By 7:00 p.m., they'd gone. By 7:30 p.m., the four of us packed up the untouched cookies, biscuits, fruit, cheese, and orange juice, and I helped load them back into the car. My hosts were embarrassed, but it didn't bother me one bit.

That's when I learned that Ms. Green had reserved a table for two at a local restaurant. She smiled very sweetly when I said I'd rather sit at the bar. A happily married man must keep up appearances. We had a wonderful dinner and a fine conversation, and I felt almost apologetic when I called my wife that night to say I had been on a dinner date.

I would see Ms. Green a few more times as the campaign unfolded, and each time I'd get a big hug and see that sweet smile. I never told her that a handful of other fund-raisers in rural Texas towns turned out the same way. Failed fund-raisers aren't something a candidate concerned about appearances wants to advertise, but they happen. People will always turn out to have a look at the governor candidate. Not so for an unknown CPA running for comptroller. Sometimes you come home empty-handed. But if you are lucky, you get a fine dinner date with the likes of Ms. Green, and a friend for life.

Diversity and Gay Marriage

Diversity was the order of the day when I arrived at Exxon in the 1980s. It kind of surprised me, frankly. I expected Exxon to be concerned with producing oil and making money, not creating a diverse workforce. And Exxon wasn't alone: All my friends who took jobs with big companies that summer found the same thing. None of us objected, but many of us found it mildly perplexing. Why would big companies—all of them—be so magnanimous when their job is to make money?

It wasn't until I joined PwC years later that I had my "Aha!" moment.

I was sent to a training session, and diversity was on the agenda. The instructors zeroed in on the business imperative. Talented people, the kind who run businesses, have a tendency to see talent when they see themselves. In other words, a white man who is looking to hire someone might unconsciously look for the best white man he can find. He may overlook a better employee for no reason other than the other employee has different skin color, or is a woman, or is gay.

Consider the implications for a company's profitability. Let's say a division manager is free to hire anyone he wants, and let's say that manager has an unconscious bias toward hiring people who are just like him. If he is a white man, he will hire the best white men he can find. When he's done, he'll look at his team and believe he has the most competitive team in his industry.

Now imagine that there's a rival manager who's comfortable hiring and working with people who look different and who come from different backgrounds. This second manager will hire the very best people he can find, not just the very best white men he can find. In so doing, his team will be more competitive.

And it goes beyond individual talent. Walk into a meeting where everyone likes sports, for example, and you'll hear sports analogies being used to help the team grapple with business issues. Walk into a meeting where some people like sports, but others like literature, and still others like history, and you'll hear all sorts of analogies and experiences being used to grapple with business issues. It will be a much richer conversation, and much more valuable ideas will emerge.

One of the older PwC partners at the training session recalled the time when his office admitted its first female partner. The regular partners' meeting had become quite a boys' club, and when a woman joined for the first time, the culture inside the meeting changed dramatically. The pattern of speaking (and thinking) was completely shaken up. Participants were more thoughtful, more professional, and more thorough. And the quality of the decisions they made together was much better.

In the PwC training session, as we spent the day talking about diversity in this context, it became crystal clear to me that diversity has an amazing impact on the quality and success of a business. Once the instructors had explained the issue to me in terms I could understand, I immediately became a champion of diversity in the workplace.

In fact, I became a big supporter of diversity not just in business but in all things. Diversity contributes to the quality and success of any human endeavor. One PwC partner from Malaysia, Khoo Eng Choo, said, "We will find unity in our diversity." Eng Choo was a pretty cosmic thinker, and although I admired him, I sometimes didn't understand him. But on this point, I got it.

Almost every big business in America now takes diversity very seriously, and they have programs to ensure that their workforces are truly diverse. If you work in a big business for a long time, you can't help but come away with a genuine trust and respect for people because they are people. You stop focusing on men versus women, or white versus black, or straight versus gay. We're just people.

....

Just as our attitudes toward diversity and political correctness have evolved over the years, our attitudes toward gays and gay marriage have evolved as well, and I am no exception. Near the start of my campaign, when Jason first asked me about my opinion on gay marriage, I told him that when I was thirteen my father didn't sit me down and say, "Mike, this is the year you have to pick whether you like boys or girls." When I came of age, there was no question that for me it was girls! From my first real crush on a brown-haired girl in third grade to my wife Suzanne, whom I adore, there's been no doubt for me.

(Continued . . .)

I'm sure it's the same for boys who are drawn to boys and for girls who are drawn to girls. As far as I am concerned, we're far more alike than we are not alike, and as such I see no reason to deny gay couples the same marriage rights and benefits that Suzanne and I, as a straight couple, have thoroughly enjoyed over the years.

Around the time New York first recognized same-sex marriage, I was traveling and I picked up the Sunday edition of the *New York Times*. The marriage section was full of announcements from gay couples who had waited a long time for this moment. Reading their announcements gave me warm feelings about my own marriage: The announcements reminded me of how much Suzanne and I enjoyed our wedding day, and how much it meant to us to have friends and family come out and show their support. Contrary to the prediction from some politicians, seeing gay couples announcing their commitment to each other did not pose a threat to my marriage. Instead, I hoped the new marriages I was reading about would be as long and as joyful as ours.

15

....

The Republican Candidates

While I was trotting around attending candidate forums, and having quite a lot of fun doing it, the Republican primaries were well under way. They had become a spectacle, and needless to say, I was studying the Republicans with great interest.

There were four Republican candidates running for comptroller.

Debra Medina was a small-business person from Wharton who was about my age and who had run for governor as an independent in the previous election cycle. She did well in that race, and she seemed like a good person, but she had surprised everyone by turning up as a Republican comptroller candidate.

Raul Torres was a CPA from Corpus Christi who had been a member of the Texas House of Representatives. He campaigned as an outsider and as the first CPA to run for state comptroller. He also seemed like a good person, and I was hoping he would win so that Texas would have its first CPA as comptroller, whether that was Mr. Torres or me.

Harvey Hilderbran was a state representative from Kerrville and about my age. He was tall and handsome, he had good ol' boy charm, and he had a reform agenda in mind. He didn't have any accounting or finance experience to speak of, so I wasn't afraid to run against him. But he seemed like a reasonable fellow, he looked the part, and I figured he'd be the hardest to beat.

Glenn Hegar rounded out the field.

The youngest of thirty-one Texas senators while in office, Glenn Hegar's landowning family helped him win a newly created Texas House seat when he was in his early thirties. As he described things, "a new state representative seat opened, and he had some time available,"[1] so he stumbled into office. He didn't seem to have much interest in what the comptroller's office did, nor was there much evidence that he was trying to figure it out. He thought Susan Combs had done a "tremendous job,"[2] which told me that Hegar wasn't a serious leader. Hegar's only work experience, other than helping in the family farming operation, had been serving in the Texas legislature. Yet on the stump he told everyone that serving in the legislature "in no way, shape, form, or fashion qualifies a person in and of itself to be comptroller."[3] Problem is, he never said in a substantive way what did qualify him to be comptroller.

My team had assumed the race would go into a runoff between Hilderbran and Hegar because they were sitting legislators who had access to big corporate money. Many of the newspapers endorsed Hilderbran because he'd paid some attention to the job he was campaigning for. Hegar, in contrast, didn't seem to care. But the Republican Party higher-ups had Hegar sponsor the anti-abortion legislation that Wendy Davis filibustered against. This would no doubt cause the hard Right to swoon over Hegar. It looked to me as though the political machine had maneuvered their man into position.

The more interesting, or should I say disturbing, statewide contest was for lieutenant governor. Everyone (including Team Collier) was paying very close attention because the outcome of that race (for the most powerful position in Texas politics) would tell us just how far the Republican Party had careened to the right. As a Texan, I was far more concerned about the lieutenant governor race than I was about the comptroller race, even though I was a comptroller candidate.

There were two main combatants in the Republican lieutenant governor primary: David Dewhurst and his Tea Party–backed rival, state senator Dan Patrick. Dewhurst had been a successful businessman before entering politics. He is a likable, intelligent, hardworking man with sensible ideas. He tried to run for United States Senate in 2012, but he was taken down by Ted Cruz, a smartest-kid-in-the-class lawyer who titillated the hard Right of the party with fiery, substance-free nonsense. Dewhurst was left badly wounded, so Dan Patrick, also a fiery, nonsense-peddling opportunist, went for the kill.

In stark contrast to Dewhurst's career as a successful business-man, Patrick had driven his business into the ground[4] before stumbling into a demagogue's utopia: talk radio. He went on to become Texas's worst state senator, according to *Texas Monthly* magazine, for being an unhelpful ideologue and bully.[5] Even my Republican friends were appalled by Dan Patrick's campaign. One called it putrid. Dan Patrick was clearly the wrong man for the job, but only ten percent of Republicans in Texas participate in the primaries, and these are the voters who seem to be most easily taken in.

In a close race, Dan Patrick won the primary. In a strange way I felt that this was a good sign, because it had to mean that Democrats would win the general election come November.

....

In contrast to the lieutenant governor race, the Republican race for comptroller seemed almost inconsequential. But it wasn't without some interesting moments.

The Associated Press ran a story that Hegar had filed an incomplete (and therefore misleading) financial disclosure form with the Texas Ethics Commission.[6] Every politician and candidate for office has to file a statement showing, among other things, where their money comes from. Hegar didn't disclose that his wife was a high-powered attorney who brought home a lot of bacon. I figured Hegar didn't want Republicans to know that his wife was a trial attorney. He filed a revised form, but only after he was caught.

Then, near the end of the primary season, Hegar put his first advertisement on TV. It showed him at a gun range firing an assault weapon, saying very little about the comptroller's office. He then ran a second commercial that featured his children saying what they wanted to be when they grew up. The commercial ended with Glenn saying that he wanted to be the comptroller when he grew up. I think he missed the irony.

....

The week before the primary, both Hegar and I attended a candidate forum in The Woodlands, about forty-five miles from my home in Kingwood. I arrived at the event and was surprised to see the venue full of Republican-red buttons and banners and signs and clothing. (I shouldn't have been surprised since The Woodlands is a very Republican enclave.) It was like going to a college football game at the home stadium of a rival whose school color is red. There was an unmistakably arrogant vibe in the room. Until then, all the candidate forums I had attended had been hosted by Democratic organizations, which were much more fun and friendly and not the least bit caustic.

Mr. Hegar was the only Republican candidate for comptroller at the event. I didn't know whether he would be my ultimate opponent, but still I felt very uneasy about meeting him in person. This politics thing was so new to me. Hegar wasn't uneasy at all, however. He was smiling broadly as people came up to the table he had set up against the wall, along with all the other candidate tables, where he spread out push cards, buttons, and who knows what else.

I didn't have a table at the event, and I was glad I didn't. I was reminded of the hideous scene from an energy merger and acquisition conference where accounting firms were allowed to set up tables in the foyer to sell their wares. One of my competitors had a table manned by a doofus who just stood there, occasionally fiddling with something on his BlackBerry to appear busy. Nobody at the conference cared about him or his accounting firm. He was just standing there looking like a doofus. If I'd had a table at this uber-Republican event, I would have been the doofus.

When it came time for candidate speeches, I moved to the front, as did Hegar, and I introduced myself to him. He seemed genuinely pleased to meet me, and he treated me as if I was doing a generous service to my community, but not as someone he had to worry about even slightly. Hegar knew that as a Republican, all he had to do was win his primary. If he did, he could go back to the farm and hang out with the family for a few months until he was sworn in as comptroller. I, of course, wanted to make things much more difficult for him if I could. But in our brief and pleasant conversation, none of that came up. It was just a few "Nice to meet you" exchanges, and then it was time to get ready.

When they lined us up, Hegar and I stood next to each other. As we stood together waiting for our time to speak, he stepped out of line and sat in a chair in the corner. It looked kind of odd, but then I realized that he didn't want people to notice that he wasn't the tallest candidate. Hegar might not know much about finance or accounting, but he displayed a prodigious talent for politics, having the savvy to sit in the corner when his opponent was taller than he was. Maybe that's what qualified him to be the chief financial officer of a $100 billion operation.

We were told we each had two minutes to speak and Hegar would go first. When he took the stage, he began by saying that he was from Hockley, a little town near Katy, which is so small that if you blink your eyes you might miss it. He said he was a sixth-generation Texan. He said he'd married a woman who was also a sixth-generation Texan. They have three children, and boy, it's hard to believe how fast they grow. He said he wanted to be comptroller. I don't remember him saying anything else.

As I listened, I felt my brain starting to go numb.

When it was my turn, I told the crowd that I, too, wanted to be our next comptroller. But rather than just babble about my hometown and family and sixth-generation Texan, I turned my attention to the key issues we face as a state: We must invest in education, transportation, and water; we must not become addicted to debt; and we must not raise taxes. We were falling well short of these objectives, I said, and we needed a real CFO. I touched on my resume and the steps I would take to drive results, and I thanked everyone and asked for their vote.

My sense was that this audience of pure Republicans was completely indifferent to me and my pitch. They might have noticed that I had talked about the issues and Hegar hadn't. But they'd also clearly noticed I wasn't a Republican and Hegar was, and therefore I wasn't even supposed to be there. The applause was polite, but the body language and facial expressions told me that my talking about the issues had taken time away from their Republican heroes talking about a whole lot of nothing.

I didn't know it at the time, but that brief showing at The Woodlands—with Hegar saying nothing and me trying to discuss the issues—would be representative of the entire general election campaign.

I descended the speaker's platform when I was finished and realized that I had to squeeze between Hegar's little campaign table and the crowd to find my way to the exit. As I walked past, I reached out to shake Hegar's hand, and I said, "Good luck on primary day."

He smiled broadly. "Thank you. And best of luck to you!" Just then his smile turned sly, and I knew exactly what he was thinking: Fighting against the political machine is futile.

As I walked to my car, I had three thoughts: I was happy this event was over, I don't like politicians, and I would rather fight the machine than be beholden to it.

....

Early voting brought the first opportunity to see my name on an official ballot. It was an eerie feeling but also an exciting one. Zach, Demi, and I drove to a polling place near the campaign office at lunchtime and walked in together. We told the monitor at the door that we were Democrats, and she directed us to the Democratic election judges who set the process in motion. I handed the judge my driver's license, she looked up my name, and she had me sign the register. She had no idea I was on the ballot, which surprised me. Here I was running for a powerful statewide post, just a few places down from the governor, in my own hometown, and the Democrat running the primary had never heard my name. I was beginning to see how much effort goes into building name recognition in a state as massive as Texas.

As we were walking back to the car, Zach told me that a man had approached him and asked him whether he should vote Democrat or Republican. Zach said he pointed to me and said, "Well, that guy is my boss, and he's a Democrat." Evidently the man had looked at me and then said, "He looks honest. I'll vote Democrat."

....

On primary election night, Hegar did so much better than Hilderbran that he was teetering on winning without a runoff. After a day or two of haggling over recounts, Hilderbran ultimately conceded. In his graceful concession statement, he said that he was pleased that Hegar was going to implement Hilderbran's reform agenda, the Taxpayer Rights Plan.[7] I found that to be comical. When in politics does the loser "donate" his platform to the winner because the winner didn't bother to develop his own platform in the first place? That's machine politics for you.

I watched the primary returns that night at my parents' home in Georgetown. They had been enjoying watching the campaign unfold, and when I was in the Austin area I often stayed with them, having made a note to spend more time there, win or lose, because none of us are getting any younger. As the evening wore on, I found it difficult to conceal my distress at what I was seeing on TV. Hilderbran had a platform, he was sensible, and he was endorsed by many of the newspapers. As far as I could tell, Hegar did nothing and pretty obviously knew nothing, and several of the newspapers had dismissed him for that reason. But Hegar was a Tea Party darling, with anti-abortion credentials and gun range ads and "Vote for my daddy" TV commercials. And on that basis he was going to win.

I went to bed that night thinking that Texas politics was a complete waste of my time.

Unfortunately, I woke up the next morning as determined as ever to fight. If I could help bring a competitive political environment to Texas—if Republican voters had to concern themselves with whether their nominee would win the general election—then Republicans would never have nominated the likes of Glenn Hegar and Dan Patrick. The Republican primary outcome told me that we needed political competition now more than ever, so I knew I'd better get out there and keep fighting.

16

·····················

The Collier-Brigham-Smith #1

For months leading up to the primary, Jason had hoped that Hegar and Hilderbran would find themselves in a runoff election. They'd have to exhaust their campaign war chests fighting each other, and there would be high negatives around whoever emerged as the winner. Instead, Hegar had won outright, and that sent Jason into a deep funk about my prospects for success.

He called me a day or two after the primary. "Look, Mike, there is no way you are going to win. I think you should consider changing course."

I didn't like the sound of that. But I knew that Jason knew a whole lot more than I did, and he'd never failed to give me excellent, honest advice.

"You're going to get beaten badly," he explained, "and that will be the end of your political career. Dead before you even get started. If you are serious about politics, you should turn this campaign into your preliminary bid for Houston city controller. You were going to start there anyway, right? So think this over: The incumbent you had planned to run against is term limited, and it'll be an open seat in 2015. You are now a Democrat, and that will serve you well in Houston city politics. You could raise $1 million for this election, spend every penny of that money on TV commercials in Houston, and develop a reputation and a fiscal-responsibility message that voters will remember when you launch your bid for Houston controller in 2015."

My reaction was swift and visceral: Absolutely no way.

I reminded Jason that the general election was a long way off and that anything could happen between now and then. Plus, now that I'd discovered how poorly Texas as a state was managing its money, I'd become committed to working on the problem at the state level. Once committed to a course, I'm as stubborn as a mule. What was more, taking money from people to fund a statewide campaign and using it to secure a municipal office was the kind of slippery maneuver a politician would do. Nope. Not even going to consider it.

I suspected that Jason had discussed this with other members of the team before calling me, and I thought it best to let everyone know where I stood. So I sat down and wrote a strong note to everyone on Team Collier. I told them we were going to run this race, starting immediately, as if the election were two weeks out and we were twenty points down. We were not going to give even a moment's thought to the idea that we couldn't win. I quoted a famous nineteenth-century general: "My center is giving way, my right is in retreat, situation excellent, I attack!"[1]

The memo seemed to brighten everyone's mood. I was learning that, more than anything, consultants want to work with candidates who refuse to lose.

....

Early the next morning, I was taking a walk through my neighborhood when a friend who was driving to work pulled up next to me, rolled down the window, and said, "Hey, Mike, I like how you're running your campaign!"

"How's that?" I asked.

He said, "You aren't doing anything!"

He wasn't being sarcastic. Since I hadn't put anything up on TV (there was no need, considering I had no primary challenger), he must have thought that I was playing possum or something. Of course, my strategy wasn't to play possum. I had just sent out a note to the team saying that we would steal the initiative and never give it up. But the incident caused me to think, *Just what can I do to steal the initiative?* The press wasn't interested (yet) in the comptroller race, so we weren't getting any newspaper coverage. The state is so large that you can't physically campaign with much impact—or at least not as

Fixing Our Broken Property Tax System

Texas doesn't have an income tax, which is terrific. Instead we rely heavily on a property tax system, which is a headache. But just because it's a headache doesn't mean we should get rid of it. Unless we want an income tax (we don't), or a European-style value-added tax (we don't), or a greater than twenty percent sales tax (we don't), then we have to make the property tax system work.

Contrary to popular belief, the property tax is a purely local tax. The state of Texas does not—

- Collect one penny of property tax;
- Spend one penny of property tax;
- Set any property tax rate;
- Perform a single property tax appraisal; or
- Settle a single property appraisal dispute.

Every one of these tasks is done locally, for the benefit of local governments. Properties are appraised by one of more than 250 appraisal districts around the state. Appraisal disputes are settled by local appraisal review boards. Tax rates are set by local entities such as school boards, city councils, and county commissioners. The taxes are then gathered locally and used for local purposes.

There are a few things the state can do, acting through the legislature, to influence the process. The legislature can write the rules on appraisals and appeals so that those rules are uniform across the state. They can exempt certain properties or parts of properties, such as agricultural lands or homesteads, to achieve a public policy goal. They can even place limits on how high local authorities can set the tax rates, if they think locals can't be trusted.

All of these state powers fall under the heading of protecting taxpayers from abuse and keeping the system fair. Otherwise, property tax is all about local, not state, government.

And that's the way we want it! Texans have a strong preference for keeping things local. We elect our school boards, our city councils, and our county commissioners, and they report to us. We can go to the board, council, and commissioners court meetings. We can demand explanations. We can raise our voices. And we can throw the bums out if they do a bad job or squander our money. That's our job, not the state's job. We don't need or want Austin's overreach into our affairs.

In that light, the state has only one role as far as I am concerned: to keep things fair.

Unfortunately, the track record of the Republicans running our state at keeping things fair is absolutely pitiful.

State law is supposed to protect property owners from an unfair appraisal. The law is called the equal and uniform statute, which says that if a property owner can show that someone else's property is comparable to his, yet his property is appraised at a higher value, his property value should be lowered accordingly. The concept is fabulous, and we should keep it. But the law is poorly written (some say intentionally so), and property owners with the money can hire a legal team to "game the system" and have their property value reduced to ridiculously low levels.

Here's how it works: Say you own a large downtown skyscraper and your appraisal district says your property is worth $500 million. You go out and find a property on the other side of town—older, uglier, and in a worse location—that is appraised at $400 million. You sue your local appraisal district, and your lawyers do their best to stretch everyone's imagination to claim that your property is comparable to the other property. Therefore, it must only be worth $400 million too. Because the law is vague, courts often rule in favor of the property owner and against the appraisal district. Often the appraisal district will give in for no other reason than the judge might very well require the district to pay the legal tab for the property owner.

It happens all the time, and it's very well documented. Some call it the property tax death spiral, because once your building is knocked down to $400 million, someone with a $600 million building across town points to your building, and he gets his knocked down to $400 million. And around and around it goes.

It's brutally unfair, and everyone knows it. If the law—for example—tightened up the written definition of "comparable," this wouldn't happen.

(Continued . . .)

But the law is very poorly written, and Republicans in the legislature refuse to fix it, thanks to campaign money from the owners of the large commercial and industrial properties. Even Rick Perry tried to fix the problem, but the legislature just won't budge. Republican legislators come cheap in Texas.

In 2006, the largest appraisal districts in Texas estimated that the property tax loophole was $4 billion annually.[4] That's $4 billion more that homeowners and small businesses had to pay each year because the big corporate property owners were exploiting the loophole. And that was a decade ago. Many observers believe that the problem has gotten much worse.

If the appraisal district estimation from 2006 is accurate, and if the problem has indeed gotten worse, then the state is failing miserably in the one role it has regarding property taxes: keeping them fair.

If you want to have a really good laugh, listen to the nonsensical spin that politicians use to defend themselves. First, they say that commercial and industrial properties are, in fact, appraised at market value (although they never offer proof of this). Then—and here is where it gets hilarious—they argue that because properties are already valued properly, we don't want laws to ensure that they be valued properly! And the owners of the big corporate properties shell out hundreds of thousands of dollars to protect this loophole, while at the same time they say there isn't a loophole to protect.

An old, grizzled auditor once told me, "Mike, I get lied to for a living!" Well, I cut my teeth as an auditor, and I know when I'm being lied to. Until lawmakers address this issue honestly, they are only mocking their fellow Texans when they talk about property tax reform.

And that's exactly what happened in 2015 when the Republican legislature gave the average Texas homeowner a whopping $10 per month property tax break, one that will vanish as property values continue to rise, leaving the multibillion-dollar loophole available to their corporate paymasters wide open. Some Republicans then had the audacity to characterize their work as "true property tax reform."[5] It was a head fake as far as I am concerned, and a disgraceful one at that.

....

In addition to closing loopholes and making the system fair again, state officials should roll up their sleeves and address one of the most painful and
unfair situations we face regarding tax policy in Texas. There are areas in
the state where incomes simply aren't keeping pace with property values,
making it harder and harder for people living in these areas to meet their tax
obligations on homes they bought a long time ago. That means tax burdens
crowd out other, more important responsibilities (like sending their children
to college) in a way that's patently unfair.

Imagine that you bought a house many years ago, raised a family there,
and want to stay because you love the home and your friends live nearby.
But you happen to live in a high-growth area where property values are skyrocketing. On the one hand, your wealth is increasing (a good thing) because
your house is growing in value. On the other hand, your increasing wealth is
noncash, yet you need cash to pay your tax bill. This situation completely
turns the tables on the whole notion of tax fairness.

Homeowners who're stuck in this situation and who want property tax
relief are not being unfair or greedy. If the goal is to keep things fair, then
the Republicans who run this state should roll up their sleeves and solve
this problem. They would find a way to help people who are the hardest hit
without opening up another avenue for bad actors to game the system, and
without starving local governments of much-needed revenues.

Such a solution would be complex, and it would require input from
experts and concerned citizens. A comptroller who is willing to fight for ordinary Texans would take the lead and propose meaningful, fair, honest reform.
A comptroller who is weak, or who doesn't want to ruffle feathers, would do
nothing. And that is exactly how we find things in Texas today.

a down-ballot candidate running for a position few people knew or cared about. And although I had an e-media team sending out email and tweets and Facebook posts for a growing list of followers, I would have to move mountains to get twenty-six million citizens and something like seven million voters to take note.

That's when something Bill White had told me many months earlier flashed into my mind. He said when he'd first run for Houston mayor, he knew that nobody knew who he was. So he ran TV ads early in the campaign so that when he knocked on doors, people would say, "Hey, you're that guy on TV, aren't you?"

I started to think, *Well, what if I did the same?*

I called Jason, who said absolutely not. He said there was no way people would remember an April TV commercial on Election Day. Dave and Bob, my TV team, were in complete agreement with Jason. It was way too early to run TV ads; people who knew politics would think I was a goofball. The answer was no.

But then Bob called me back the next day. He said, "You know, I've been thinking. Even though it's too early to make an impression on voters, sometimes an early TV commercial can stimulate media coverage and campaign contributions."

"How much does a TV buy cost?" I asked.

"If we focus on just one media market, and if we run the ad with enough intensity that it punches through, it will cost something like $300,000. We could go cheaper, but if people don't see the ad several times it won't have any effect at all. So we would run that ad during the evening news for about three weeks. With any luck, the newspapers will pick up the story, and we'll get some exposure outside of Houston."

I decided to call my retired CEO donor to see what he thought. He had experience with TV ads, and he was also my largest contributor, so I wanted him to participate in the decision. He agreed that it was a very high-risk strategy but that we shouldn't be afraid to take risks. We could also do some polling before and after the media buy, and we could use what we learned to shape the campaign going forward.

He then asked the key question: "Mike, if you do this, how much of your war chest will you burn up?"

"All of it," I told him.

I mulled it over, and then I decided to run the ads. It would mean that the campaign would be broke with six months to go. As risky as this seemed, doing nothing seemed even riskier. I called the team to inform them I was moving ahead with the ads. Their response was better than I had hoped. Working for a candidate who takes risks must be better than working for a candidate who limps to a loss.

....

We started thinking about what to put on TV. My idea was to hammer Hegar on something really stupid he had said on the campaign trail. During the primary, he had recorded some of his stump speeches and posted them on YouTube. Zach had dutifully kept up with the postings, and he showed me a clip of Hegar making a presentation to Tea Party members in East Texas where he said this:

> I don't like the property tax, never have. I think we should replace it. I think we should replace it with a consumption-type tax, a sales tax per se. Somebody the other day asked me how much money was involved, what were the steps involved. And I said, "Steps? You just do it!"[2]

When Zach first played me the tape, I was astounded at how ridiculous it sounded. Getting rid of the property tax in Texas and replacing it with a sales tax is a terrible idea, one that candidates have been using for years in an attempt to mislead voters. To those who hate the property tax, replacing it sounds like a great idea. But to replace the property tax with a sales tax, we'd have to triple the sales tax from 6.25 percent to more than 20 percent.[3] Many Texans (including many Republicans) would pay more taxes overall, and such a high sales tax rate would ruin our retail economy.

I saw this as a chance to show Republicans, including Tea Partiers, that they were being duped by their own candidate. And we had Hegar on tape, so he couldn't pretend he hadn't said it.

Dave and Bob pulled together a TV spot that did the job, we wired the money, and in a few days we were blanketing the Houston media market.

In making the decision to risk our war chest on an ad this early in the election cycle, I felt like the oil company executive making the decision to drill an expensive, exploratory well. So I nicknamed the media buy the "Collier-Brigham-Smith #1" (as in the three of us who worked together each day in the rented campaign office) just as one names an oil well. We held our breath and waited to see if we were going to strike it rich.

It was an eerie feeling to be walking to the kitchen to grab some potato chips before the news and hearing my voice and seeing my face on TV. My neighbors started calling Suzanne to say how much fun they were having watching the campaign unfold.

....

Reaction to the TV commercial was swift.

Several newspapers in the state took note of our aggressive style and wrote about the property tax issue. A theme running across several of the newspaper articles was that it was very unusual for a down-ballot Democratic candidate to attract any attention in a state-wide race.

On the flip side, I heard comments from political pros saying that I had made a terrible mistake in running ads this early. Some called to tell me as much.

A third reaction, which was the most encouraging, was that Democrats were delighted to see a Democratic candidate with a very hard-hitting message playing such an aggressive game.

We took a quick poll in the Houston media market before and after the ads ran, and we found that they were effective. I called several of my financial supporters and walked them through the polling data and what it indicated, and before long, my donors wanted me to run more early ads in Austin and San Antonio as well. Some began writing checks specifically to help air the ad.

I felt we had struck oil with the Collier-Brigham-Smith #1. Since the success of the ad had helped me raise far more money than it cost to produce and air it, I no longer had to apologize to critics who questioned how I'd spent my war chest. And suddenly, my profile among the party faithful was beginning to rise.

17

....

The Money Game

Now that we were past the primaries and into the general-election phase of the campaign, and I knew who my competition was, I started calling on political action committees (PACs, as they are called) to say that now was the time for them to make a decision in the race. Did they believe that an accountant (and political outsider) or a rice farmer (and political insider) would make a better Texas comptroller?

It was at this point in the journey that I began to see just how rotten our political system is in Texas.

I had spoken from time to time with Bob Owen, the government affairs director of the Texas Society of Certified Public Accountants (TSCPA). Texas has never had a CPA in the comptroller role, and the TSCPA actively encourages CPAs to run for public office. Therefore, as a former PwC accounting partner, a Texas CPA, a member of the TSCPA, and a nonpolitician determined to "take politics out and put competence in" to the state's top accounting role, I assumed the TSCPA should support me.

I was being naive.

Bob is a terrific guy. We got along wonderfully, and he was very open. But the true nature of Texas politics emerged from those discussions. If I had run as a Republican, I have no doubt that I would have enjoyed TSCPA's full and enthusiastic support. But because I was running as a Democrat, the TSCPA struggled to bring themselves to support my campaign. I called Bob several times, and I contacted a number of fellow TSCPA members asking them to write a letter on my behalf. I worked very hard to secure TSCPA's financial support and endorsement because I thought it would be politically very damaging otherwise. At one point, someone close to the situation whispered in my ear something I had heard from another PAC: If Republicans saw evidence that TSCPA had supported a Democrat, retaliation in the legislature would rain down on them.

To be clear, Bob never said this to me directly. He told me the difficulty in getting the TSCPA to fall in behind me was because most TSCPA members are Republicans. But I had a very strong suspicion that if TSCPA got behind me in a big way, Republicans in the legislature would settle the score. As a CPA, the last thing I wanted was for politicians in Austin to retaliate against my own profession. In the end, the TSCPA played it safe: They contributed equally to both Hegar and me, but they withheld their endorsement from either of us. As a member of the TSCPA, and bowing to the sad reality of Texas politics, I think they made the right decision.

The only time I was truly angry with the TSCPA, with anyone on the campaign trail, for that matter, was when they ran a special election edition of the monthly newsletter, sent to every TSCPA member in the state, singing the praises of CPAs who had the courage to run for public office. Feature-length articles with flattering photographs of the candidates, none of whom was running for anything more consequential than state representative, were lavishly included in the magazine. I, on the other hand, who was running for the top financial executive position in the second largest state in America, as a corruption-fighting CPA and the first ever to serve as our top accountant and fiscal watchdog, was excluded. Not one word was mentioned of me or my campaign.

I came within inches of withdrawing from the TSCPA and publishing a very angry letter I had drafted. Instead, I called Bob and let him have it. Bob was embarrassed, but he did what he had to do. He was kind enough to devote a few words to me in the next edition, buried in a long article, but he felt bound to remind all the TSCPA members that my campaign was doomed from the start.

When voters reflexively choose one party, regardless of the candidate, corruption becomes inevitable. Republican politicians in Texas are delighted that the TSCPAs of the world don't attempt to break this cycle.

....

As time went by, I kept picking up the same vibe from other PACs, some of which told me very directly that they could not risk retaliation. One PAC director said, "Mike, you are clearly the most qualified candidate for the job. But Hegar will remain in the Senate if you beat him, and I can't afford to be looking into his 'baby blues' if he finds out I contributed to your campaign."

Texas Association of Business. Texas Oil and Gas Association. Real estate lobby. Automobile dealers. Dentists. Petroleum landmen. You name it. Every business-oriented political action committee landed in the same spot. I concluded that political action committees don't throw their weight behind the right person for the job—they throw their weight behind the candidate with the highest likelihood of winning. If you are a PAC and you have cash, that's how you get what you want in Austin. If you are a Republican and you need cash, that's how you raise it and stay in power. If you are an ordinary Texan, you are screwed.

If that's not corrupt, I don't know what is.

It wasn't just PACs. An attorney I had gotten to know said he would like to support me because he thought I would be a great comptroller, given my technical background. But he was representing a client with a matter before the comptroller's office, and he told me that if his name appeared on my campaign finance report, the current comptroller would rule against his client. That comment spoke volumes, I thought.

I was on the phone with another individual donor who was retired but who used to work as a lobbyist. We hit it off, and so I started talking about the dilemma I faced in raising money from political action committees as a Democrat in Texas. He told a story from many years ago, when the PAC he worked for had given a large donation to a certain US senator's opponent. He got a call from one of the senator's people saying that the senator would be flying through Dallas and was demanding a meeting. The lobbyists dutifully went to Dallas, and after a few polite opening comments, the senator said: "I help my friends and I crush my enemies, so you guys better rethink your contribution levels."

Another story I heard along the way had to do with Ann Richards's run for governor back in the early 1990s. Richards, a Democrat, was expected to lose the election to Republican Clayton Williams, an oilman from Midland. But Clayton made a shocking and highly offensive remark about women and rape while the cameras were rolling, and Richards campaigned hard on Williams's gaffe. She won an upset victory, and even though the race was over, PACs fell all over themselves to pump cash into her campaign account.

It went on and on, story after story, like that.

....

On several occasions, the press asked me whether a candidate for comptroller should take campaign money from individuals or companies with business before the comptroller's office. My answer was always that I would take money from anyone who would give me money. If donors wanted good government, I was their man. If they wanted a monetary return on their investment, I wasn't. The more interesting question, I thought, would be who would give me money when it came time for my reelection.

Thus, with a very clear conscience, I called on a high-powered tax consultant known for making large contributions to the comptroller. I will call him Slim. With the exception of the Oval Office, I've seen every kind of executive office imaginable, from the wealthiest financial magnate's to the executive suite of a Fortune 500 CEO. But I had never seen anything like Slim's office. It was unbelievably large and, obviously, unbelievably expensive. Slim looked like any other accounting firm partner. We're about the same age, although he looks much more athletic than I do, like a runner or a tennis player. He was soft spoken, had a generous smile, and seemed sincere. He was friendly, and we hit it off immediately. We spent the first few minutes comparing notes on mutual friends in the accounting world, which was a very pleasant diversion from the campaign. We had plenty to talk about, two veterans of the public accounting world, but time was limited, and he politely let me shift gears and walk him through my campaign thesis. I talked about roads and education and avoiding debt and so forth. Occasionally, he would utter a crisp "You're right" or "Boy, I sure agree with that."

I knew that Slim was close to all the Republican politicians, but I was pleasantly surprised that he didn't diminish our conversation by dropping names, thumping his chest, or making snide remarks about Democrats. Only once, in reference to improving public education, did he say something along the lines of "Yeah, Rick and I were talking about that just the other day."

I was impressed. It was Slim's subtle way, I thought, of making the point that Rick Perry was not as extreme as people had come to believe. I recall thinking in that instant that perhaps the push and pull of politics drives even the likes of Rick Perry to say and do things that might not be in their heart. Yet I felt zero sympathy: Politicians who want to lead, more than they want the job, don't fall into that trap.

After a while, I asked Slim whether he had met my opponent, Glenn Hegar. He said he hadn't and didn't really know that much about him.

That's when I surprised Slim and said I was going to ask for his support.

I told him that I understood he would need time to think about it because he was a staunch Republican and I was a Democrat. But I felt that his clients certainly wouldn't object to a comptroller who had the technical skills to do good work and make compliance with state tax law more manageable. I reminded him that Glenn Hegar didn't know the first thing about accounting, and I said that it was inconceivable to me that anyone involved in state taxes, whether that was a consultant like Slim or a corporation trying to comply with complex tax law, would prefer a rice farmer with no accounting experience over a former PwC accounting partner.

As I made my case, every muscle in Slim's body went rigid. His eyes squinted, his mouth twisted. He turned slightly in his chair, almost involuntarily, as if to ward off a hard punch in the face. I had never seen anyone physically cringe before that.

I made it easy on him and said I would like to come back in June to work out the details. "Yes, let's meet again in June," he said, and we were all smiles as I left his office.

I did not believe for one second that he would support my campaign.

When June came, nobody in Slim's office would return my call. When the campaign finance reports came out, I learned that Slim had written a big check to Glenn Hegar.

Believe it or not, the following are the facts:

- There are no limits to the money a consultant can charge clients for accounting services in Texas;

- There are no limits to the money a consultant can give to the comptroller's campaign;

- The comptroller has the power to rule on tax matters and can even overrule an administrative law judge; and

- Because we are a one-party state, nobody in Texas other than fellow Republican politicians can independently inspect, or cause to be independently inspected, the work of the Texas Comptroller of Public Accounts.

As I will discuss later, it became clear to me that the Texas Constitution should be amended to create a Texas Inspector General who is completely removed from politics and who has the authority to inspect the work of any state official, including the comptroller. The louder politicians yelp and bawl at such an amendment, the harder Texans should fight for it.

....

It became clear that campaign finance is one reason that Texas has always been a one-party state: the party dominated by people with deep pockets, largely at the expense of the rest of us. Learning that was irritating, but not demoralizing. My mission was to wake up enough concerned citizens to fund a campaign to knock the politicians who sell their influence out of office. It was an inspiring challenge.

18

....

Meeting with the Tea Party

It was about this time that I had the most interesting meeting of the entire campaign. I met with three leaders of the Tea Party movement in Houston.

A friend of mine who is active in the Tea Party had told me that members of the organization wanted to meet with me. They were fighting a war on a number of fronts, one of which was throwing out entrenched politicians who served their own careers rather than serving "we the people." My friend thought that perhaps we had something in common. So I happily agreed to the meeting, although I didn't really expect them to like me very much.

I told my friend that as a precondition to meeting, everyone would have to agree that we would discuss only our state's finances and the role of the comptroller. We would not go near any of the hot-button social issues such as abortion and immigration. The Tea Party contingent agreed, and on that basis we finalized the meeting details.

I have very mixed feelings about the Tea Party. I recall reading about them when they first came together. They held themselves out as being against government corruption and waste, and I agreed completely with them in that regard. It seemed that they were reacting to a feeling of powerlessness caused by a political system that is rigged in favor of special interests and against the little guy. Banding together, and demanding to be heard, seemed like the right and patriotic thing to do. At the time, I liked them, and I even thought that perhaps I should join them.

But as time passed, the Tea Party changed in ways that left me feeling cold about them. They adopted social issues that aren't relevant to fiscal policy, and they became far more emotional than rational. They also never attempt to actually solve problems. Ted Cruz, for example, was the darling of the Texas Tea Party because of his emotional rhetoric, and because he was the consummate outsider (although he tried his darnedest to become the savior of the insiders in the presidential contest, confirming my suspicion that the only thing Ted Cruz is truly passionate about is the ascendency of Ted Cruz). Cruz never gave me any specific proposal that I could analyze. I am an analyst by nature, and emotional rhetoric lacking any detectible substance does nothing for me. That's how I had come to view Ted Cruz, and that's how I had come to view the Tea Party.

But I thought, *Let's go see them anyway. Maybe I'm missing something.*

....

Zach and I arrived at the meeting about fifteen minutes early. Right on time, two men roughly my age came into the conference room and introduced themselves. One was pleasant, the other angry. I couldn't tell whether the angry one was angry by nature or whether he just didn't like Democrats. The pleasant one made small talk while the angry one glared silently at me. Then the third Tea Partier arrived.

Now that everyone was assembled, we exchanged business cards and took our seats. I quickly got the impression that the third Tea Partier was the leader of the group. He opened the meeting by attacking President Obama on something he had read in the newspaper, the details of which I don't recall. I interrupted to remind him that we were there to talk about Texas finance and the comptroller's role. He then launched into a second diatribe about how President Obama was intent on ruining our country. Again, I reminded him that we were there to talk about Texas finance and the comptroller role. He tried two or three more times to make this an Obama-bashing session, but I held my ground.

Finally, we got into Texas finance. We started by discussing property taxes. I opened by saying that the proposal to eliminate the property tax and replace it with a sales tax was a terrible idea that politicians have been mischievously peddling for years in exchange for votes. Before I could articulate my reasoning, the leader shot back with the kind of absolute certainty that is available only to the ignorant: "Sales taxes are better than property taxes. The more you buy, the more you pay taxes."

I knew instantly that this was not going to be a meeting where we explored differences of opinion in a thoughtful way.

I asked, "What does retail consumption volume have to do with consumption of state services? Is there a correlation between retail consumption and demands on our public schools? Is there a correlation between retail consumption and water consumption? Is there a correlation between retail consumption and use of transportation infrastructure?"

I wasn't trying to argue, I was only running a pressure test to see if he had any idea what he was talking about. He didn't. He just glared at me.

I then went on to explain that property taxes, as much as we don't like them, allow for local control of school districts and counties and cities and so forth. There is a single property tax roll that every local government authority uses (e.g., a listing of every property and its appraised value), and the elected (local) board members of each government unit calculate a tax rate to apply to that property roll to fund their operation. These rates, in combination, add together to become the total tax we pay, for most of us through our mortgage escrow account. In this way, the whole process of raising revenues to fund the local governments is simple and can be handled by local officials.

"No different than sales tax," fired the leader.

I corrected him by saying that property taxes are collected locally, whereas sales taxes are collected by the state. If we switched to a sales tax model, the state would have to collect all the money and then allocate it to every school district, city, county, MUD, fire district, hospital districts, you name it (there are four thousand political subdivisions in Texas), based on budget submissions. In other words, loss of local control.

My Tea Party friend countered that every local government could collect its own sales tax. I told him that that wouldn't work. A sales tax system that provided for local revenue needs would create enormous differences between poor and rich political subdivisions. For example, a county with an outlet mall would collect far more in sales taxes than a county without one.

"So if any school district or county wants more sales tax, they can open their own outlet malls," he said.

"Then we'd have way too many outlet malls," I said, "and none of them would make any money, and that would be a calamity!"

I was clearly irritating my Tea Party friend.

I then explained to them that property taxes were about $45 billion per year,[1] and we'd have to raise the sales tax to twenty percent or more to cover that revenue. That would hurt our retail industry, perhaps ruin it, because out-of-state merchants would have such an advantage over Texas merchants that everyone in Texas would do their shopping in Louisiana, or Oklahoma, or online.

"And yet Dan Patrick and Glenn Hegar have convinced you guys that this somehow would be good for you," I said.

That comment earned me even angrier glares, so I suggested that perhaps I could walk through the rest of my agenda and then see if we had anything more to talk about.

One of them stopped me by saying—shouting, really—that they were *not* interested in talking about anything other than how much we hate government, hate taxes, and need to shrink government until it no longer exists. Unless I was prepared to discuss that, he said, we had nothing to discuss.

I had planned for something like this. "Why don't we try something," I said to the leader. "Why don't you guys finish the following sentence for me: The thing I like about Texas is small government, and—?"

They all stared at me for a moment, not quite knowing what to say.

"The thing I like about Texas," I said, "is small government, and—great schools."

To my delight, the Tea Partiers' faces softened.

I took another run at them. "The thing I like about Texas is small government, and—?"

They looked back at me, puzzled, and I said, "How about great roads?"

Again, they agreed.

"How about water infrastructure?"

Again, they agreed.

I said, "You see, gentlemen, that's my agenda. We must invest in education, in roads, and water infrastructure, we must not become addicted to debt, and we must not raise taxes. That's going to be very hard work, so we need a real chief financial officer who knows what he is doing. Otherwise we don't stand a chance. What's more, I hate corruption, and our state is rotten to the core. A comptroller who knows what he's doing, and who isn't an entrenched career politician, can really clean things up."

My Tea Party friends did a complete 180 on me. I could see in their expressions that suddenly they liked me. *Perhaps*, I chuckled to myself, *they were thinking that I am the accounting version of Ted Cruz!*

But then we turned our attention to public education, and that's when things went to pieces again.

I began by walking through the numbers. Texas is at the bottom of the heap in terms of our investment on a per-student basis. Our output statistics are abysmal. Businesses are complaining that they can't find skilled workers. And young people will soon be roaming the streets because they can't find any good-paying jobs. Crime is almost certainly going to rise. It's a vicious cycle that will lead to a very painful future if we don't do something about it.

That's when my Tea Partier friends pounced.

"You can't just throw money at the problem!" one shouted.

"I haven't said anything about throwing money at the problem. Maybe we can spend less money and get better results. Maybe we have to spend more money to get better results. My point is that we need results-oriented leadership. We need leaders who will give us a plan that will make public education work for all Texas schoolchildren, including the poor ones, and then we need to have the courage to fund it."

"I don't know if you know this," said the leader, "but our SAT scores would look much better if we excluded all the schools and all the students in the inner cities."

"I haven't seen any statistics separating inner-city from non-inner-city student achievement," I said. "But I'm not sure it's relevant—unless you're suggesting that we just toss all the inner-city students into the Gulf of Mexico."

That made the leader very angry, and he reached into his pocket and pulled out his money clip. He shook it in my face. "This is the only thing *those* people want from me!"

This meeting ends right here, I thought. *I'm not going to waste my time discussing anything with a bigot.*

"This is a conversation I'm not willing to have," I said, and I began to stand up.

It was very tense in the room, and I looked over at Zach, who was sitting next to me and I'm sure trying not to vomit. Before I could leave, however, one of the Tea Partiers, the pleasant one who hadn't said anything yet, changed the subject by asking what I thought about school choice.

I settled back into my chair and took a deep breath. I said that I agreed conceptually that market-based solutions often produce better results than bureaucracy-based solutions, and we should avail ourselves of market mechanisms whenever and wherever they can be made to work. "But I've never seen a credible proposal for injecting market solutions into public education that'll effectively deal fairly with all five million students coming at us."

I went on to highlight my point by posing a series of hypothetical questions. Let's say we went with school choice in Humble ISD (where I live), starting in the fall. We've got two high schools, a half-dozen junior high schools, a few dozen elementary schools, and tens of thousands of students. When do parents decide which school to send their children to? What information will the schools give parents so that they can make their decision? What if they change their mind during the school year? How will budgeting, planning, and teacher assignments work when enrollment is dynamic? How will we manage facility utilization if head count shifts between schools? What will the transportation plan be?

My Tea Party friends just looked at me, knowing that they didn't have the slightest idea how to answer any of my questions.

"Go ask Dan Patrick or whomever how school choice will work," I continued. "I'd like to get my hands on a real plan and analyze it in order to see if it does a better job educating our five million children than public schools can do, at their best. Until then, we've got to get public schools right, and that takes dynamic, experienced leadership, and commitment to traditional public school success. And if we can find a way to get our money into the classroom to increase teacher pay, reduce class size, and not waste money on administrative overhead, I believe Texans are willing to pay it."

As I was speaking, in the back of my mind I was thinking that politicians like Dan Patrick have railed against public schools for a long time—not because they know what they are talking about, but because it whips their Tea Party voters into a frenzy. Now, they've painted themselves into a corner. They have to either propose a credible alternative to public schools (which they obviously cannot do), or they have to "amp up" the misinformation campaign to avoid being held accountable for botching the most important thing they were sent to Austin to do.

I was hoping that this would be the end of the meeting. But it wasn't. The angry one looked at me and said, "It all comes down to parenting, and there is nothing we can do about bad parenting."

"Well," I started, "whether those kids have good parents or not, they will be ours to deal with if they aren't self-sufficient, so we've got to teach them."

"I don't agree," the angry one said angrily.

No surprise there, I thought.

At this point, it was clearly time for us all to stand up and walk away.

A few days later I called my friend who'd arranged the meeting and asked what kind of feedback he had gotten. He simply said, "Well, Mike, they just don't like Democrats."

A response of remarkable depth, I thought.

Paying for Our Highways

When Rick Perry was first elected governor, Texas ranked nineteenth out of fifty states in terms of "lane" miles per person, a measure of the adequacy of a state's transportation infrastructure. By the time he left office, we had declined to twenty-third.[2] Our highways are becoming more dangerous, and our cities have become among the most congested in America.[3] In oil country, the state wanted to use gravel to fix the farm-to-market roads that the oil companies had ripped up. Our highways are becoming ugly, and when a friend of mine from New York City came to Houston recently to make a speech in front of hundreds of CPAs, the first thing he mentioned was how horrible our traffic was.

We are clearly not on the right path, and everyone knows it.

During the campaign, I had an eye-opening discussion with a member of the Transportation Alliance, a Who's Who of developers, construction companies, and other high-profile Texans. According to the member, we're not only chronically underinvesting in transportation in the state, but we've just about run out of shovel-ready projects close to our urban core(s). We've been cutting corners for so long that we haven't done the front-end work on constructing new roads, work that takes years to complete. In other words, when congestion finally brings us to a complete stop, we'll have to wait years for solutions. It's like a train wreck happening in slow motion, and it's going to be very, very painful for all of us.

It's just heartbreaking that it has come to this.

When my family moved to Texas in 1975, we were immediately struck by how beautiful, safe, and plentiful our Texas highways were. Now, when you drive between Austin and Dallas on I-35, you'll maneuver slowly through painful, dangerous, and ugly construction, where you won't see any work being done. Another friend of mine in local politics told me that one of the tricks politicians use to make it look like they are building roads when they aren't is to set up cones, start redirecting traffic, and dig up old concrete. After creating the impression that things are under way, they'll just let it all sit for months or even years.

When I look at Texas highways today, I believe it. Weeds are growing between the "temporary" barriers that go on for miles and miles and miles.

(Continued . . .)

The highways are ugly, broken up, and dangerous, and commute times are absolutely dreadful. Businesses will stop moving to Texas because our roads are awful, to say nothing of how frustrated and angry we Texans are that the quality of our lives is being compromised.

....

The root problem of our transportation crisis in Texas is that the funding mechanism that worked so well for many years, and which was working brilliantly when my family moved here in 1975, is now broken. We decided long ago, as citizens of a proud state, that we would have great roads and that we would share the cost of those roads based on usage. Every motorist would pay a small per gallon tax on the fuel he or she consumed, with the fee adjusted as needed in order to make sure we had enough money for great roads. It doesn't get any simpler, or fairer, than that.

But in the 1990s, Texas politicians stumbled onto a reelection formula that consisted of promising to reduce or eliminate taxes while saying nothing about the slow and steady decline in highways that would follow, or the mountain of debt they would incur in order to delay the day of reckoning.

Politicians didn't reduce or eliminate the motor fuel tax, but they froze it at $0.20 per gallon. Over time, due to inflation and changing fuel-efficiency standards, that figure has effectively been reduced. While we're still paying $0.20 per gallon, some observers have called for a $0.10 increase to $0.30, thus helping restore a funding mechanism that is fair and that once worked so well.

Instead of a sensible motor fuel tax, many politicians in Texas favor toll roads. I absolutely hate toll roads. As far as I'm concerned, they represent double taxes: You pay the toll to the state, and you also pay the tax on the fuel you are using. Every time I drive through a toll plaza, I daydream about a great big sign with flashing neon letters that reads *The toll you are about to pay is a tax, courtesy of the Texas legislature.* That would get folks' attention. And when we rely on public–private partnerships to build our toll roads—in other words, when some big construction company is making a profit off our toll payments—that makes my blood absolutely boil.

Our highways ought to be funded by a motor fuel tax, one that every motorist pays, to keep the system as fair as possible. We never should have frozen the motor fuel tax, because now we are relying on sales tax, oil and gas severance tax, public–private partnerships, tolls, and an absolute mountain of debt to pay for our roads and bridges. We use so much debt, in fact, that our credit rating may become shaky.

If we had the wisdom to adjust the motor fuel tax so that we had enough money for excellent roads again, we could reduce the sales tax by a like amount so that there would be no overall increase in taxes. Just like that, we would have a tax system that was simple, transparent, that got the job done, that didn't overly rely on debt, and we wouldn't have to raise taxes to get there. Why our so-called conservative leaders can't see this is beyond me.

19

....

Convention Madness

A few weeks before we held our Democratic convention in Dallas, the Republicans held their convention in Fort Worth. I didn't bother to pay much attention to it, although I did note that when the Republican platform was issued, it contained some astonishing planks.

The platform contained a plank calling for "reducing taxpayer funding to all levels of educational institutions."[1] In the history of politics, few planks in a party platform run so counter to the interests of the members of that party. If members of the Texas Republican Party were all affluent, I could see the logic. They would be in a position to fund their children's education from private schools through universities, and so they wouldn't be at a loss. But the majority of Republicans, just like the majority of Democrats, are working men and women who depend on public education to give their children a fighting chance at success.

Furthermore, when I think about income inequality, I immediately gravitate to the cost of higher education in Texas. The simple fact is that in 1990, tuition, fees, and room and board at public four-year universities in Texas amounted to fifteen percent of median household income. By 2010, it had grown to twenty-nine percent.[2] It represents a terrible burden on working- and middle-class families.

The fact that rank-and-file Republicans willingly support measures that work against their interests is just baffling. But their willingness to vote against their own interests creates enormous opportunities for the demagogues lurking in the shadows of the party. Case in point: Also on the platform was the proposal to eliminate the property tax ("We support the abolishment of property taxes"[3]) and replace it with higher sales taxes ("We believe the most equitable system of taxation is one based on consumption"[4]), against which I'd just argued with the Tea Partiers.

There were other aspects of the Republican platform that were eye popping. I heard all about them at a retirement party for a PwC tax partner at an upscale restaurant in Houston. A number of fellow PwC partners and retired partners came to celebrate that night. Suzanne and I were there, and since I was in the middle of a statewide political campaign, I attracted a fair amount of attention.

One of the attendees was a retired partner from Dallas who had just driven to Houston directly from the Republican convention. She was a delegate, and she was furious. She simply could not believe the platform that had just emerged, particularly the uncompromisingly hard line it took on women's rights and on gay issues. She was angry and a bit lost. She had been a Republican all her life, and she had reached a point where she couldn't stomach what her party was forcing on the more moderate element of the party.

She was not aware that I was running for comptroller as a Democrat, but someone pointed me out. She immediately marched in my direction, introduced herself to me (we had never met; PwC is a big firm), and pledged to help me win the election.

As the retirement party moved into the dining area, Suzanne and I were seated at a table filled with some of the staunchest Republicans PwC had ever produced, spouses included. Because I was calling and bugging everyone for money with great persistence, I had been a minor nuisance to everyone at the table. I braced myself for a long evening with a lot of potshots taken at me for being a Democrat.

But I was pleasantly surprised. They treated me wonderfully. Their curiosity about my campaign, as well as the fact we'd all known and liked one another in a prior life, softened their harsh stance against me and my party. In fact, they all said they planned to vote for me.

Then something very unexpected happened while we were drinking our wine and enjoying the conversation. One of the spouses said, with pride, that she had been a big fan of LBJ. Suddenly, for the briefest of moments, there was nostalgia for a bygone era when it was okay to be a Democrat! Many times on the campaign trail I would hear how fondly some older folks remembered Lyndon John-son, John Connally, and Sam Rayburn. But this was different. It felt as if, for a moment, my friends were granted a reprieve from some strange, mandatory indifference to the less fortunate. It didn't last for more than the blink of an eye, but it served as a reminder that most Texans, no matter what party they identify with, have Chris-tian empathy in their hearts. Imagine, I thought, if Texans voted for Democrats who were fiscally conservative but allowed them to act on their human compassion.

Awakened from my reverie, one of our dinner companions turned to me and asked, "And what do you think about secession? We'd be so much better off if Texas were its own country again, don't you agree?" Two or three others at the table agreed that we should secede, that we have everything we need to be an independent country, probably the most unbelievable country on earth. They said it with such mat-ter-of-factness that for a moment I thought they might not be joking.

I simply said, "I don't support secession."

....

My retired PwC partner friend from Dallas turned out to be a big help in the campaign. She introduced me to as many as fifty people, all of whom were Republicans and many of whom became campaign con-tributors. She held a fund-raiser in Dallas that was well attended and thoroughly enjoyable. As a former tax partner, she offered technical advice on how to improve the comptroller's office, much of which I tried to use on the campaign trail.

I greatly appreciated her enthusiastic support, not least because it was a clear indication that rational Republicans are simply not going to tolerate being controlled by the irrational hard Right of their party forever. I've always believed we should do what's necessary to make our society better, not worse, and I've always believed that it takes great skills to achieve this important objective without overtaxing or overregulating the system. I had abandoned the Republican Party because their politicians were far more likely to pander to the militantly anti-everything right wing of their party than to provide enlightened leadership. The reaction of these hardened retired PwC partners and their spouses to me that evening was proof that I was on to something. We as Democrats just need to keep working to get our message out.

....

Coming into the campaign, I had three very real dreads. One was speaking in front of TV cameras, but I was relieved at how quickly I got used to it. Another was debating my opponent, and I knew that date would come.

The third was making a speech at the Democratic convention.

I was given a ten-minute slot, and we were planning a two-minute introductory video. This meant I had to write an eight-minute speech that was as motivating as I could make it without wandering too far away from my message. I thought about the speech for a long time, but when it came time to write it, it took less than an hour. I sent it off to Jason, and he turned the edits around by the next day. He called me to say that I had written a good speech.

I knew that the speech was good, but I didn't know if I could deliver it. By now I had made a number of stump speeches to small crowds, and my stumping was coming along fine. But I had never given a political speech to a large crowd. It was televised, which was another first, and I was to use a teleprompter, something I had never done before. To say I was nervous is an understatement.

The convention itself was great fun. It took place at the Omni Hotel in downtown Dallas, a relatively new hotel that was bright and spacious. Conventions themselves are mostly caucus meetings, and there must be a hundred caucuses within the Democratic Party. Each senate district held a caucus meeting, and there are thirty-one such districts. Then there are the geographic caucuses such as West Texas and East Texas, and the issues caucuses like the women's caucus and the LGBT (Lesbian Gay Bisexual Transsexual) caucus. It took two full days and dozens of meeting rooms to accommodate all the caucus meetings, and when folks were not meeting, they gathered in an enormous common area with booths and food stands where there were always hundreds of people milling around. And of course there was the main convention hall, which served as a meeting place for some of the caucuses prior to the televised speeches.

My role during the convention, other than making my big speech on big speech day, was simply to mill around and talk to people. It was a fun couple of days, because when people figured out who I was (they didn't often recognize me until I introduced myself), they were very happy to speak with me. And like all the other candidates running for statewide office, I was allowed to walk from meeting room to meeting room, where the presiding officer would stop the meeting to recognize me so that I could make a small speech. I enjoyed this aspect of the convention because everyone treated me so graciously, and I was amazed at how many times I heard the words "Thank you."

But I also made several rookie mistakes. I walked into the West Texas caucus and made a big deal about a trip I had made to Midland and Odessa and how warmly I had been treated. But I didn't mention that I had also gone to Amarillo and that I had been treated beautifully there as well. Some of the folks I'd met from Amarillo were in the room, and I didn't recognize them. I caught my mistake only after I had said good-bye and started for the door. I dashed back to the podium, admitted my mistake, and begged forgiveness. Not a mistake I'll make a second time.

Another mistake happened when I met someone from a small town in a part of the state that I was very familiar with. I told the person that I loved her part of the state and that I spent a lot of time in a neighboring town, which I liked best of all for several reasons. The look I got could have killed me. A politician never divulges a preference for one city over another.

As I walked around meeting people, I began to relax a little about my speech, which I was to deliver early in the afternoon of the last day. The biggest speeches—Wendy Davis, Leticia Van de Putte, and Joaquín Castro—took place the night before the end of the convention, so that they could be viewed in prime time. I wasn't the least bit disappointed at my placement; I had no experience, and I had no idea how it was going to turn out. Better to have a less prominent spot.

The night before the speech, I went back to my hotel room around 8 p.m., made sure that I had just the right amount of food in my system, and relaxed before I went to bed. I practiced the speech several times before lights out, each time reading from a printout I had been carrying with me for a few days. I made notes here and there, just as I'd done in the old days when I was playing trumpet and preparing for a concert.

I went to sleep around 10 p.m. but awoke at 3:00 a.m. It was clear that there would be no more falling back to sleep, and I might as well just keep practicing the speech. So I went over it several more times, making slight adjustments to speed and emphasis, and by breakfast time I was feeling good.

I was scheduled to make the speech in the early afternoon, so I spent the morning walking around the convention, talking to folks, and trying not to wind myself up into a ball of nerves. It was the same feeling I used to get in high school when my band director would make me play a trumpet solo from the fifty-yard line at halftime. I would spend the entire day in a haze of anxiety, trying to project an outward appearance of calm. As the moment approached, fight-or-flight waves of panic would come over me, but when I actually started to play I would feel complete exhilaration. I learned to love it. And nine times out of ten, I played really well.

But that was a long time ago, I thought. The thrill of anxiety giving way to exhilaration is for young men. I didn't like the feeling this time around, not one bit.

At 1:00 p.m., I made my way into the green room, which reminded me of the holding pens at a rodeo. It had Astroturf on the floor, waist-high fencing to corral everyone in, a table with water bottles on one end, and chairs strewn all over the place. Several speakers were there, including Democratic luminaries like Congresswoman Sheila Jackson Lee and former head of the Texas General Land Office (and gubernatorial candidate) Garry Mauro. I introduced myself to Congresswoman Lee, whom I found surprisingly gentle and soft spoken (unlike the fiery speaker you see on the stump), and I said hello to Commissioner Garry Mauro, whom I had met once before. Garry was scheduled to speak right before me, and he was thumbing through his speech, which he had carried in a manila folder. He suggested I sit down next to him, but I told him I was too nervous to sit.

Garry said, "Look, just talk slow. That's all it takes. You'll look like a pro."

I had my doubts that I would look like a pro, whatever I did.

When Garry was introduced and walked onstage, I was called to the on-deck circle to speak just after him. Garry's talk seemed to last for hours. It wasn't his slow talking that made it seem like an eternity: It was because I was shaking like a leaf and just wanted it to be over.

But then, hearing my name, I charged out to be greeted by hundreds of enthusiastic people, and my nerves went completely calm. The moment I stepped onstage, I was exhilarated, having more fun than I had ever had in my life.

Dang if it wasn't just like my trumpet days.

Despite the spotlights, I could see friends in the crowd, and I was tempted to point to them from the stage. But I didn't: National politicians always seem to make fools of themselves pointing to folks in the crowd, and you just know they are faking it.

In the speech, I stated right off the bat that I was new to politics and new to the Democratic Party, but that I had signed up with the Texas Democrats because we were the pro-business party. I made the case that if we don't invest in roads, water and transportation infrastructure, and schools we will fail to thrive economically. I also pointed out that I thought the Republicans were corrupt thanks to many years of absolute control of the state and that we needed an outsider to come in and clean things up. And I made it clear that my opponent, Mr. Hegar, lacked both the qualifications and the experience to do the job.

I also decided to add a little snarky humor to the speech. I said we needed "a comptroller who can count to twenty without taking his boots off." The crowd loved it, but I heard some gasps from the audience. I guess folks didn't know that I could be so aggressive. High time they found out, I thought. I also poked fun at something Hegar said on the campaign trail that Zach found on YouTube. Someone had asked Hegar why he wanted to be comptroller, and Hegar said, "I just want to drive the boat for a while." So I said, "I got news for you, Glenn, there's more to being comptroller than hopping up in the governor's lap and pretending to drive for a while!" The crowd loved it.

My voice was strong, and I delivered my laugh lines just as I had rehearsed them. I finished with a strong ending, and that was that; it had gone well, and it was behind me.

....

I had a chance to study the video of my performance a few days after the convention. I had bobbled one of the very last lines, but only slightly, and overall I was pleased with the words, I was pleased with the sound, and I was pleased with the crowd's response. But I was very disappointed in how I looked. I had never seen myself in motion making a speech, and I was mortified at how nervous and fidgety my hands were. *I guess you have to start somewhere*, I thought.

For the rest of the campaign, I would often hear folks say, "I heard you at the convention." And it was obvious to me that after the convention speech, more and more Democrats knew who I was and were paying attention to what I had to say.

A short while after the convention, I ran into a Republican friend who'd watched the speech. "You sounded like a Republican, talking about fiscal responsibility and all," he said. At the same time, I was informed that another Republican friend blurted out during the speech, "Collier sounds way too liberal, and I'm not going to vote for him!"

I guess it's all in the eye of the beholder.

20

....

The Watchdog Tour

Shortly after the convention, I got two calls. One was very good news, and one was very bad news—at least for me. I'll start with the good news first.

Will Hailer, executive director of the Texas Democratic Party, called, and we met at a coffee shop in Austin to talk about our movements going into the summer. He said that if I was willing, the party would be happy to organize an around-the-state Watchdog Tour in July. We had been receiving invitations to speak at candidate forums and Democratic club meetings, but campaign appearances were sporadic and for the most part only in the major cities. So needless to say, I jumped at Will's offer.

One of the biggest surprises (disappointments) of the campaign was that the chambers of commerce around the state did not want to meet with me. Despite the fact that I was campaigning on a platform of "taking politics out and putting competence in" to the state's top accountant role; despite the fact that I had the strongest business resume of anyone who had entered the race; and despite the fact that my opponent was a rice famer, career politician, and political wheeler-dealer (i.e., the last person you want serving as the financial cop), only one chamber of commerce in the state, out of the two dozen we approached, invited me to speak to them. The reason was simple: Chambers don't want to hear from Democrats.

So Will's offer to organize a Watchdog Tour was exciting news. At least, that's what I thought until I realized, with a deep sadness, that it would take me completely away from our annual Port Aransas beach week with my wife's family.

For the first time I began to sense the cruel irony of being in the political arena. Your family and friends are cheering you on because they want what's best for you. Some may actually want to see you in office. And you let yourself be pulled into the arena because you want to make them proud and because you want to do good work for everyone's benefit. So you jump in, only to find that your work takes you away from the very people you're doing it for in the first place.

I started feeling very sorry for myself that I was going to miss beach week at Port Aransas. Imagine, I thought, what it must be like for real political leaders, the ones who win and who are given enormous responsibility. It really makes you wonder why on earth anyone would voluntarily do this.

I love the beach, Port Aransas, and time with my family. But I agreed to do the tour as proposed. Later that evening I called Suzanne to break the bad news. I expected her to be angry. To my surprise and relief, she said she understood and that the rest of the family would understand as well. That was welcome, but it did little to compensate for the awfully sad, almost homesick feeling that I got when I thought about it.

....

And then there was the bad news—at least, bad for me.

Right after my convention speech, Jason called to tell me that he had taken a full-time job in Washington, DC, which meant that he wouldn't have much time to devote to my campaign. I was happy for Jason; I think he's a talented person, not to mention a very good guy. But I wasn't quite sure what his departure might mean for Team Collier.

Of course, at this point Jason's work was largely done. He had taken me from a standing start, helped me build a team, coached me on how to run a campaign, and stayed with me every step of the way as we hammered out our message and style. From here up to the election, it was mostly just executing the strategy we'd worked out, and I felt that with the help of the other very skilled members of the team, we'd be okay.

Jason suggested that I hire a campaign manager, and Will Hailer thought I should too. But Zach thought it was a bad idea. His reasoning was simple: As a down-ballot candidate, I would never have enough money to build a field operation that could knock on doors and turn out the vote. I would be riding Wendy's and Leticia's coattails for that. We were already doing everything we needed to, and a campaign manager, in Zach's opinion, would be a waste of money. And I certainly didn't want to hire someone just to watch me work.

Besides, I had come to value Zach and his advice implicitly. I had hired him to help me with call time, and at first his job was just to make lists and handle follow-ups. But he listened to every conversation, and he gave me pointers along the way. His advice was always spot on, and as we got to know each other, he started offering advice on other aspects of the campaign, like how to improve my stump speaking, which events to attend, which issues to work with, and so forth. Before long, I would not make a move without first consulting Zach. I trusted him completely, and because we didn't need to run a field operation, I decided that Zach could be my campaign manager as well.

It was one of the best decisions I made during the campaign.

....

A lot of candidates incur big overhead expenses, and I had decided that I would run a very low-overhead operation instead. So even when planning the Watchdog Tour, I simply refused to spend money unless I knew that it would directly impact voters. We paid for our own lunches, and we drove my Ford Escape, through the night if we had to, in order to save on airfare. We stayed in very inexpensive motels, and only essential staff would travel. And I kept people off the payroll. I enjoyed managing the financial aspects of the campaign, frankly, because it was very much like running a low-overhead, high-impact consulting business.

I did, however, decide to bring a press attaché onto the team to pick up where Jason was leaving off. Chaille Jolink, who was available and living in Austin, agreed to come on board for the last few months of the campaign. Chaille knows the press, knows the legislature, and knows communication strategy: In short, she was a huge help. When she started, I gave her a very simple goal: Make sure I win the endorsement of every newspaper in the state. Beyond that, I hoped that she could help me get into the newspapers with stories, articles, and so forth.

Not only did Chaille help me secure the endorsement of every major newspaper in the state and several regional papers, but she also did an excellent job sifting through all my op-eds and tweets (I write every day, in massive quantities), separating the wheat from the chaff, which Chaille is very good at. She made sure I stayed in character and didn't make any serious mistakes.

So with the slightly revised Team Collier in place, we were ready to start planning the Watchdog Tour in earnest.

....

It took the party about two weeks to organize the tour, and there was nothing to do but make fund-raising calls. Since it was early July, nobody was interested in talking politics or speaking with a candidate. I left two straight weeks of voice mails, and it was two of the most painful weeks of my life.

Around mid-July Keegan Bobholz, a young party staffer who would be on point to help me with the tour, sent the schedule over to Zach. The tour started near my home in Kingwood, and in fourteen days we were to make campaign appearances (and do a few TV interviews) in this order—Houston, Sugarland, Bryan, Waco, Killeen, Georgetown, Austin, Elgin, San Antonio, Gonzales, Hondo, Laredo, Rio Grande City, Brownsville, McAllen, Corpus Christi, Sinton, Victoria, Port Lavaca, Pearland, Lufkin, Nacogdoches, Texarkana, Longview, Paris, Tyler, El Paso, Alpine, Odessa, Midland, Lubbock, Abilene, and Fort Worth.

We signed off on it, and I braced myself for a two-week odyssey.

On the Border

First of all, I love driving in South and West Texas and along the border. I love the people, the scenery, the food, the air. I feel happy when I'm there, and not the least bit afraid. Business is booming in parts of the border region, and Republican politicians are a disgrace to all Texans when they insult the region's inhabitants and risk business vitality by wearing flak jackets and camo and sitting in military vehicles for the Houston and Dallas newspapers.

....

When making my donor calls, occasionally I would run into a buzz saw: Someone would be furious that illegal immigrants weren't paying their way. They demand services, the argument goes, but they don't pay taxes.

I would try to explain that everyone who lives here, legally or not, pays the same state taxes as everyone else: When they buy things, they pay sales tax, and if they live under a roof, they pay property taxes. Not only does everyone pay state taxes whether they are here legally or not, but also the federal government is making a huge profit from illegal workers. That's because many have fake social security numbers: Employers withhold taxes, but the workers never claim the benefits. The Social Security Administration estimated that in 2010, undocumented workers paid in $13 billion to Social Security but collected only $1 billion.[1]

We are foolish to bring students into Texas, watch them earn their graduate degrees in technical fields, and then force them out of the country. We must be the dumbest people on earth to do this. This isn't just my opinion: I heard it often during the campaign, and most often from Republicans.

As for economic migration, the business community is strongly in favor of guest worker programs because, frankly, we need the help. Guest workers provide an invaluable service, producing profits for Texas businesses, and everyone knows it. I believe Texas businesses should always hire Texans first. Then immigrant workers can fill in the gaps as needed.

As for children born to illegal aliens: Their parents are paying property and sales taxes, so they ought to be allowed to go to school here. And since they are raised here and educated here, I can find no reason that suggests our society will be better off by throwing them out. Some on the hard Right want the children of illegal immigrants gone, but most of us welcome hard-working, law-abiding, tax-paying, and friendly neighbors.

When I made these arguments about taxes and education to people, sometimes they'd tell me, "I hadn't thought of that." But I would also some-times hear "I see where you are going, and I just don't like them here." That answer always left me feeling cold.

....

As for security on the border, we need to do the job right. Every Texan I spoke to told me they wanted to know truthfully what's going on. Keeping a very tight lid on border security operations while scaring Texans into thinking the border is a war zone doesn't cut it.

Not once since Texas started spending $1 billion on "protecting our bor-der" has any politician, agency head, or inspector general briefed the public on what we were doing and whether it's working. Unbelievably, lawmak-ers stripped language from the legislation requiring the Texas Department of Public Safety to provide regular updates as to their performance; they aren't required to tell anyone how they are doing until 2017.[2] In other words, we're spending hundreds of millions of dollars on what may very well be a law enforcement goat rodeo along the border. We deserve to be better informed so that we can hold our leaders accountable.

While campaigning, I spoke with law enforcement officials living in the border towns, and I heard again and again that there is very poor coordination among agencies. Local agencies are involved. State agencies are involved. Federal agencies are involved. If all these agencies are not tightly coordi-nated—and I suspect they are not—then we're wasting millions, if not bil-lions, of dollars. And we still may not be securing the border. Texas officials need to start giving us the whole truth: what steps they are taking to coor-dinate law enforcement activities and intelligence, how the money is being spent, and what kind of results we're actually getting.

....

(Continued . . .)

During the 2014 election cycle, Dan Patrick hoped to use the border to frighten people into voting for him. He developed a TV commercial that opened with footage of armed militants traveling in a convoy, dressed in Middle Eastern garb, and gesturing angrily at the camera. Then Patrick said in the background, "While ISIS terrorists threaten to cross our border and kill Americans . . ."[3]

It sure looked to me like Patrick was using footage from the Middle East to scare the dickens out of Texans. I suppose he was probably following the lead of Rick Perry, who hoped to terrify the easily terrified and get himself elected president. Speaking to the Heritage Foundation in Washington, DC, Perry had this to say about the border situation (I did not attempt to translate Perry into English; he actually said this):

> *Because of the condition of the border from the standpoint of it not being secure and us not knowing who is penetrating across, that individuals from ISIS or other terrorist states could be, and I think it's a very real possibility that they may have already used that. We have no clear evidence of that, but your common sense tells you . . .*[4]

Okay. It's one thing for Rick Perry to make this stuff up as he goes. Texans figured Perry out a long time ago, and mercifully, the rest of America figured him out in time too. But it is quite another for Dan Patrick to frighten people with a blatantly dishonest TV commercial.

Right after the campaign I went back to Patrick's TV ad—the one that showed ISIS terrorists threatening the Texas–Mexico border—to see if I could figure out where he got the footage. I found the exact footage that Patrick used in his TV commercial. It was a military assault on Fallujah, about thirty miles from Baghdad in Iraq, in a documentary made by Journeyman Pictures. The name of the documentary is *Inside ISIS and the Iraqi Caliphate*.[5] It had nothing to do with Mexico, or Texas. It was all a cruel hoax, and Dan Patrick was the jerk who perpetrated it.

When the most powerful politician in the state can be so deliberately deceptive, our policy will become an embarrassing mess.

....

I had been struggling to make a good political speech, and at the start of the tour I was still hammering away at the arguments as to why I should be comptroller and discussing the financial issues we faced as a state. People who came to hear me speak were very polite and would compliment me on my qualifications for the job. They would say the word "refreshing," and they would thank me for running for office. I'd take questions, and then people would applaud politely and head home.

It wasn't until Killeen that I relaxed a bit and allowed some humor to enter the proceedings. And that's when I made my big discovery: The audience in Killeen didn't head home when we were finished. They lined up to have their picture taken with me. I had seen lines form to be photographed with Wendy, but I really didn't expect to see anyone form a line to have their picture taken with me, and until now, very few people had. But for some reason, this Killeen audience saw something more in me, and I attributed it to my use of humor.

I've always been a bit of a stand-up comedian. From my earliest days in elementary school, I have enjoyed making people laugh. I never outgrew it. But I learned at PwC that there needs to be a balance between humor and serious work, and I trained myself to find that balance. In the professional world, I would keep many of my one-liners and zingers to myself. Restraining your impulse to be funny in the business world is a good thing.

But what I learned during the tour—first at Fort Hood, and increasingly as I stumped in city after city—is that politics calls for an entirely different balance. More humor is better, and since I enjoy humor, I found myself enjoying the stump speeches more and more. I could always tell whether a dash of humor here or there was having an impact on the crowd: If so, a line would form to take a picture with me. If not, folks would simply file out and go home.

I noticed something else. Whenever I heard the word "refreshing," it was usually on a day when a line didn't form. It was as if refreshing and entertaining were mutually exclusive. So I worked on my stump speech, trying to make it both refreshing and funny. By the time the tour was over, I had made quite a lot of progress, and people were taking my picture at almost every event. And I was certainly having more and more fun.

I started telling the story of the politician who was campaigning out in West Texas and who, because he was a Democrat, was having a hard time getting people to pay any attention to him. One day, at a cattle auction of all places, he jumped up onto a mound of dirt to make a speech. He attracted plenty of attention because the mound he had jumped on wasn't dirt after all. A crowd of cattlemen gathered around to see what this fool was up to, and as he sank up to his ankles in you-know-what, he made his speech. It was a good one, too, about investing in education and roads and water and not getting addicted to debt and not wasting tax money.

When he was finished, one of the cattlemen yelled, "I never thought I would listen to a Democrat making a stump speech." The politician hollered back, "I never thought I would give one from a Republican platform!"

I must have cracked that joke a thousand times, and the Democratic crowds loved it. Never once did anyone realize I had borrowed it from a Ronald Reagan speech, with the political parties reversed.

....

If you are running for governor, you tour the state in an airplane. If you are running for lieutenant governor, you tour the state in a motor coach. As comptroller, I toured the state in my 2013 Ford Escape. When I bought it, I nicknamed it Landslide, and we had a blast driving the wheels off it.

A typical day on the tour would start with a free breakfast at an economy motel, the kind where you drive up to your room and the air conditioner is half in and half out. We survived, but barely. Then it was off to a morning meeting with local activists. Keegan would arrive about twenty minutes before the event to set up a small podium with my logo on it and flags that would stand against the wall behind me. This always made for a good picture.

I wanted to arrive on time because that's my training as a business consultant, but I learned along the way that the attendees would rather see the candidate arrive ten minutes late because they wanted to visit among themselves first. When I got there, I would shake everyone's hand and visit for a few moments before making a fifteen-minute stump speech. After that, I would open to a few minutes of questions. Then picture time and more hand shaking, and we were usually finished within an hour of the advertised start time. Then we'd head to the next town.

The audiences varied in size from just a few people to as many as fifty local Democrats, depending on the time of day and on whether they had already had several visits from other candidates (our visits were more than a little disruptive, and I always appreciated it when people left work or put down their chores to come to an event). Sometimes the press would be there, and we would start or finish the event with an interview. I learned that when the TV cameras arrived, you dropped everything and did your interview. The audience never minded the interruption, and the TV team was delighted because they didn't have to waste time waiting. They'd find a way to take some shots of the candidate speaking to the crowd or shaking hands. The interviews were always very friendly and fun. Why was I in town, why was I running, why should the citizens of the local community care about my race? I was nervous at first, but after doing it several times, it became second nature to me.

The distances between events depended on which part of the state we were in. In East Texas, the towns are relatively close together and we could comfortably do four events in a day. But in West and South Texas, the distances are enormous, which meant three or more hours between events. I did all the driving, much to Zach's chagrin. And since I had made tens of thousands of phone calls before the tour, I felt I was entitled to two weeks of no phone calls: just enjoying driving around the state and meeting people at campaign stops.

It had rained in many parts of the state before we started our tour, and because the state was in such a drought condition, the vegetation gobbled up every bit of it, gathering strength to come back to life and making midsummer look almost like spring. I had never seen such beautiful scenery in my entire life.

In a few places, like the Big Bend area and parts of the Hill Country, Texas is spectacular to behold. But for the most part, Texas beauty is as understated as it is unmistakable. I had seen a lot of the state before my campaign, but most of what I'd seen had been from a car window on one of the major interstate highways. As I used the state highway system to crisscross Texas on my tour, I was thrilled to see that beyond the interstate highways, our beautiful countryside just goes on and on and on.

Some of the happiest memories of my life, from back in my high school days in Central Texas, were when I would play my trumpet in Doc Gamble's Happy Oompa Band in little towns near my hometown of Georgetown, places like Walburg, Theon, Jarrell, and Corn Hill. I hadn't spent any time to speak of in real Texas towns like these since I'd gone off to college and become a city slicker. It warmed my heart immensely to be back in the countryside, meeting so many joyful (and colorful) people and calling up some great old memories of a simpler time in my life.

This trip also marked the first time I had been to Laredo, Big Bend, and the Rio Grande Valley. We made the long drive from Laredo to the Valley, hugging the Mexican border as we went. Sometimes the Rio Grande was in sight, but often not. It was nothing like I had come to expect. If you live in Houston, images from the border are pumped into your TV set by Republican politicians in their attempt to frighten Texans into thinking the border is a war zone full of flak jackets, military equipment, and camouflage nets. I saw nothing of the sort as we drove. Occasionally we'd see a green-and-white border patrol car, and we saw plenty of Texas Department of Public Safety black-and-white sedans that appeared to be driving in circles. But otherwise, everything seemed calm, and the day was sunny and the landscape beautiful.

The Big Bend area juts way south and west, coming to a point and nestling next to Mexico. It's mountainous, and it's beautiful. The rains had turned everything green, and the sky was an unbelievable blue with white clouds distributed liberally across it. We drove through Texas's own Marfa, a legendary artists' retreat, and we saw the comical Prada store (actually a "pop architectural land art" installation, according to the artists who created it) that sits on a stretch of desert highway, all alone but fashionable nonetheless. And we stopped in Alpine, the community that services parts south, and had a nice visit with local Democrats who treated us wonderfully. I had a strong desire to move there one day.

The Rio Grande Valley, or "the Valley," as it's called, was very impressive. The main highway that connects McAllen and Brownsville and parts in between was new, wide, busy, and there were new office buildings, fancy restaurants, car dealerships, you name it on either side without interruption for miles. I was delighted to see that the Valley, which my geography teachers had described way back in my Pennsylvania days as some of the best farmland in the world, was also becoming an exciting economic powerhouse. The fact that Republican politicians go out of their way to paint a frightening picture of the place just to keep their supporters frightened and ignorant seems almost criminal to me.

....

The most memorable moment of the tour came when I drove through Port Aransas between campaign appearances and spent the night with Suzanne and the boys and the beach-week gang. I pulled into the driveway of the rented house sometime after dinner. I heard talking and laughing as I got out of the car and reached for my suitcase, but it stopped abruptly. I heard someone whisper, "SH!" as I climbed the wooden stairs to the main entrance of the beach house, knowing that whatever was about to happen would be fun. Suddenly the door swung open, and there stood the entire family, young and old alike, wearing matching "Collier the Watchdog!" T-shirts and howling and barking like a pack of wild dogs. It was a wonderful greeting and a wonderful, although sadly brief, visit.

I spent the night, and then I hit the road at 6:00 a.m. the next morning. I met up with Zach and Keegan at the next campaign stop, and from there we kept plowing ahead.

I drove something like five thousand miles in those two weeks. When I am a very old man and can't remember any other aspect of the campaign, I'll remember seeing the entire state from behind the wheel of Landslide in the summer of 2014. The days went by incredibly fast, and we had a wonderful time.

21

....

Late Summer Doldrums

After the Watchdog Tour, we took one day off and then went back to the campaign office to make phone calls. We were near the end of summer, with vacations wrapping up, and we discovered the hard way that nobody seemed the least bit interested in politics. We called and called and called, leaving messages by the hundreds, and made almost no progress. The trend continued through August, which turned out to be the hardest month of the campaign psychologically. But I knew that each phone call I made, even the ones that ended in a voice mail, was a small brick in what I hoped one day would be a large and sturdy foundation.

I suppose it's the accountant in me that tolerates drudgery. I took comfort in the fact that I would only have to run my first campaign once.

I decided that I would also use this quiet time to study my opponent and prepare for Labor Day, which I hoped would signal the start of a vigorous campaign season.

In interviews he had given (and posted to YouTube) during the primary, Hegar had been very forthcoming about his education and career leading to his campaign for comptroller. He told a Tea Party crowd that he didn't study accounting in college because it would take too long.[1] He told another interviewer that he had considered becoming a minister, but "a new state representative seat opened up, and it happened to be at a crossroads and I had some time available,"[2] so he ran for the office. He told another interviewer that after serving in the legislature, he wanted to move on. A friend thought he should run for agriculture commissioner, but since he liked "economic numbers,"[3] he decided he'd like to be comptroller. Another interviewer asked what qualified him to be our state's top accountant, and he said that the hardest thing he had to do in finance was convince his dad and his cousin to hold off on buying some expensive equipment.[4]

I recognize that few people really care about the comptroller position, and Hegar didn't seem to care all that much either and didn't plan to campaign for the job. He had won the Republican nomination. Now all he had to do was wait for this "electing thing" (my words) to blow over.

I didn't know whether to laugh or cry.

I had taken just the opposite approach. In the business world, you do your homework, you develop a meaningful point of view, and you communicate it as clearly and effectively as you can. We refer to that in business as leadership. One of the worst things that anyone can say about you in business is that you are an "empty suit." From the earliest stages of the campaign, I'd felt the pressure to know what I was talking about. What would my friends and business colleagues say if I campaigned on lofty platitudes but otherwise had nothing real to say?

The fact that I had done so much homework—and that I had a point of view worth listening to—helped me in the press. The newspapers took an interest in me and my campaign, and writers who followed state politics signed up to receive my emails and tweets so that they'd know what I had to say about such things as property taxes and quarterly revenue estimates. I tried my best not to sound partisan, but rather to explain technical matters in a simple and meaningful way.

Without exception, the writers who commented on the race were very complimentary of me and of my qualifications for the job. They weren't all that kind to Hegar, who wasn't saying much of anything.

Early in the campaign, we hammered Hegar on wanting to replace the property tax with a sales tax. In August, we dug through his legislative record and found that he'd had a chance to close a massive loophole in the property tax laws that allows owners of commercial and industrial properties to game the system in a way that homeowners can't.[5] The largest of the appraisal districts calculated in 2006 that this loophole cost honest taxpayers $4 billion per year, every year.[6] But Hegar, as chairman of the Senate Finance Committee, killed a bill designed to close the loophole. Why? Because he received $160,000 of campaign money from the folks who wanted it dropped, such as the Texas Association of Realtors, the Texas Apartment Association, the Texas Chemical Council, and the Texas Oil and Gas Association.[7]

We also discovered he was telling people on the campaign trail that because business was booming, he had voted to give tax money back to the taxpayers in what he called across-the-board tax cuts. What he didn't tell anyone is that big companies, not individuals or small businesses, got all the breaks. It went to the owners of big businesses in the form of franchise tax relief,[8] and when one class of taxpayer gets some relief, the rest end up paying more. As far as I am concerned, Hegar should have been telling people that he let taxes increase for the people who live and work here while he helped cut taxes for the big corporations.

Then we found a video clip of Hegar answering questions about education spending at a Tea Party meeting where he openly displayed his education-cutting bravado. When the legislature met back in 2013, after everyone could see that the massive cuts in education from the previous session hadn't been necessary, they bowed to popular demand to restore funding, but they only restored half the cuts. (That didn't stop some of the Republicans from dishonestly calling this a historic increase in public education spending.) While most Texans wanted the cuts restored, the Tea Party faithful (strangely working against their own interests) did not. So during the primaries, when a Tea Party interviewer grilled him about whether he would put more money into education, Hegar showed his stripe. He said, "Someone the other day asked whether we put more money into education. No, we didn't. There's no way you can spin that. No, we didn't. But I was not ashamed to say we didn't. I was proud to say we did not."[9]

That remark was the smoking gun for Texans who thought the 2011 education cuts were a deliberate expression of the hard Right's insistence that we starve public education into oblivion.

So, as we wrapped up August, I not only felt that I understood the issues and was ready to campaign hard, but I also felt that I knew my opponent. He took campaign money from big corporations to keep the property tax loophole open, costing the rest of us more than

Half-Truths and Bad Tax Deals[1]*

How many times have we heard Republican politicians tell us that they know how to create jobs? Seems like every time they put a tax deal together, whether it's a good deal or a bad deal for hardworking and retired Texans, they tell us that it was necessary to create jobs. Too often, however, the tax deals they put together are really meant to benefit the big corporate lobby, leaving hardworking and retired Texans to pick up the tab.

A case in point is the massive cut in the business franchise tax that was passed by the Republican legislature (HB 32) and signed into law by our Republican governor just last year.[12] This maneuver will cause hardworking and retired Texans to pay higher property taxes, tolls, and fees. And while Republicans claim that they did it to create jobs, they ignored the fact that they could have cut the property tax and the sales tax and created just as many jobs—maybe even more jobs—by putting money into the pockets of hardworking and retired Texas families.

Here's the deal: When the eighty-fourth legislature convened in January 2015, they believed they had more money than they needed. They had to decide which group of taxpayers would receive a tax break. The legislature had several options, of which three were seriously considered. One, they considered reducing the sales tax (something every Texan and every Texas business has to pay). Two, they considered reducing residential property taxes (something every Texas homeowner has to pay). Three, they considered reducing the business franchise tax (something only large companies have to pay).

It won't surprise anyone who follows Texas politics that big companies came first. While the Republican legislature gave homeowners a tiny, temporary property tax break (worth about $10 per month for the average homeowner)—nothing more than a head fake—they gave the biggest tax breaks to the biggest companies by reducing the business franchise tax. As for a sales tax break, which would have put money in every Texan's pocket? Republicans in the legislature said forget it.

---

1 *Originally published in a slightly different version as: Mike Collier, "Collier: Half-Truths and a Rotten Tax Deal," *Austin-American Statesman*, 18 August 2015, http://www.mystatesman.com/news/news/opinion/collier-half-truths-and-a-rotten-tax-deal/nnLf3.

The saddest part is that many of the biggest winners in the Texas tax-cut sweepstakes don't live in Texas. Fewer than half of the top fifty business franchise taxpayers in Texas happen to be Texas companies. Companies like Apple Computers, Cisco Systems, Anheuser-Busch, General Motors, General Electric, Nestle, Microsoft, Xerox, and Siemens were among the biggest winners, and they aren't headquartered here. Even many of the investors of the Texas companies on the top fifty list, companies like ExxonMobil and AT&T, live outside Texas.

Anyone who knows finance understands that the largest companies doing business in Texas are owned by investors who live all over the world. So when it came time to decide who would enjoy the tax cuts, the Republicans in the legislature refused to give preference to taxpayers who live, work, or have retired right here in Texas. Instead, Governor Abbott demanded (and Lt. Governor Dan Patrick happily delivered) tax relief for thousands, if not millions, of corporate investors who don't.

Imagine driving up our debt, which is what Republican politicians in Texas have been doing for years, while giving preferential tax breaks to investors who don't live here. The governor's business franchise tax cuts will put money in the pockets of investors in California, New York, Ohio, Massachusetts, and every place you can imagine. Is he going to demand that these investors step up and pay off Texas's enormous debt when it comes due?

And what about thousands of small businesses in Texas who pay the sales tax but who don't pay the business franchise tax? Since businesses making less than $1 million per year don't have to pay the franchise tax, thanks to Republican politicians, they got exactly $0 tax relief.

Republican politicians in Austin say that the franchise tax cuts were needed to create jobs. In fact, cutting the sales tax or the property tax would have created jobs—perhaps even more jobs—because more of that money would have stayed right here in Texas.

And therein lies the problem with a one-party political system when the party in charge is controlled by big business. What if Texas had real political competition, with combatants who understood finance and economics, who were thoroughly pro-jobs and who knew from experience how to create them, yet who were not controlled by big corporations? We would have a much different dialogue in Austin, and hardworking and retired Texans would get a much better deal.

$4 billion per year. He bragged about cutting taxes, concealing the fact that big corporations got the break, while small businesses and working Texans didn't see a dime. He told voters he wanted to eliminate the property tax, but he didn't tell them the sales tax would go through the roof. He refiled his ethics forms to include his wife's income after being called out by the newspapers.[10] He stated publicly and repeatedly that his career in politics thus far in no way, shape, form, or fashion qualified him for the comptroller job. His campaign was being financed to a large extent by the corporate lobby and consultants who bring tax matters before the comptroller.[11] He was proud to have cut public education spending. And he was going to hide from voters through Election Day if he could, hoping Texans never found any of this out.

I was frustrated that my opponent, who I strongly believed was the wrong man for the job, was not going to come out and fight. He didn't have to, because the political machine that controls Texas was going to install him. It didn't help that he was sending a constant barrage of Christian inspiration to his followers through e-media, a technique that some Republican politicians have adopted to the chagrin of Texans (including Christian Texans) like me who believe in the separation of church and state.

....

Hegar was not alone in refusing to campaign. The Republican candidates for lieutenant governor and attorney general were refusing to campaign as well, and rumor had it that both were even refusing to meet with the press. Having won the primary by appealing to the very hard Right of the Republican Party, they must have known that they couldn't openly campaign for the general election. If they did, Texans might find out just what they intended to do in office, and they knew we would never tolerate it.

On the one hand, I found their behavior to be anti-democratic in the extreme. Voters really deserve to know what their political leaders have in store for them. As I've stressed, single-party systems bring out the very worst in people. The party becomes obsessed with power; it becomes as indifferent to policy as it is indifferent to democracy.

I was frustrated, but I didn't let it get me down. In fact, I found it energizing. Democracy thrives on competition. Competition is the only thing that a political machine fears. The harder I worked to create competition, the greater the service I was rendering to my neighbors. And my neighbors—even my Republican neighbors— were cheering me on.

....

About this time, former governor Mark White called to check in. He wanted to know what I was going to do to keep people awake and focused on the race.

"I'm going to campaign hard on education, because—"

That's when Mark White pounced.

"They'll be dead asleep! Education puts voters to sleep! You're the CPA; you have the know-how to stop corruption. You know how to make taxes fair, and you can bust these yahoos for giving away tax dollars through corporate welfare. That's how you gotta fight this fight, Mike. Let folks know that these Republicans aren't working for ordinary Texans; they're working for the special interests. Voters will believe you—you're a Price Waterhouse man!"

I knew instinctively that Mark White was right. My gut told me that Texans didn't see education as a Democrat versus Republican issue. In fact, some teachers were Republican, despite Republicans' open hostility to public education.

I'd also had an eye-opening, if not comical, experience with voters out in West Texas. We had been hearing that folks in Midland and Odessa were unhappy with school funding, so we ran a TV commercial that showed Hegar bragging about education cuts. We conducted polls before and after the commercial. As we expected, voter agitation toward education policy went up, but to our stunning surprise, so did support for Hegar! It was an absurd outcome, but it taught me a powerful lesson: Some voters are more concerned about keeping their party in power than they are about making sure their party is serving them well. You could rile folks up by showing them that Hegar was proud to cut education funding, but their reaction was to turn out for Hegar. Republican Party first, policy second. That's what we're up against in Texas.

So I decided that although education is one of the most important problems we face in Texas, I wasn't going to spend much time campaigning on it. For the balance of the campaign, I would attack the Republicans in general, and my opponent in particular, as being soft on corruption, unfair on taxes, dishonest with voters, and determined to escape scrutiny.

With limited campaign money, I knew that was going to be a real challenge.

22

....

Labor Day

Labor Day weekend is an important weekend for Democratic politicians. Labor unions all over the state organize picnics and events, and any hardworking Democratic candidate worth his salt attends as many of these as possible.

I have become a big fan of the unions in Texas. This is partly because I come from the corporate world, and I understand how forces inside companies sometimes drive reasonable people to do unreasonable things. Simply put, greed can overwhelm judgment. And unions play a role in keeping things in balance.

I had the good fortune of meeting Ed Whitacre on the campaign trail, author of *American Turnaround: Reinventing AT&T and GM and the Way We Do Business in the USA* (New York: Business Plus, 2013) and former CEO of AT&T (and of General Motors, having been appointed to the job by the Obama administration after the 2009 meltdown). Ed described in his book how, as CEO of General Motors, he drove to the United Autoworkers headquarters and called on the union's president, unannounced. Ed told the UAW president that they had to work together to fix the company—and they did. And that's precisely how I view the relationship between labor and management.

I was proud that the AFL-CIO endorsed me, and I made a promise that if elected, I would have a union representative on my immediate staff. I wanted someone nearby who understood the issues faced by working men and women in the state, and I wanted to make sure that my policy decisions or recommendations would be balanced in this regard.

I found the Labor Day events to be as emotional as they were joyful. My grandfather, with whom I was very, very close, was a maintenance foreman at a chemical plant north of Pittsburgh. My earliest political memory was my grandfather telling me he was "for Lyndon Johnson, because President Johnson was for the working man." I distinctly remember thinking, "How could anyone not be for the working man?"

My appreciation for unions comes from my upbringing, but it also comes from my love of history and the accounts I've read of labor conditions during the Industrial Revolution. Back then, labor leaders weren't saints, but they had courage, and they fought hard. They achieved a balance between labor and management that allowed a middle class to emerge in America. I doubt we would have had a middle class, or the prosperity we take for granted in America, were it not for the labor movement of the last century.

Attending Labor Day events as a Democratic candidate for office, I had the terrific feeling that my grandfather would have been very proud.

Occasionally, my Republican friends would tell me that their party is for the working man, too. I suspect that the majority of Texas Republicans are working men and women themselves. But Republican policies in Texas decidedly favor the corporate lobby and the wealthy who keep the Republican politicians in power. Their refusals to allow the minimum wage to keep up with inflation, to even consider expanding Medicaid for the working poor, to give us great public schools, to ease the cost of college education, or to close big corporate tax loopholes: These are all policies that work hard against working people and the middle class in Texas.

One of the most striking examples of public policy that works hard against the middle class is Texas's refusal to allow the minimum wage to keep pace with inflation. On the downside, raising the minimum wage causes some employers to automate and reduce payroll costs. But automation and the impact it has on jobs is a fact of life in a capitalist system. On the other hand, allowing a company to pay less than a living wage results in a transfer of wealth from taxpayers (i.e., the middle class) to the company's shareholders. If a company can supercharge its profits by paying people less than a living wage, then the support (such as food stamps, earned income tax credit, publicly funded health care) that the rest of us provide that company's poor workers is nothing less than a subsidy for the company's owners paid for by taxpayers. To say that refusing to adjust the minimum wage for inflation is somehow conservative, as Republican politicians routinely do, simply isn't right.

....

The Houston and Beaumont Labor Day events took place on Saturday, and the Corpus Christi Labor Day event was a brunch on Sunday. I drove from Beaumont to my beloved Port Aransas, which is just outside Corpus Christi, and checked into a hotel. I was hungry, and I was starting to feel lonely after more than a year of campaigning. So rather than simply buying gas station food and going to the motel to sleep, I decided to drive around Port Aransas and find a restaurant that had good food, a cold beer, and people.

I discovered a restaurant in Port Aransas I had never heard of and liked the atmosphere. There was live music and laughter coming from a bar upstairs, and I decided to walk up after dinner and have a look. There I found a family reunion in progress with a group of cousins who hadn't seen one another in some time. They were about the same age as me and my cousins, one of whom (also named Michael) had died unexpectedly a few months before. I couldn't attend Michael's funeral because of the demands of the campaign, so I watched these strangers from a distance and with a very heavy heart.

At one point one of the cousins stood next to me at the bar to order another beer, and before long, she started talking to me. Others wandered over, and they were very friendly. My mood brightened, and they invited me to join them at a karaoke bar down the street. I said not one word about the fact that I was the undisputed karaoke champion of Kingwood, but I tagged along, and I stood in the crowd and listened to one cousin after another sing their heart out. I stayed for a half hour, but it was enough to take my mind off the campaign, and my poor cousin Michael, and how lonesome I was for my family and friends.

This was the first time I started daydreaming about having the campaign behind me.

....

The next morning, the Sunday before Labor Day, I awoke very early and in a cold sweat. It occurred to me that Hegar might use Labor Day to come out of hiding and launch his public campaign and that he would make a big announcement that he was proposing some sort of Taxpayer Rights Plan. Of course, he didn't actually have such a plan, but his primary opponent, Harvey Hilderbran, had developed one, and he'd pledged to pass it on to Hegar. I suspected Hegar would use Labor Day to make a big splash and announce his (or rather, Hilderbran's) big plan. I would then be reacting to something Hegar had done rather than maintaining the initiative. This was a risk I was not willing to take.

So I sent a note to the team saying that we needed to launch our own plan, one that had the words "taxpayer" and "rights" in it (because that's the name Hilderbran had given his plan). We decided to repackage the ideas and reforms I'd been talking about already on the campaign as my "Protecting Taxpayer Rights" plan, and we wanted to announce it before Hegar had a chance to announce his.

Response from the team was positive, although I hunted Jason down and asked his opinion, and he said it was overkill. He thought Hegar would remain silent all the way to Election Day. But he didn't see any reason not to play it safe by launching a media blitz around my plan. So we scrambled and issued our Protecting Taxpayer Rights plan the next day.

The Labor Day event in Corpus Christi was a real joy. Becky Moeller, president of the Texas AFL-CIO at the time, is originally from Corpus, so she drove from Austin and was one of the speakers. I grew to really enjoy Becky over the course of the campaign. She's not a very big person, but when she speaks she packs some punch! She's pleasant, always on the side of the working man (and working woman), and direct. And she can make a wonderful, sassy, inspiring speech. I was delighted when she told me at one of the events that she saw how hard I was working to win the election and that she wanted someone that worked this hard on the side of the union men and women in Texas. I wish all my Republican friends could spend five minutes with Becky. They'd see what I see in the labor movement for Texas.

Another speaker was Wesley Reed, a retired US Air Force pilot and candidate for US Congress. I was proud to know Wes, and I thought for sure voters in his district would have the wisdom to elect a veteran and true patriot to serve in Congress. Wes's incumbent opponent, Congressman Blake Farenthold, a conservative talk radio personality turned do-nothing Tea Partier, won thanks to gerrymandered congressional districts that ensure Republicans, even the likes of Blake Farenthold, can go to Congress and do nothing for Texas.

My speech was fun for me, but I never seem to blow the doors off when I'm behind other speakers who know how to fire up a crowd. I'm just the accounting type, I suppose. Still, I enjoyed the event very much, and the folks there treated me wonderfully. Every time I would visit a union hall for a campaign event, I came away feeling inspired. Our state is great because working men and women made it great. Shame on us if we ever forget that.

Gerrymandering[1]*

Politicians of both political parties use partisan gridlock and divisiveness to keep their jobs. If they compromise on anything, they risk losing their seat in the next primary. That's because congressional districts are carefully drawn to be reliably Republican or reliably Democrat. The party in charge of each state draws them that way for the sole purpose of remaining, forever, the party in charge. Whether government works or not is of secondary concern.

The framers of the Constitution were silent as to gerrymandering, such as it is known. When the practice first appeared, it seemed a bit odd but generally benign. The courts did not feel the need to block it in a muscular way.

But gerrymandering is no longer benign. Technology has turned it into a malignancy. Computing horsepower gives the party in charge the data it needs to draw congressional districts with a precision the earlier courts could never have imagined. The ruthlessness of this precision has obliterated our politicians' capacity to compromise. Since compromise is the *sine qua non* of representative democracy, we must act to end gerrymandering or our government will never work to our satisfaction again.

Let's say you live in a Republican congressional district (for the purposes of this thought experiment, you could choose either party). Let's say you run for office and win. Once in office, you are confronted with policy choices that call for compromise. You want what's best for your country, so you cast your votes accordingly. You sleep well knowing you've made wise trade-offs to achieve the greatest good.

But soon you return to your reliably Republican district. To your horror, you find that you are criticized for conceding to Democrats' demands. An ambitious Republican challenger runs against you and tells the Republican voters in your district that you cannot be trusted to represent their views. He wins, and you lose. He then goes to Washington and refuses to compromise, lest someone overtake him as he has overtaken you.

---

1 *Originally published in a slightly different version as: Mike Collier, "Gerrymandering No Longer Benign," *San Antonio Express-News*, December 27, 2015, http://www.mysanantonio.com/opinion/commentary/article/ Gerrymandering-no-longer-benign-6720035.php.

Now imagine that your congressional district comprises an equal number of Democrats and Republicans. Once again, as a thoughtful person, you understand and act on the need to compromise. Soon you come home to your district and face challengers from both parties; each argues that you failed to represent their views. But neither challenger has the votes to ultimately win your seat unless he can synthesize the varying points of view in your district better than you did. He will only win if he can articulate more persuasively the reasons for the choices that must be made.

In short, the winner will not be the kind of hyper-partisan belligerent we have representing us today; *the winner will be the statesman*.

Ending gerrymandering is the sole and essential means of ending gridlock in Washington. Ordinary Americans, once again, can make a vital contribution to the success and longevity of our constitutional democracy by raising their voices and demanding an amendment to the US Constitution ending gerrymandering once and for all.

Precious few national politicians will vote to propose such an amendment, because it will make their work much more difficult and their jobs much less secure. But that's one more reason we the people should act. We want our congressmen and congresswomen to feel off-balance. We want their jobs to be difficult, because effective government is difficult. We want only the true statesmen among us to survive the long haul.

Article V of the US Constitution says that two-thirds of the states can call a national convention for the purpose of proposing an amendment. If three-fourths of the states ratify the amendment as proposed, the amendment will become the law of the land. We don't have to wait for the US Congress. We can act.

23

....

To Get Along, Just Go Along

I awoke on Tuesday after Labor Day ready to hit the campaign trail hard. As it turned out, Jason had been right, and Hegar didn't make any big tax plan announcement. In fact, he seemed to remain silent altogether. It was the start of the final push, yet it seemed like he was hiding somewhere, calculating that if he opened his mouth, voters might start wondering who this guy was and what he was running for. And that couldn't be good for his chances.

So we redoubled our efforts. Now that the election was close at hand, potential donors had started taking my calls again, and more money was coming my way. Donations, some quite large, arrived from people to whom I had never spoken, but who'd received a voice mail from me months earlier. I had asked Zach to pull together a list of the one hundred most important Democratic donors in the state, and I was pleased to see that many of them had started contributing to the campaign. It was very encouraging.

But I could see from the size of the donations that in their judgment, their money needed to go to Wendy as a top priority, with smaller amounts going to down-ballot candidates like me. At the time, the press was suggesting that Wendy's team may have been actively discouraging donors from giving money to anyone but Wendy.

If they were, I can't say that I blame them; I was seeing just how hard it is to get people to pay any attention to the election, much less a down-ballot candidate. I would go out of my way to speak to store clerks, hotel attendants, and other people I encountered on the road, and ask them if they were following the elections. It was stunning how little interest there was in the elections on any level. People lead busy lives, and politics to many is just background noise. It was clear to me that by Election Day we'd be lucky if ordinary voters knew who Wendy Davis was, much less the rest of us. I started to wonder whether I should stop everything I was doing and just campaign for Wendy and Leticia. In retrospect, that's what I should have done.

To the extent that donors allocated money to me—and for the most part, they did so in small amounts—I took that to mean that they were glad I was running and they wanted to encourage me to keep fighting the good fight. Some told me that they were going to help me not because they thought we were going to win (although some polls suggested we might pull off an upset), but because they wanted to get to know me for future reference. Regardless of the form of their support, even when that support was directed primarily at Wendy, I was sincere in my appreciation.

....

September brought TribFest, a three-day gathering on the UT campus in Austin for everyone who is someone in Texas politics. There are big speeches from big politicians (like Ted Cruz and Wendy Davis) and panel discussions for the little people like me. It is sponsored by *The Texas Tribune*, an online newspaper devoted to Texas politics.

Evan Smith, the CEO and editor-in-chief of *The Texas Tribune*, called me into his office a few weeks before the festival while I was visiting two of his reporters. I had met Evan many times, and I found him to be very well informed, smart, and entertaining. He had interviewed me on a live broadcast back in April, and we had a fun time sparring on matters related to Texas finance.

I had already accepted his invitation to participate in TribFest, and Evan was trying to decide where to place me on the program. I told him that I thought I should be a keynote speaker, which he got a real kick out of. He then straightened me out, saying that I should be thinking in terms of participating on a panel. He showed me a draft of the panels and asked me which one I might like to be on. I immediately seized on the Transparency in Budgeting panel because it was the only panel devoted to the work of the comptroller.

I could see the pained look on Evan's face when I told him my choice.

A week or so before the event, Evan called to say that he had a small problem on his hands. Hegar, he said, was going to sit on the Transparency in Budgeting panel, but he was refusing to appear if I also sat on the panel. He told Evan that he didn't want to create what would amount to an unofficial debate.

I laughed pretty hard when Evan told me that, and I wondered whether Hegar grasped the irony: He was blocking a person who could bring transparency to a panel whose subject was transparency. Evan, an intelligent man, saw the irony, but he still had a problem on his hands: Hegar was a state senator, and it would create a problem for Evan to ignore the demands of a sitting official. I could tell that Evan thought this was political peevishness, but my sympathies were with Evan, who has an important job to do. I told him I would think about it.

It didn't take me long to decide. I sent Evan a long, rather spirited email, telling him that there was no other panel at TribFest that made the slightest sense for me to join, that the Transparency in Budgeting panel was the only one that was germane to my efforts as comptroller candidate, and that if Hegar didn't budge, I would just skip TribFest. Some politicians live or die when it comes to speaking at such events. I could not have cared less. Unlike Hegar, I had campaigning to do.

But Evan called Jason and twisted his arm, and Jason called me and twisted my arm, and by the time all the arm-twisting was done, I had agreed to sit on a panel on energy policy called Deconstructing the Boom. Energy policy wasn't even remotely related to the work of the comptroller, and I didn't think for one moment that it made any difference to me and my campaign, but I had a great deal of respect for Evan, and I figured if he wanted me to participate enough to call Jason, I might as well do it.

On our call, Evan asked me if I had written the spirited email he received from me, and I told him that yes, I had. He then asked if I had written the op-eds that had appeared under my name in various newspapers, including *The Texas Tribune*, and I told him I had (with only a little editing support here and there). I also told him that I write

Water

As I campaigned around the state, Texas was in the midst of a historic drought, stemming from 2011, the driest year ever on record for the state, and the crisis was acute. Refineries were jittery about their ability to keep running. Farmers and ranchers were having a terrible time, losing cattle and crops and millions of dollars. Some residents had to start drinking recycled (read: toilet) water. Folks were mortified to see their golf courses turning brown and their lake homes becoming gulch homes.

It was a terrible drought, one that dragged on for months, and the longing for rain was physically painful. Some creeks and tributaries had gone completely dry. Aquifers that supplied whole cities were dangerously low (although some Texans, like then–attorney general Greg Abbott, had no qualms about drilling their own water wells to keep their lawns lush and green while further threatening the general water supply).

I frankly had a hard time believing it would ever rain. I couldn't look outside without my eyes hurting. I swore I would never complain about a rainy day again.

Texas experienced an awful drought in the 1950s, and our leaders knew that without fresh water for drinking and bathing and irrigation and industry, we'd never become a prosperous state. They wisely set out to construct dams and do the other things that can turn an arid state into an economic powerhouse. In the ten years following the great drought of the 1950s, Texas built 2,700 dams that today help manage just under half of our state's water needs.[1] That was a time when politicians did more than try to make headlines with publicity stunts. They actually solved problems.

At one point on the campaign trail, while someone on the phone was giving me an earful about our water problems, I heard that Richard Fisher, the president of the Federal Reserve Bank of Dallas, had made a speech about water. His speech was on YouTube.[2] Fisher had always struck me as the epitome of Texas swagger without the arrogance that I find so off-putting, and I figured his speech would be worth listening to.

Texas has a water problem, according to Fisher, and we need to deal with it now. I already guessed this, but what surprised me as I listened to his speech was the magnitude of the problem. Over the next fifty years, our

(Continued . . .)

population would likely double (as Fisher put it, Americans would have to deal with 46.3 million Texans!). But over the next fifty years, if we didn't take steps now to expand our water supply, it would actually shrink from seventeen million acre-feet per year to 15.3 million acre-feet. I whipped out my calculator and ran the math: Our water infrastructure supplies seven-tenths of an acre-foot per person today; by my 105th birthday in fifty years, it will only supply three-tenths.

Fisher then went on to say that Texas will have to invest $231 billion over the next fifty years to solve the problem. That's $4.6 billion per year, every year, for fifty years! He must have gotten the crowd's attention with these eye-popping figures. I later learned that he got all his information from the Texas Water Development Board.

I was hoping he would provide some insight on where he thought we'd get the money. Would he go so far as to say we shouldn't cut key business taxes—something the Republican candidates were promising their campaign donors they'd do—until we had a plan to fund our water needs? Would he suggest we close the commercial property tax loophole which, when last evaluated in 2006, was driving a $4 billion underpayment of taxes?

No, Fisher didn't suggest anything of the kind. Instead—to my disappointment—he implied that we could simply borrow the money. I suspect that he didn't really mean it, because he didn't come out and say it. That would be irresponsible, considering Texas is already deeply in debt. So instead he simply noted that Texas has an AAA credit rating. He noted that we only owe $3.1 billion in water debt. He pointed out that other countries have been loading up on cheap debt. There was no mistaking his suggestion: We don't actually have to pay for our water supplies; we can make our children pay for them!

Fisher was speaking to a so-called conservative audience who, like the politicians they elect, (1) hate taxes, (2) hate debt, and (3) hate anyone who says that you have to choose one or the other. No point in causing an uproar among conservatives with responsible talk, Fisher must have thought.

Sometimes voters will get angry, for example when they are tortured by a long drought. They will demand action from a recalcitrant legislature. That's exactly what happened in 2013, during the thickest part of the drought, when the legislature got off its duff and introduced and passed the Texas State Water Fund Amendment (Proposition 6). The constitutional amendment passed by voters down the line created two funds that were financed using $2 billion from the Rainy Day Fund to use as collateral for new low-interest loans, credit enhancement agreements, deferral of interest obligations, and funding for government entities that develop and manage water supplies. But as I listened to Fisher, I began to doubt that this small step represents the kind of bold move Texas needs to avoid an economy-choking water crisis.

But by the time the legislature met again in 2015, it had started to rain again. Lakes filled up and lawns turned green. So the eighty-fourth legislature postponed any serious move to address the long-term water needs of our state.

And the problem goes beyond supplying water to a fast-growing state. According to the American Society of Civil Engineers, Texas has earned a D– on maintaining its dams. There are more than seven thousand dams in the state of Texas, and according to the Society, more than one thousand of them are so poorly maintained that they pose a "high hazard (probable loss of life)." Additionally, over seven hundred of them are graded as "significant hazard (potential loss of life)."[3]

Our so-called conservative legislature ignored this too.

my own campaign literature and speeches (and, for better or worse, every word of this book).

Evan paid me the highest of compliments: "Hmmm. I figured Jason did all your writing for you."

I guess that's how modern politicians do it. I read somewhere that Woodrow Wilson did his own writing (speeches, letters to foreign leaders, etc.), and that he did it by banging away at the keys of his personal typewriter. I'm no Woodrow Wilson, but we do have at least that in common.

....

I was the only Democrat on the Deconstructing the Boom panel. The rest were Republicans: a commissioner from the Texas Railroad Commission (which regulates the oil industry), two US congressmen, and one state representative. I didn't know any of them.

To prepare myself, I got caught up on my reading, and I spent some time calling friends in the energy arena. I hadn't "talked shop" in months, and it was a real pleasure getting my head back into the business I love.

The panel was a nonevent, although I had some fun showing off that I knew more about the oil business than they expected from a Democrat. A couple of times, the other panelists found themselves agreeing with me before they remembered that I was the enemy and that it was important that they make me look stupid. I didn't give them any openings.

At one point, I told them that one of the reasons I was championing quarterly revenue forecasts was the possibility of a commodity price downturn. We wouldn't have much warning if it happened, and in the new shale-dominated oil industry we didn't know how a price collapse might affect state revenues. "I'm an accountant," I said a couple of times, "and it's in my nature to worry about this stuff."

One of the panelists, also an accountant in a prior life, tried to embarrass me, I suppose, by blurting out, "I'm an accountant, but I'm not worried!" It had that condescending "Republicans don't have to worry because we are the miracle workers!" feel to it. I remember thinking that he was going to look pretty stupid if the price of oil were to fall (postscript: shortly after the panel discussion, the price of oil fell like a rock and triggered the worst Texas oil recession in memory).

At one point, the moderator asked for everyone's view about lifting the ban on oil exports. The Republicans were all for it, but their justifications were glib to say the least. They hadn't thought their positions through at all, and in my view they were just mouthing what the oil and gas lobby expected them to say.

Instead, I jumped in and talked about the changing production mix from heavy crude to much lighter shale oil, the impact this might have on Gulf Coast refineries primarily geared to handling heavy crude, and the way all of this had to inform any decision about lifting export bans. The panelists all nodded their heads in agreement, but they seemed a little off balance. I could tell what they were thinking: *Wait a minute; I'm not supposed to be agreeing with a Democrat.*

We then talked about the regulatory environment. When it was my turn to speak, I could see the commissioner of the Railroad Commission glare at me, expecting the Democrat to take potshots at her agency. Instead, I said that ours was the best regulatory agency in the country and that I'd had recent firsthand experience dealing with the commission. While I was at Layline, a neighboring processor had pumped highly concentrated poison gas into the ground, where it migrated to one of our old wells and started leaching to the surface. While it wasn't our gas, Layline crews had to work in very dangerous conditions to seal the well. We worked as a team, including Railroad Commission personnel, and we got the job done without any loss of human life. I was impressed with the commission's professionalism, and I said so on the panel.

I went on to say, however, that we needed more engineers at the Railroad Commission because as the industry grows, the commission's ability to keep pace will be compromised. Heads on the panel started bobbing, but the chairman took it as a slight. Her dander up, she aggressively defended her commission, but then she settled down a little and said that if anyone in the audience knew of any good engineers, please let the commission know . . . implying, of course, that I was right.

I decided to rest my case.

At the end of the panel, the moderator asked whether we had left any issues out. I had already rankled the Republicans by being a Democrat who was knowledgeable about the oil and gas industry, and I guess I could have left well enough alone. But I was having too much fun, so I raised my hand and said that we ought to consider touching briefly on water. I could see heads nodding in the audience. The panel that had come before us, I was told, had talked about finding a way to reduce the demands the oil and gas industry was placing on our state's dwindling water resources, and I thought we should take up the subject.

At this, the Republican panelists jumped all over me as if I had called their firstborn child ugly. We do *not* have a water problem, they informed me, thanks to the great leadership of Republicans and blah, blah, blah. I was embarrassed for them, and I decided not to fight back.

....

Later that day, I ran into a friend who'd attended the panel on Transparency in Budgeting. She said that Hegar didn't have anything meaningful to say, other than some crack about how big the darn budget was, and how it will make your darn eyes glaze over. My friend reported that the moderator actually had to remind Hegar that he was running for a statewide office.

24

....

Showdown at the *Dallas Morning News*

From the minute Hegar won the primary, our campaign began calling for a debate. We even rented a billboard in Hegar's hometown that read: *Glenn, why aren't you Texan enough to debate me?* It had the desired effect of giving us some headlines, and we had fun with it on Facebook (which was the intent), but it didn't influence Hegar. He remained absolutely silent on the question of whether he would debate, just as he had been silent about most aspects of the comptroller role. Why expose yourself to voters when the political machinery had successfully maneuvered their man into place?

We wanted to make hay over debates, but we knew it wouldn't be good enough for me to call for a debate and have Hegar simply ignore me. Someone needed to formally invite us to debate so that we could have an official record of Hegar refusing, giving me a blunt instrument to use against him in the press. In searching for someone to host a debate, however, we ran into the same problem I was having with getting the support of chambers of commerce, the Texas Society of Certified Public Accountants (TSCPA), the PACs, and the others. Everyone knew that Hegar would say no, which meant that an invitation to debate would be seen as giving me a weapon, which meant that extending an invitation could lead to retaliation, which meant that there would be no invitation.

One civic organization that advertised itself as conservative but nonpartisan wanted us to debate, but they fell short of issuing a formal invitation. Rather, they maneuvered us into doing back-to-back interviews. I went first, and Hegar went second. Each interview was thirty minutes long. I was happy with my performance. I have no idea how Hegar did, but I guessed that he talked about his family and the fact that he was a sixth-generation Texan and other nonsense.

A few weeks went by, and no endorsement came from the organization. It was a very prominent organization, and it seemed out of character for it to remain silent. I knew one of the panel members who'd interviewed me and Hegar, so I called him and asked what was going on. He said I had scored better than Hegar on all decision criteria, but they were not going to endorse me because I was a Democrat.

I reminded my friend that his organization was nonpartisan. "That's right, we are nonpartisan," he said. "But we're not going to endorse a Democrat."

Each time I heard someone duck and run for cover because I was a Democrat, I grew more proud to be a Democrat. And I became more determined to make sure the whole world knew it.

Finally, as September turned into October, we got our debate invitation. YNN is a cable TV network in Austin, and Paul Brown was a TV journalist at YNN who covered state politics. He had interviewed me twice during the campaign, and I found him to be well read and a good interviewer. He was the one who finally called for the debate.

Now we were in a win-win scenario. In the unlikely event that Hegar would debate me, he'd lose. In the likelier event that he'd ignore me, we could point out that he was refusing to debate the issues, and we could make his refusal stick.

We would end up waiting a very long time before Hegar finally accepted the invitation.

....

I was pleased with my fund-raising, and I even felt I was keeping up with Hegar. Republicans can easily raise money from special interests because special interests believe that the Republican will win, whether they are good for the state or not. So they write the check, and after Election Day they tell the officeholder what they want him (or her) to do. The Democrat, in contrast, isn't likely to win, so special interests don't waste their money. If the Democrat slips in by accident, the special interest can give the Democrat money after the election. Which means the money needed to help a Democrat win the election must come from concerned citizens who want reliable leaders. That was how I was raising my money, and it's much harder work. Still, I loved fund-raising because it always made me feel that I was not in this fight alone.

The highlight of the last two months of the campaign was riding the circuit and speaking with the newspaper editorial boards. These were very satisfying meetings because the boards were well informed, and they wanted to get into details. This was the kind of setting I was most comfortable in: a conference room, a small, well-informed audience, and a technical discussion. I left each interview feeling very upbeat, and in the end, I secured the endorsement of every major newspaper in the state and several regional papers.

The *Austin American-Statesman* editorial board told me and Hegar that they wanted to meet both of us at the same time, and in the same room. I was nervous about the encounter, not because I doubted that I would come out the winner, but because I had been spending hundreds of thousands of dollars on TV ads around the state telling everyone how thoroughly unfit Hegar was for the job. I figured he'd be angry, and I dreaded being in the same room with him. To my relief, but not to my surprise, he no-showed the interview.

When the time came for the *Dallas Morning News* interview, I expected to sit with the board alone, as usual. But when I pulled into the parking lot, I saw a car with a government license plate and a "Hegar for Comptroller" bumper sticker. I thought for sure it must be Hegar's car, and I braced myself for an encounter. As I entered the building, I found Hegar sitting in the waiting room, and he seemed just as surprised to see me as I had been to see him. The newspaper had invited us to interview at the same time and didn't tell me. This was going to be interesting indeed.

At first, Hegar was friendly. We had a few minutes together before the interview, and he welcomed me to sit next to him in the waiting room. It must have been obvious to Hegar that I didn't particularly want to be there. He might be a nice guy, and if it weren't for politics, we might be friendly toward each other. But he is a backslapping politician who carries the water for the corporate lobby, and I just didn't—and don't—have time for that. And now, thanks to the miracle of Texas politics, he was the frontrunner for an essential office, to which, as far as I was concerned, he would contribute nothing.

So our conversation was strained but polite as we were led into the conference room and introduced to the editorial board. The first question came at me, and it was about how I would reform our state's revenue forecasting methodology. I walked through the details of my proposal to update our forecasts every quarter, and the board nodded approvingly and took careful notes. I spoke for less than two minutes but I got my entire point across.

The board then asked Hegar what his plan was. What came next seemed almost like a *Saturday Night Live* skit. Hegar rambled on about all kinds of topics, some related to revenues, some not, and to me at least it made no sense whatsoever. After what seemed like five minutes of this meandering, one of the board members asked, "So, are you saying you would, or would not, change to a quarterly system?"

Glenn answered, "I will do a top-to-bottom review of the agency."

Honestly, you can't make this stuff up.

At another stage in the interview, one of the board members asked how many people worked for the comptroller. Hegar said it was something like five thousand. I corrected him and said it was 2,500. Hegar shrugged it off, but near the end of the interview, long after the subject had changed, Hegar came back and said, "Mike is right, the agency employs 2,500 people." In business, such a thin grasp of details would ruin an executive's reputation, and my brain was starting to go numb again in disbelief. I wanted to blurt out, *This is not some college-level mock business competition, Glenn; we are interviewing for the job of chief financial officer of a $100 billion operation.*

The entire interview went that way, and I became angry that someone so utterly disengaged would put himself forward for this position.

As we were getting ready to leave, one of the board members asked if we were planning to debate. I quickly answered that a cable TV station in Austin had proposed a live debate and that I was waiting for Glenn's response. That set Hegar off, and he started muttering under his breath: something about what a negative campaign I was running, how I had been hounding him for refusing to debate, how he was going to have to put up with this for how many more days now?

It was such an awkward moment that one of the editors offered to walk me to the elevator while the other editors held Hegar back to make small talk. That way we wouldn't have to stand in the elevator together. I was thankful that they were experienced at dealing with competing politicians.

A few days later, the *Dallas Morning News* strongly endorsed me.

25

....

Rigged, at Almost Every Turn

It was shortly after the *Dallas Morning News* interview that something amazing happened out of the blue: Hegar announced that he would accept the invitation to debate. I just about fell off my chair when I heard the news.

YNN had given us eighteen different dates and times to choose from, beginning in early October and extending until just before Election Day. I accepted all the dates except two. Hegar said he needed time to work on his schedule, which I found amusing given that there were few signs he was actually campaigning. It seemed as if Hegar woke up each morning, crossed another day off the calendar, put his feet up on his desk, and asked, "When's this dadgum election gonna be over?"

He ultimately chose the last time on the last date, surely just to get the press off his back. In other words, we would debate right before the election, after half the voters had already cast their ballots in early voting. Pretty slick move by a professional politician intent on keeping voters in the dark. In any event, we were going to debate! But it was still a few weeks off, so I had to just keep putting one foot in front of the other on the campaign trail until the big day finally arrived.

....

Late September brought the Texas Taxpayers and Research Association (TTRA) annual convention in Austin. I looked forward to that speech as much as, or perhaps more than, any other speech in the campaign because these were the people—I assumed—who would be most interested in what I had to say. I would know a number of audience members, and I would be able to speak on a technical level.

The previous year's conference had featured a panel discussion that included all the candidates for comptroller—all the Republican candidates, that is. A friend of mine texted me from the event, asking why I wasn't there. He even approached the president, Dale Craymer, and asked why the panel was limited to Republicans only. Dale told my friend that he didn't want the conference to become too political. I thought that was a dodge; he could have invited me to a separate slot. But I didn't mind. Back then I wasn't quite ready to go prime time, having just entered the race.

But I did call Dale right after the conference and introduced myself. We hit it off, and with Dale's help, I participated in several long discussions about tax policy in Texas at the TTRA offices. It turns out that there was a range of technical problems in the comptroller's office that needed to be fixed, from lack of coordination to delays in policy pronouncements to defects in the dispute resolution mechanisms. With Dale's help, and with the help of several specialists Dale kindly introduced me to (and several attorneys and accountants I knew from my professional life), I developed a comprehensive reform agenda for the comptroller's office, which I posted on my website. Jason had predicted that this reform agenda would never come up during the campaign, and he turned out to be right, but as a PwC man, I knew that I needed to show the tax world that I had done my homework.

At one point, I had a conversation with fellow Democrat Bill White about "knowing your stuff" on the campaign trail. He hadn't read my reform agenda, although he seemed pleased with the broad strokes I outlined for him on the phone. But he said something very interesting to me. He said I should learn the job, prepare a reform plan, and campaign on the issues. If I did so, the business community would appreciate what I was doing, I would enjoy the campaign more, and I would be prepared to govern if elected. But he said that a reform agenda wouldn't affect the outcome of the election. The election would turn on how people felt about their respective political parties on Election Day, and the comptroller candidate couldn't really influence that.

I thought his advice made sense, but I didn't take it to heart. As far as I was concerned, I was running to win, not just to ride my party's coattails.

Ultimately I would find out that Bill was dead right. I'm happy I didn't know that at the time.

....

When the day of the TTRA speech came along, I was ready. I had published my reform agenda, and I heard no complaints from the handful of folks who read it. The audience would be filled with tax experts, both corporate employees and consultants. I looked forward to showing them that I had done my homework and that I would be a good comptroller.

I delivered the speech on my reform agenda without a hiccup, but I noticed an unmistakable vibe in the room as I spoke, one that was particularly unwelcoming. At one point, I emphasized that the comptroller could do a better job with small businesses that had a hard time complying with Texas tax rules. A friend of mine who was in the audience later told me that when I said that, some folks near the back of the auditorium laughed out loud. The audience, it turns out, were the big corporate guys, and they didn't have the slightest interest in small businesses. I also began to suspect that they didn't have the slightest interest in a Democrat, no matter how qualified he might be. I had the distinct impression that the folks in the room, all big corporate guys and their consultants and lawyers, wanted a comptroller they could manhandle. They didn't want a comptroller who was qualified and who would take politics out of the job. What good is a comptroller if he can't be bought?

....

Zach told me about something funny that happened after the speech. He was standing next to the chairman of the TTRA, who'd listened to my speech in its entirety. When I had finished, he looked at Zach and said, "Your boss did a good job. Who wrote his speech?" I found the statement as hilarious as I did telling. First of all, I didn't have a written speech. I had only a three-by-five index card to remind me of the topics I wanted to cover and their order. But the chairman figured somebody wrote my speech, because that's standard practice in politics (particularly when it comes to substance). I thought to myself, that's precisely why so many politicians are such pitiful leaders.

....

There was a brief question-and-answer session after my presentation, and someone asked me whether I had a point of view on "private letter rulings," which are rulings by the comptroller's office as to whether a specific taxpayer, facing a specific tax issue for which the law is unclear, would have to pay taxes or not. In Texas, private letter rulings aren't made public, and they aren't allowed to serve as precedent for other taxpayers in a similar situation. I hadn't been confronted with the question before, and I didn't have an answer ready (which I told the questioner).

I was aware of the fact that the incumbent comptroller had a history of failing to clarify the tax rules, and that she'd refused to let prior rulings from the comptroller's office serve as a guide for other taxpayers. I had assumed that she was just incompetent: Any comptroller worth their salt would take steps to update and clarify the rules and to allow their decisions to set a precedent. At least, that was my naive point of view at the outset of the campaign.

But I began to suspect something more sinister was happening. Refusing to make private letter rulings public or otherwise allow them to set precedent left the power to decide a taxpayer's tax fate in the hands of the comptroller. That, I realized, could be very good for the comptroller's campaign fund-raising. If the rules aren't clear and if precedent is never set, then the comptroller gets to make the final decision as he pleases—which means that companies better pay a consultant a huge fee, and the consultants better give the comptroller a huge campaign contribution.

Clear rules, reliable interpretation, and allowing resolutions to set precedent: These might be things a competent comptroller would do, but they would make it much harder for a comptroller to shake down companies (through their consultants and PACs) for campaign cash.

Not everyone would immediately leap to this conclusion. Some might argue that cynicism has gotten the best of me. I have to wonder about that myself. But after many months of seeing Texas politics up close and personal, and after years of service as a financial auditor and due diligence expert, there was no mistaking the risk. And as I will discuss later in the book, this risk can be managed in a way that is win-win for everyone, on so many levels, if Texas has a muscular, and fiercely independent, Inspector General.

....

As we were leaving the TTRA event, I thought I saw Brint Ryan, the consultant who shells out big money to his favorite comptroller candidate—and it looked to me as if he'd listened to my speech.

Within a day or two of the conference, Hegar posted a detailed reform agenda on his website. It was silent as to sixth-generation Texanism, family, and faith, and it was technically useful, so I figured Hegar hadn't written it. My guess was that Brint Ryan had heard me speak, decided that he'd better not take any chances on people figuring out his candidate was a know-nothing, had his staff write a reform agenda, and had Hegar publish it as his own. At least that's how it looked to me, and I never encountered any evidence that Hegar had even read his own reform agenda, much less understood what any of it meant.

26

....

Corruption

It was late in the campaign, and I tried my best to call attention to the role a corruption-fighting comptroller ought to play in Texas politics. Shady behavior involving the state's Major Events Trust Fund and the Texas Enterprise Fund provided the backdrop.

The Major Events Trust Fund is a pool of state money available to help communities host very large events. Assume a group within a community wants to host something like the Super Bowl, the Olympics (if that day ever comes), or Formula One racing. Before officials can use state money to lure the event to Texas, the community must submit an application. Imagine a situation where the locals don't want the noise, hassle, and traffic congestion of a major event, but the state uses its financial muscle to bring the event to town anyway. That would be government overreach and not something anyone in Texas would tolerate. So the law is very clear: The city council or the county commissioners or both have to vote to bring the event to their town. And the organizing committee, duly authorized by the city or county, must submit a valid application.

Formula One races are spectacular and draw huge crowds from around the world. Texas's outgoing comptroller, Susan Combs, was widely known to be a Formula One racing fanatic. So Combs, who was both comptroller and the state official in charge of the Major Events Trust Fund, sent a letter[1] to the folks at Formula One, which was run by Bernie Ecclestone, the controversial European jet-setting racing mogul, saying that the state would be sending $25 million, presumably once each year, preceding each race event in Austin. The letter was dated May 10, 2010.[2] The problem was that the organizing committee with authority to apply for the funds wasn't created until June 2011.[3] Without an application, payments to Formula One would be illegal.

A top state official, Texas General Land Office Commissioner Jerry Patterson, was suspicious of the whole deal and brought it to the attention of Attorney General Greg Abbott. Abbott responded with a long opinion letter saying that yes, in order for state money to fund an event, the process must be initiated by the local authorities, who must submit an application. In his letter of May 18, 2012, Abbott amazingly sailed over the fact that in the case of Formula One, no such application existed. He simply made reference to a statement from Combs's office saying "that every action taken to date . . . has been fully compliant with . . . the statutes . . ."[4]

Abbott's look-the-other-way response must not have been good enough for Patterson. If everything had been done legally, then Patterson wanted to see the organizing committee's application with his own eyes. He informed Attorney General Abbott that he had submitted requests under the Texas Public Information Act to the City of Austin, to Travis County, and to the Texas Comptroller of Public Accounts demanding to see the application. None was produced. Abbott amazingly responded to Patterson that a letter existed, signed by none other than Bernie Ecclestone in May 2011, stating that he chose Austin based on an application, according to a brief submitted to Abbott by Combs.[5] Good enough, right?

Wrong. The organizing committee that supposedly submitted the application as of May 2011 wasn't formed until June 2011.

Perhaps Bernie can be forgiven if he got his dates a little confused. He might have been distracted by a bribery scandal[6] involving Formula One that would ultimately cost $100 million, payable to a German court, to make it all go away.[7] If Texas is going to get in bed with EuroSport jet-setters who write $100 million checks to European courts to make bribery scandals go away, what's the big deal with a few mixed-up dates on official documents?

Tell that to Stephanie Richmond, one of the original members of the organizing committee that was purported by Bernie to have submitted the application. She resigned from the committee and signed a sworn affidavit that no such application was submitted.[8]

That news didn't sit well with a local attorney, who brought the evidence to Attorney General Greg Abbott's office, this time in a letter to Assistant Attorney General Jack Hohengarten.[9] Hohengarten amazingly wrote back that the comptroller is not required to verify whether supporting documents such as applications exist.[10]

And that was precisely my point. If the comptroller doesn't check to make sure payments are legal, who will? I don't care whether the state writes a check for a $5 box of pencils, or pays a bunch of Euro-weenies $25 million, the comptroller's job is to make sure all the *t*s are crossed, all the *i*s are dotted, and everything is legal. And if you looked closely at Formula One, you would see that that was NOT happening in Texas.

One might ask why the comptroller, the state's top accountant and fiscal watchdog, would also be the manager of a fund capable of giving away $250 million of taxpayer money. It's a great question, because it's a stupid arrangement. As I said many times on the campaign trail: If your watchdog is a deal maker, you ain't got a watchdog!

After studying the issue, I campaigned hard on taking the Major Events Trust away from the comptroller. It was a clear conflict of interest.

Hegar's response? He would keep the Trust in the comptroller's office, but he promised he wouldn't misbehave.[11] That's the kind of non-answer that would get a real CFO fired. And Hegar never said whether, if elected comptroller, he would demand to see the application. In contrast, I said I would demand to see it, and if it didn't exist, I was not going to make an illegal payment to Formula One.

If the whole Formula One debacle wasn't sordid enough, the Texas Teachers' Retirement System (TRS) had invested more than $100 million in Bernie Ecclestone's private European company, Delta Topco (which owns the Formula One Group), about the time the Major Events Trust Fund mess was unfolding. Ecclestone's bribery scandal had already hit the papers when TRS made the investment, and Delta Topco had just canceled its planned initial public offering (never a good sign).[12] But TRS plopped down $100 million anyway.

What are the odds that the comptroller, who is supposed to be our state's watchdog, would investigate TRS's $100 million investment in

Formula One when she was, at the same time, putting a deal together with state money to bring Formula One to Austin?

None, as far as I am concerned. And that's precisely the problem in Texas.

....

The other scandal that hit the papers about that time involved the Texas Enterprise Fund, which was intended to provide support for start-up businesses in Texas. For years, Governor Perry had doled out the money in the fund to companies who failed to apply for funds or who had failed to produce the jobs they were expected to produce.[13] Some critics say the fund was used to hand out money to top donors who had been involved in fund-raising for Perry. After the 2014 Republican primaries, the Legislative Audit Committee finally instructed the state auditor to look into the matter. State Auditor John Keel issued a scathing report[14] that was in the newspapers for a couple of days, but that didn't seem to bother Texans much at all.

I campaigned hard on the report and against the structural problems in our government that it revealed. For one, there was the timing of the audits. The state auditor's office does not have free rein to investigate: It has to wait for the Legislative Audit Committee to tell it what to look at. The members of the committee, all Republicans, must not have wanted to look into Perry's activities until he was a lame duck. Otherwise Perry could easily have settled the score. That's how one-party systems work.

Another clear structural problem was the fact that the comptroller, who is supposed to be the state's top fiscal officer, had let the funds flow as Perry had instructed, rather than reviewing each transaction and insisting that everything be in order.

I immediately issued a statement saying that the comptroller's duty is to make sure every payment is proper, and that as comptroller, I would make whatever changes were necessary to the state's accounts payable system in order to protect taxpayers. I said this would go a long way toward halting corruption in Texas.

Hegar, of course, was as silent as a church mouse.

....

Another deal made the newspapers late in the campaign, one that makes me wonder whether there's any limit to the financial nonsense an unchecked one-party machine can perpetrate on an electorate who is kept largely in the dark.

Two construction companies had joined forces to build the southern half of State Highway 130, which runs from Austin to Seguin, just outside San Antonio. The state condemned the land[15]—meaning they took possession of private property using their constitutional power to do so—and the construction companies built the highway at a cost of \$1.3 billion.[16] They borrowed the money, and for the next fifty years the state and the construction companies were set to share the toll revenues. The companies' share of the toll revenue is meant to pay interest on the debt, and then to pay off the debt. The rest is meant to be profit that the companies can keep for themselves.

That means that those of us who use the highway will not only pay for it twice (we'll pay our tolls while we also pay the motor fuel tax), but we will pay millions more than the actual cost of the highway, because our money will flow to the construction companies as profit. These types of arrangements are called public–private partnerships, and they are the most expensive form of financing possible. Politicians like public–private partnerships because they create the illusion that someone else is paying for the highway. In fact, taxpayers (and our children) are paying more money than if we had just built the highway ourselves. It's a disgraceful misrepresentation of the facts as far as I am concerned.

I'm a capitalist, so I understand the proposition: The construction companies were taking a risk that people might not use the highway. Thus, they demand profits as a reward for taking the risk. If people don't use the highways, and the construction companies don't make enough money to pay back the debt, they should lose the highway.

In the case of SH 130, the construction companies took the risk, they built the highway, and then nobody came. Did they lose the highway? Texas bailed them out by subsidizing its use by trucks[17] and truckers who otherwise wouldn't pay the toll. If the state bails out the construction companies, did they really take a risk to begin with? Are they really entitled to profit, at our expense?

I made the case on the campaign trail that if we had a real chief financial officer—if we had a comptroller who knew what he was doing and was concerned about reform, rather than a career politician using the job as a stepping-stone—we wouldn't have this kind of nonsense in state government. Voters would then have much more confidence that their tax money wasn't being wasted.

....

If there is one thing I know from my work as an accountant, and having learned how to evaluate financial controls in a large corporate setting, tone at the top is essential to maintain financial control. If there are irregularities in the executive ranks, there are problems through and through the organization. I don't need a State Auditor, or Public Integrity Unit, or Performance Review, or whistle-blower, for that matter, to tell me that with Formula One, and Major Events Trust, and (before that) problems with our cancer research funds, and (after that) problems with major contracts, and payments to employees for not working, and government-paid trips to the rodeo—all at the hands of our state's top Republican leaders—corruption and abuse is running rampant through our state government. And it's aided and abetted by a Republican political machine that keeps everything completely under wraps to avoid embarrassing the party and jeopardizing its iron grip on power.

Texas Needs an Independent Inspector General

Having campaigned hard on bringing Texas Performance Review back to the comptroller, I decided near the end of the campaign to speak to Representative Donna Howard of Austin, whom I had gotten to know on the campaign trail, about drafting enabling legislation. Even though she was very supportive of my campaign, she hesitated to say that she would support giving performance reviews to the comptroller. I didn't press the issue, but I went off and wondered what it meant.

After I'd considered everything I had learned about performance reviews under comptrollers Bullock, Sharp, and Keeton Strayhorn, I finally realized that I was being naive about the whole thing. I had in mind that the performance reviews would be objective, independent, and not political. But it occurred to me that nobody on Planet Earth expects the comptroller to be any of those things. I knew I would be the exception, but why would anyone believe me?

Most comptrollers use the office to continuously raise campaign money and position themselves for lieutenant governor or governor. Protecting Texans' interests is not their top concern. Donna's not-hard-to-discern hesitation was that giving the comptroller the power to do performance reviews would be giving an ambitious politician an extraordinarily powerful weapon. The result could be a political nightmare that would do more harm than good.

I trust Donna's judgment and her sincerity completely. I knew exactly what she was thinking; she didn't have to spell it out for me. I decided that bringing back performance reviews wasn't exactly right. We needed something much more audacious.

As I was considering what this new and improved approach should be, it occurred to me that Texans don't have a single independent, objective audit or inspection of our state government. Not only are the performance reviews led by the legislature, but also the state auditor reports to the Legislative Audit Committee (all Republicans). And that's a terrible arrangement.

So I decided that if I were elected comptroller, I would do the unthinkable. Rather than try to secure legislation giving my office the power to conduct performance reviews, I would champion a constitutional amendment to

(Continued . . .)

create an Inspector General for the state of Texas. I would take power away from the office I was seeking.

Specifically, I would assemble an ad hoc committee of experts in the field of financial control, fraud detection, and efficiency, and ask them to design the agency. To ensure independence, the agency would be overseen by a commission whose members would be appointed not by politicians, but by the senior partners of the largest accounting and law firms in the state. That would keep the commission completely out of the politics business. The commission would then appoint an Inspector General who, among other attributes, would have no political history or aspiration. In fact, a law saying that the Inspector General could never run for office or serve in state government without the legislature's unanimous consent would seem very much the right thing to do.

The budget for the Inspector General would be set in the constitution as a fixed percent of the total state budget and not subject to a reduction by the legislature or governor (to prevent politicians from killing it, as they effectively killed the Travis County Public Integrity Unit). And the Inspector General would have unlimited access to every person and every part of the state and could conduct any audits and reviews he (or she) saw fit.

A muscular, nonpolitical Inspector General with complete autonomy would strike terror into the hearts of hundreds of politicians and state officials in Texas. This type of office would bring corruption to an absolute, screeching halt. And it would set the standard for fiscal management for all states—perhaps even for the United States!

As committed to this course as I became, I didn't see the need to add this idea to my campaign in 2014. It was too complex an idea, and it would have come too late in the game. I loathe politicians who break their promises, but I couldn't imagine that anyone would denounce this initiative as a breach of trust. I would reduce the power of the office I sought, not enhance it, and I would be leading Texas to an innovative solution to a problem that vexes iron-rule one-party states: How do you police the politicians when the politicians control the police? We could solve that problem, and once solved, every government in America would copy it.

27

....

The Down-Ballot Boys

As we got close to Election Day, Sam Houston, the Democratic candidate for attorney general, suggested that the two of us travel together and hit some of the rural communities in East and West Texas. I thought it was a great idea, and we started making plans.

Sam and I had become friends almost immediately when we first met during the primary season, and our paths had crossed again and again as we traveled to candidate forums and Democratic club events around the state. Sam always suggested we carpool, but I had a strong preference for traveling alone (alone, of course, meaning me and Zach). So our interactions were limited to standing together before or after speeches or talking on the telephone.

Sam had run for statewide office before. In 2008, he ran for Texas Supreme Court and did better than any other Democratic candidate on the ballot, coming in at just under fifty percent of the vote against a Republican incumbent. It wasn't enough to win, but it gave Sam invaluable experience at running a statewide campaign. I knew that I could learn a lot from Sam.

And he is a terrific person. He is friendly, respectful, honest, affable, and humble. He is a lifelong Democrat and unashamed of it. He was respectful of President Barack Obama and had the audacity to admit it on the campaign trail. Despite the fact that I had considered myself a Republican for many years, Sam treated me wonderfully. There wasn't a single topic that came up that we disagreed on. Sam would have been a terrific attorney general, one who brought a work ethic and a Texans-come-first mind-set to the job.

Sam campaigned hard on the fact that he wouldn't use the office simply to grandstand and pander like his predecessor Greg Abbott had done. Abbott was famous for saying that as attorney general, his job was to come to work, sue the Obama administration, and then go home. Few people challenged his sanity, despite the fact that he lost (or abandoned) more than half his cases and burned up millions of taxpayer dollars to pull off his stunts. As far as I was concerned, Abbott was the quintessential headline grabber. I had met Abbott once many years earlier when he was on the Texas Supreme Court. He was the guest speaker at a Financial Executives Institute dinner meeting, and I found him to be serious, thoughtful, and mature. But as attorney general, he seemed to transform into an unalloyed political huckster. My faith in Abbott as a principled leader who put Texans' interests ahead of his personal ambition collapsed. I knew that Sam would never have operated that way. He would have gotten up in the morning, thought about what was best for our state and the people who live and work here, and he would have simply done his job.

Now that Abbott was vacating the position to run for higher office (no surprise there), Sam's opponent, Ken Paxton, was hiding from the press and refusing to campaign because he had repeatedly ignored a securities law (one that he'd helped pass in the Senate), and he was headed for indictment. Paxton was not disputing the charges,[1] but he was the Republican nominee for attorney general, which meant that it didn't matter. Hide from voters and let the political machine finish the job. Paxton was even quieter than my opponent Glenn Hegar.

Both Sam and I found our silent opponents to be thoroughly disrespectful of Texas voters. We also knew that we had to do everything we could to turn out the Democratic vote, so in early October we hit the road and ran up through East Texas together, making as many stops as we could. Sam had his right-hand man Jacob with him, and I had my right-hand man Zach with me. My old college friend Cameron—the Texas Oracle, as I now called him—came along as well to help out, paying his own way, of course.

Steve Brown, who was running for railroad commissioner and who was the only African-American on either statewide ticket, joined us for several stops. Steve was a pleasure to campaign with, and his campaign theme was similar to the message that ran through every

Democratic candidate's campaign: Let's not let big corporations call all the shots in Texas. Steve believed at least one independent person should sit on the Railroad Commission—someone who isn't controlled by the oil and gas industry—to help regulate the oil industry.

I made my career around the oil and gas industry, and I love it and I respect the people in it. But I believed that Steve was exactly right. We don't want the regulators to be owned and operated by the industry they are there to regulate. Steve offered voters a very sensible choice: someone who is an ordinary citizen, not an industry insider, on the Railroad Commission to ensure that we stay ever vigilant so as to maintain our excellent safety record. Having at least one independent citizen on the commission made good sense to me, and I had hoped that Steve would be elected.

....

Despite the repetitive feel of these last campaign stops, the crowds, who were the hardiest of the party faithful, were wonderful to us. They thanked us for running and encouraged us onward. The three of us and our small parties got along wonderfully, and it was by all accounts a terrific experience. When I'd started the campaign, I'd never expected to feel quite this sense of fraternity with my fellow down-ballot candidates. It was welcome indeed.

On one of our very last campaign stops together, when Steve and Sam and I were taking turns at the podium, I decided to try something different. Rather than make the same fifteen-minute stump speech that I had made at least a hundred times by now, I launched into something new. I made the decision moments before I took the stage, which meant I hadn't had a chance to even rehearse it. But it was a topic I had spent a good deal of time thinking about, and since we were close to the end of the race, I thought I would experiment.

The crowd was very friendly and numbered about seventy-five people. We were meeting in a community center deep in the Piney Woods of East Texas. It was a sunny, cool afternoon, and everyone at the meeting was upbeat. Broad smiles could be seen everywhere you looked. There were political signs, homemade cakes, and lemonade, red-white-and-blue was everywhere, and it had the feeling of an old-timey country political rally. Since my all-time hero is Abraham Lincoln (I'd read at least a dozen books about him, and I'd seen the movie *Lincoln* more than ten times), I organized my thoughts to sound as much like Lincoln as I could manage, particularly his 1860 Cooper Union Speech, which I think is one of the most interesting political speeches ever given. So, just for the thrill of it, my little off-the-cuff speech went something like this:

> Today I'd like to talk to you about the Texas miracle.
>
> Republicans would have you believe that they have been in charge for twenty years, that they are terrific leaders, and that as a result, Texas is a miracle.
>
> As an accountant, I love to analyze assertions. I have analyzed the three assertions embedded in this claim, and I found the results very interesting. And I'd like to share them with you now.
>
> The Republicans assert three things. First, they assert that they have been in charge for twenty years. Second, they assert that they are excellent leaders of our state. And third, they assert that Texas is a miracle.
>
> Let's test each of these assertions, shall we?
>
> Let's start by testing the first assertion: that Republicans have been in charge for twenty years.
>
> This first assertion is true. A Democrat hasn't won a statewide election since 1994. While the legislature in 1994 was roughly split between Democrat and Republican, the Republican majority has grown over time, and for most of the past twenty years, Republicans have dominated Texas politics.
>
> Rather than turn to the second assertion, that Republicans are great leaders, let's skip to the third assertion: that Texas is a miracle. Then we'll come back to the second.
>
> So, what do we make of Republicans' third assertion, that Texas is a miracle?

Like assertion number one, assertion number three is also true. Texas is indeed a miracle.

Texas has over 260,000 square miles of land, more than any state except Alaska. It's a miracle!

I could tell the crowd knew where I was going, and I could see smiles starting to form.

And our land is flat and you can use almost all of it for agriculture and industry. Miraculous! And you can build as many roads and rail lines and pipelines as you want. Truly, a miracle! And we have some four hundred miles of coastline, which is miraculous! And as many deep-water ports as we like. A miracle indeed! And we have warm weather, and we have a wonderful, hardworking, and diverse population . . . an unbelievable miracle!

So, Republicans' third assertion, that Texas is a miracle, is true!

Texas! Is! A! Miracle!

Oh, I left one thing out: We have oil!

So the Republicans' first and third assertions are true. Republicans have been in charge of Texas for twenty years, and Texas is a miracle.

Now, then, what about Republicans' second assertion, that Republicans are excellent leaders, hence the Texas miracle?

Well, I hate to tell them, but that assertion is patently FALSE!

You see, every aspect of the Texas miracle: From 260,000 square miles of good land, to as many roads and railways and pipelines as we need, to four hundred miles of coast, to as many deep-water ports as we like, to great weather, to fabulous people, to an ocean of oil . . . they all came . . . before . . . Republicans! The Republicans had absolutely nothing to do with them!

Of course, you know what else came before the Republicans, don't you? *Democrats!*

Now then, having shown that the uninterrupted Republican rule for the last several years did *not* produce the Texas miracle, don't you think we ought to ask ourselves, just what has Republican leadership produced? Shouldn't we ask ourselves, what in the world are they good for?

Well, after twenty years of Republican leadership, Texas's schools are among the worst in the country.

After twenty years of Republican leadership, Texas's roads are crowded, dangerous, ugly, and uncomfortable.

After twenty years of Republican leadership, Texas is running out of water.

After twenty years of Republican leadership, Texas has become one of the most indebted states in America.

You might say, after twenty years of Republican leadership, that Republicans are . . . good for nothing!

Well, since we're talking Texas miracles, I think the real miracle is that voters haven't thrown the Republicans out yet, even though they've botched everything they've touched . . . for twenty years!

If there is *any* true miracle, my friends, it is that we live in a democracy where we can *vote*, which means we can elect Democrats, and we can get our state moving again!

So let's keep after it! Let's work a miracle! We have several perfectly good days left! Let's get out there and *LET'S WIN THIS!*

The finale produced a standing ovation, and it made the day one of the most memorable days on the campaign trail. I waved a thank-you to the crowd and shook Sam's and Steve's hands while I made my way to my seat.

Sam and Steve loved the speech and were very congratulatory.

It must have been obvious to everyone in the room how much we enjoyed our friendship, and how much we enjoyed the important mission we were on.

To run statewide as a Democrat is a hard, uphill battle. But I found it energizing and rewarding, particularly at that moment. And I felt sorry for the Republican candidates who had to use sharp elbows to win their nomination, who then had to hide from voters because they had so little to offer, and who were going to have to spend their days in office bowing to the big corporations, lobbyists, and goofballs that controlled their party.

How lucky Sam, Steve, and I were to be Texas Democrats!

....

Shortly after that, I found myself with Steve at a church picnic in Beaumont. It was an African-American church, and Steve had a good relationship with the pastor. There were hundreds of people and several candidates (all Democrats) who, under a tent on a small stage, were trying to fire up the crowd to turn out to vote. It was sweltering hot, and the humidity was smothering. But the day was wonderful. I was delighted at how appreciative the gathering was for all the candidates, including me.

As I made the long drive home that afternoon, I thought how good it would be if everyone would hang out at a church picnic, just once, where the people don't look anything like themselves. Meet the pastors, run around with the children, talk to the mothers and fathers. Seems to me it would do us a world of good if we became more familiar with one another.

28

....

All in the Family

My wife's father, Gilbert Laskowski, was born in San Antonio and raised in Del Rio, a very pleasant town on the Mexican border. Gil was quite a bit older than my wife's mother, which meant that I first met him when he was in his sixties. He died in 2004, and we all mourned his passing because we truly loved him. He was a remarkable man.

Many years ago, Gil and I drove to Del Rio to rummage through his childhood home before it was sold off to strangers. Gil's mother had just passed away, and our trip was only partly related to the house. It was also part of the healing process for Gil. Although we didn't spend any time discussing his mother, he gave me a tour of the city and his boyhood home, and there was no mistaking that he was touching all the old bases, remembering his childhood and no doubt remembering how much he loved his mother.

The stated objective for the trip was to retrieve some personal belongings Gil had stored in a tiny garage-turned-makeshift-bedroom in the backyard. Gil opened the stubbornly locked door and went straight to an old footlocker next to a small wireframe cot that served as a bed. He dragged the locker across the sagging wooden floor and opened it with great enthusiasm, almost surprised that it was still there after all those years. We sat there for more than an hour, going through what turned out to be memorabilia of his early years, the years before he was shipped off to England, before he crawled into a troop transport headed for Normandy on D-day plus six.

His face lit up as he discovered a copy of a letter he had written to the US State Department sometime in the 1930s, asking for pamphlets, reports, photographs, and whatever materials might be available about some obscure country in Africa. Even as a young man, Gil was fascinated by the world, and politics, and history. After the war, he met and married a Royal Dutch Airlines flight attendant, a similarly remarkable woman named Magda whom my children today call Oma. Gil went on to work for the US State Department, and he and Magda lived in Greece, Laos, India, and all over Africa. My wife was the third of four children, and although she was born in the United States, she lived overseas much of her life. She graduated from the American School in Kinshasa (Democratic Republic of the Congo), and because Gil had maintained his Texas residency, Suzanne went to the University of Texas. That's where we met, and the rest is history, as they say.

In retirement, Magda and Gil lived in Alexandria, Virginia, in a quiet suburb a mile or two from Mount Vernon. Suzanne and I and the boys spent most of our Christmas holidays there, and we loved it. Gil and I got along fabulously, despite the fact that he was a seasoned, brilliant, well-read, well-traveled diplomat and a lifelong Democrat, and I on the other hand was a cocky, upstart, junior Republican. It made for some tumultuous dinner conversations, particularly when beer and wine were involved (which was always the case), but we always enjoyed each other thoroughly.

Gil lived to age eighty-two, and he was smart and energetic to the very end. But as he aged, I could see that his enthusiasm for political sparring was declining. I didn't know whether it was due to old age, fatigue from years of trying to straighten me out, or his disdain for the direction of politics in America. Perhaps it was all three.

One day while President Bill Clinton was under siege over the Monica Lewinsky affair, the extended family had assembled in Alexandria. Gil and I were watching the news, as usual, while the rest of the family was getting ready for dinner. I made some wisecrack about Bill Clinton's indiscretions. Instead of taking up a spirited fight, which would have been the norm in an earlier time, Gil simply turned in his chair, looked at me, and said, softly and sadly, "Republicans have no concept of making society better." He turned back in his chair, and everyone within earshot fell silent. It was so out of character for Gil, and I felt just awful.

Gil was wrong. Yes, I was a Republican at the time, but no, I was not indifferent to the quality of our society. But his comment helped me realize that being cocky lends itself to being misunderstood. I changed my stripe that day, and over time, I even changed my party. If Gil were alive, he would be proud that I became a Texas Democrat.

....

Gil's best friend from his Del Rio days was Max Stoole, who owned a furniture store on Main Street. Unlike Gil, Max never left Del Rio, but Gil and Max stayed in touch until the bitter end. Max's daughter Elizabeth is a very active Democrat, and when she learned that I was running for comptroller, she said she wanted to help me. So she graciously invited me to several dinners and luncheons in San Antonio so that I could meet people, and I enjoyed all of them thoroughly.

One of the events was a luncheon to raise money for Planned Parenthood, with Diane Keaton as the keynote speaker. I didn't know much about Planned Parenthood, other than that they performed abortions and that Republican politicians want people to hate them. I worried a little that my turning up at a Planned Parenthood luncheon might come back to haunt me, but at this late stage in the campaign, I figured that few people were paying much attention to the comings and goings of the down-ballot Democrats. So I went.

Although I like Diane Keaton the actress, I didn't much care for Diane Keaton the luncheon speaker. The room was full of women, and Keaton was serving up stories and tall tales that were geared solely to women. At times I felt uncomfortable, like I suppose a woman might feel attending some manly event where the speakers are all men and the topics all about manliness.

In contrast to Keaton's speech, however, the brief remarks by the Planned Parenthood official hosting the luncheon made a huge impression on me. He spoke for twenty minutes, giving an impassioned speech about access to HIV testing, cancer screening, education, and all the other essential services that Planned Parenthood provides to poor women. He said almost nothing about abortion. And I came away with a much different perception of Planned Parenthood.

As I drove home to Houston that afternoon, I found myself getting angry. Politicians in Texas invest an enormous amount of time and effort trying to convince voters that Planned Parenthood is evil incarnate. In so doing, they damage an organization that does tremendous work for women who rely on their services. Planned Parenthood saves millions of lives.

It's fair to question whether public money given to Planned Parenthood is used to pay for abortions. If so, that practice should stop: Pro-life taxpayers, in my opinion, are perfectly justified in their refusal to pay for abortions. Seems to me that Planned Parenthood would be wise to separate abortion services from all the other good work that they do, thus assuaging people's concerns that their money is paying for abortions.

But for politicians to assail the whole of Planned Parenthood, for political gain and at women's expense, is just not right.

Near the end of the campaign, I got an urgent phone call from a Republican friend who heard that Planned Parenthood was funding my campaign. He had changed his mind about helping me. Evidently he couldn't stand the idea of his money commingling with Planned Parenthood's. I explained that they hadn't donated to my campaign and I hadn't asked them for money because it wasn't linked to my campaign to serve as comptroller. My friend was relieved and sent my campaign $1,000. Later, when I mentioned that I had called folks who'd donated to Planned Parenthood and asked them for money, he almost withdrew his support a second time.

My friend was not thinking rationally, but few people do when it comes to abortion. Other Republican friends suspect that Planned Parenthood stokes acrimony against politicians because it helps the organization raise money. If that's true, they should stop that practice as well. We need more rational thinking in politics, not less, and few areas of public policy are as turbulent and devoid of civil discourse and reasoning as abortion. It is a prime factor in political dysfunction in the United States, and it doesn't have to be that way.

....

I was raised a Catholic, and I think abortion is heartbreaking on many levels. But I am also an American, and I hold the Constitution to be the law of the land. While the Catholic Church forbids abortion, the Constitution as interpreted by the US Supreme Court says that under certain circumstances, terminating a pregnancy is not unlawful.

How does one reconcile these two opposing precepts?

It's not simple. In fact, Americans have been struggling over this for decades.

My personal belief is that we must respect the Constitution in all things. Our freedom as individuals is inextricably linked to our devotion to the Constitution and the rule of law. But our zeal for the Constitution, which, according to the Supreme Court, protects a woman's right to choose, does not mean we are powerless to stop abortion. It means that if we want to fully, and lawfully, live up to the expectations of a moral society, we must try to prevent abortions by preventing unwanted pregnancies. We can do that through education and contraceptives. And when confronted with the heartbreak of an unwanted pregnancy, we can do everything in our power to find that baby a loving home. Until we have done all that we can in this regard, we haven't done all that we can to stop abortion.

Which leads to a very interesting question: What have the so-called pro-life Republicans done to genuinely address the abortion crisis by preventing unwanted pregnancies or facilitating adoptions? Have they done all that they can to fund education? To distribute contraceptives? To help unwanted babies find wanting families? The answer is that they have done, and are doing, precious little.

I told many donors, Republican and Democrat alike, in one-on-one conversations, that I cannot see myself working to change either the US Constitution or the US Supreme Court to take away a woman's right to choose, to the extent the decision is made in the earliest stages of pregnancy. I would repeat what former governor Mark White said to me on the phone one day: "It's between the woman, her doctor, and her preacher." I agree with Mark White. And I don't hold this to be inconsistent with my Christian upbringing. The Sisters of St. Agnes taught me that we were all given free will. What's required of me, as far as I am concerned, is that I lead my own life and raise my own family in accordance with the Christian values that I revere. I may wish for others to do the same, but it's not up to me to force my value system on anyone else.

The Sisters of St. Agnes thought that wisecracking little Mikey Collier wasn't paying attention, but I absorbed every word they said, and their teaching that man's free will is central to Catholic ideology really stuck, and it underpins my passion for the separation of church and state. And that, in a fundamental way, influences my thinking on abortion.

....

I often wondered why the state's top accountant—why any state official, for that matter—should be required to join the abortion fight anyway. Aren't enough people fighting over it already? What could I say to influence the debate that hasn't already been said thousands of times over, by people with higher standing than me when it comes to moral, religious, and medical considerations? Surely there is a place in government for leaders who wish to focus on the job they were elected to do. Wouldn't politics descend into chaos otherwise?

As the campaign unfolded, I scrupulously avoided discussing abortion in public. Many folks were glad that I would stick to the comptroller issues and stay clear of unrelated subjects, however emotive (read: vote-getting) they might be. My opponent, in contrast, pounded his chest that he was the pro-life choice for comptroller. I found the argument absurd; on the rare occasion that I talked about abortion, it was to remind people that abortion had nothing to do with being the state's top financial watchdog.

In private conversation, it was a different story entirely. Often on fund-raising phone calls, the person on the other end of the line would want to know where I stood on abortion. In one-on-one conversations, especially when I was asking for support, I felt I owed a full and honest accounting.

During these conversations, I found almost universal agreement with my position among Democrats. But I also found plenty of agreement among Republicans, which surprised me. And I talked to many Republicans who believe that the abortion litmus test (which is not the only Republican litmus test these days) is impacting their party in a very negative way.

Occasionally in one-on-one conversations I would vent my spleen. The truth is that I think the Republican track record on abortion is pathetic. Texas women are having tens of thousands of abortions each year, and Republicans do little more than pass meaningless laws that they know won't stop it. Their laws are publicity stunts designed to round up votes, not meaningful policies designed to end the abortion crisis. This has been their modus operandi to win votes for four decades, and in that time, they have accomplished almost nothing.

Case in point, the 2013 Texas law that requires abortion providers to have hospital admitting privileges.[1] This law did nothing to stop abortions in Houston, Dallas, Fort Worth, Austin, San Antonio, and McAllen—which means it did nothing to stop abortions where most abortions take place. However, it did make it difficult for very poor Texas women who don't live near the state's largest cities to have the same procedure that affluent, urban Texans can have with much less difficulty. Facts, however, don't stop politicians from pounding their chests and (falsely) asserting their pro-life bona fides. Yet despite their so-called anti-abortion law, women in urban areas, Republican and Democrat alike, can have as many abortions as they like.

Republican politicians now (falsely) claim that their ineffective law is causing the number of abortions to decline. But the fact is that the number of legal abortions began declining everywhere, not just in Texas, long before HB2 was passed. In 1991, the legal abortion rate per 1,000 women aged fifteen to forty-four was 22.9 in Texas (2.29 percent; the national average was 2.63 percent). By 2011, the percentage in Texas had fallen to 1.35 percent (1.69 percent nationally).[2] Nobody really knows how many illegal abortions are happening; some believe that the practice is substantially on the rise. Nevertheless, the point is that politicians are crediting their 2013 law—a law that I doubt had any real impact—for a trend that has been under way for years.

What makes the whole matter thoroughly disgraceful is that champions of the law have the temerity to lie and say that requiring abortion providers to have hospital admitting privileges was meant to protect women's health. Few frauds in Texas history have been so brazen. The Texas Hospital Association spoke out strongly against the law, saying that it would not improve women's health and that it would, in fact, create an undue administrative burden on hospitals. Here is precisely what they had to say:

> THA [Texas Hospital Association] agrees that women should receive high-quality care and that physicians should be held accountable for acts that violate their license. However, a requirement that physicians who perform one particular outpatient procedure, abortion, be privileged at a hospital is not the appropriate way to accomplish these goals. A hospital's granting privilege to a physician serves to assure the hospital that the physician has the appropriate qualifications to provide services to patients in the hospital. Thousands of physicians operate clinics and provide services in those clinics but do not have hospital admitting privileges. Requiring a hospital to grant admitting privileges to physicians who do not provide services inside the hospital is time-consuming and expensive for the hospital and does not serve the purpose for which privileges were intended; rather, the Texas Medical Board is the appropriate agency to address whether physicians are delivering appropriate care to patients, as the TMB regulates all physicians. Hospitals should not be required

to assume responsibility for the qualifications of physicians who do not practice in the hospital.

Should a woman develop complications from an abortion or any other procedure performed outside the hospital and need emergency care, she should present to a hospital emergency department. Requiring that a doctor have privileges at a particular hospital does not guarantee that this physician will be at the hospital when the woman arrives. She will be appropriately treated by the physician staffing the emergency room when she presents there. If the emergency room physician needs to consult with the physician who performed the abortion, the treating physician can consult the doctor telephonically, which is often done in other emergency situations.[3]

Every time I hear a Texas politician say that the hospital admitting privilege law was intended to improve women's health, I immediately conclude that that politician is either a dunce or a liar. Some politicians act as if we live in a strange, parallel universe where a lie can turn bad law into good policy. Well, it doesn't. A lie turns bad law into a disgrace.

The hard work of stopping abortions in Texas, in my opinion, involves stopping unwanted pregnancies through education and contraception, and increasing the rate of adoption. Any politician—however pro-choice (legally speaking) he might be—who has the courage to lead Texas in this direction will emerge as the true pro-life leader.

....

One conversation stands out from the hundreds I had on the subject of abortion. It was perhaps the most memorable conversation of the entire campaign. A staunch Republican and business contact had just finished telling me in no uncertain terms that he would not support me, even though I was the best man for the comptroller job. He said that I was a Democrat, and Democrats are pro-abortion. I tried to explain my point of view, but it didn't matter. He would not budge.

But suddenly, as if to find a graceful way to end what had become a tense conversation, he lowered his voice and said, "Between you and me, I was happy with *Roe v. Wade*, because I didn't want to haul my girlfriend to Mexico if I knocked her up."

29

My Fifteen Minutes of Fame

The angel investor who helped launch my campaign called as we were headed into the last few weeks of the campaign. He had been talking to folks about me, and people seemed amazed that Glenn Hegar, the farmer, was doing better in the polls than the CPA and businessman. He wanted to know if I had considered a "closer" TV ad that stayed away from all the technical issues like property taxes and education spending and just focused on my qualifications.

I told him that I had, and that the team had given me two alternative TV scripts to consider. One was a simple script with me talking to the camera, making the pitch that we needed a CPA, not a rice farmer, in the comptroller's office. The other script had me crashing around a farm in a suit and a tie, looking very out of place and making the same point, but in a comical way.

I told my angel investor (and now trusted advisor) that I thought the farm idea was terrible. The issues we were dealing with were too serious, I was too serious, and doing a silly farm ad was a bad idea. I had assumed that he would agree with me.

He didn't. He thought the farm ad was a great idea. He said from his experience in advertising, you've got one chance to make an impression. If you can make it visually, that's best. He also said that the people who think the issues are serious are probably already reading the newspapers, but the millions of voters I needed to reach weren't, and they probably didn't know anything about the comptroller. A silly farmer ad might be the best chance to reach them—and if it was funny, all the better.

I liked his style a lot. He never insisted that he was right; he always pitched his ideas as just one man's opinion. But he had a lot more experience with TV commercials than I did, and I decided to trust his instincts.

I called the team and told them we would go with the farm ad, and they were ecstatic. Bob Doyle and Dave Heller, my TV team, as well as Jason (who was still engaged in the campaign, even though he was working full-time in Washington), had decided long ago that this was the route I should take, and although I had said "no" to the farm ad repeatedly, they kept doing all the subtle things you do to change an old man's mind. Bob even suggested that I ask my supporters' point of view, which I would have done if the most important of them hadn't called me first.

Doing the ad meant I had to find a farm. I had one donor whom I suspected would be able to help me line up a farm. I called him and told him what we had in mind and asked if he knew any farmers who could help us pull this off in a short time. It turned out that his family runs a very large farming operation near Houston, and he said we could have the run of the place. One phone call was all it took. *Much easier than organizing our first video*, I thought.

On the day of the shoot, I drove up to the farm in my Ford Escape, Landslide, dressed in one of my favorite pinstripe business suits and dress shirt with cuff links. I pretty much knew this would be the last time I would be wearing that suit, although I'd thought that once before when I'd used it to look like FDR at a Halloween party. The suit seemed indestructible. We were about to put it to the test!

Dave and the "grips" he had hired were already at the farm when I pulled up. It was quite a sight: The foreman was leaning on his Chevy pickup, gawking at the ponytails, tattoos, and earlobe holes on the young men and women lifting equipment out of a rented Subaru. They told me that when Dave had arrived from Miami, he had hopped out of his car and said, "Take me to your tractor!" I'm sure the foreman thought the whole thing was insane, but he was smiling, and I figured it was going to be a fun afternoon.

We spent about five hours making fifteen seconds of video, featuring me trying to drive a tractor, getting splashed in the face, climbing some equipment, and so forth. At one point, Dave had the idea that I walk up to a cow with calculator in hand and try to make it look as if the cow and I were talking about finance. *Seemed simple enough*, I thought. The crew mic'd me up, and we loaded the five people it takes to run the camera, sound, lights, and so forth in the truck. We came upon a half-dozen cows, and we started walking toward them. But five people with video equipment, stumbling through a pasture and making noise, scared the cows, which then turned and walked away. So we loaded into the truck, found another group of cows, and tried again. Same result.

We were running out of daylight, but we decided to give it one more try. This time, the crew stayed a few yards away, and I walked up to the small herd alone, hoping not to spook them. It didn't work. I got within twenty yards, and they started to turn and walk away. So, thinking we weren't going to get the shot, I turned to the crew and said, "Nobody wants to talk about the numbers!"

Dave stuck that shot at the back of the TV commercial. And since it aired, that's all anyone ever said when they talked about my campaign—"Hey, you're the guy with the cows!"

That's politics for you.[1]

My suit lived to fight yet another day, which is unbelievable, considering that our last shot was me getting blasted in the face with a watering hose. The water came from a sulfur-laden aquifer, to boot. We did the take twice, and I sat soaking wet, in my suit, for the two-hour return trip in Landslide. Physically, I was miserable driving home, but I'd had much too much fun that day to complain.

30

....

The Debate

Going into October, there weren't going to be too many new experiences for me on the campaign trail. With one exception: the debate. Hegar insisted that he wouldn't be available until shortly before the election, when early voting was well under way and millions of Texans would have already cast their votes. Since there was no evidence that Hegar was actually campaigning, I figured "scheduling difficulties" was code for hiding until the election was over. To say I was nervous about the debate is an understatement. As much as I wanted to win the election, I was quietly hoping Hegar would back out and save me the horror of doing a televised debate. But as the clock ticked down, it didn't look like that was going to happen.

With only three weeks left in the campaign, there wasn't much to do other than prepare for the debate, make fund-raising phone calls, and try to get my story out through the media. I was hearing from donors that they had made all the contributions they could afford in the 2014 election cycle, and I believed them. I knew how hard candidates were working to raise money, me included, and at some point the donor base simply runs out of cash. As Election Day nears, there isn't enough time to make a meaningful media buy. That didn't stop me from making fund-raising calls, though; I was determined to do all that could be done.

Of course, it didn't work that way for Hegar or Paxton. They each announced that they were so far ahead in the polls that they weren't going to spend any more money on their campaigns. To my amazement, that's when big money started pouring in for them.[1] I realized quickly what Hegar and Paxton had done: They'd signaled that they were going to win, which meant any special interest who wanted something out of them had better stump up the cash but quick. Hegar took in almost $1 million[2] in the final month, of which large chunks came from political action committees.

That's how corrupt Texas politics is.

As a Democrat, I didn't have access to big corporate money, whether it came laundered through consultants and lobbyists or otherwise. But I never felt sorry for myself. Raising money from concerned citizens was a labor of love, and by late October we had raised $1.6 million.

With fifteen days left before the election and ten days before the debate, the Texas Oracle had a wonderful suggestion. We could hop in his car and go see reporters and TV stations around the state in a final push to get the word out. Zach, my right-hand man, was a bit unhappy that there wasn't a role for him on the road, but Cameron was an excellent driver, he could handle logistics of a statewide media blitz brilliantly, and he had great political instincts. And I enjoyed his company thoroughly. He was also in a position to take some time away from work, and he was willing to contribute his time (and the cost of transportation) to the campaign. So we packed our suitcases, and we hit the road.

We decided to hit media outlets in Republican strongholds around the state as our top priority. We had about five days, and Texas is a big place. So we started in my hometown of Georgetown and worked our way up to Amarillo, hitting as many small towns along the way as we could. We then worked our way south and east through Lubbock and down to Kingsville just south of Corpus Christi. By the time we got back to Austin, we had gone three thousand miles and stopped in twenty-three towns. An article about me appeared in the local newspaper in about half the towns we stopped in, and I made it to the evening news three times. And it was great fun.

Cameron turned out to be a fantastic campaign aide. If my chat with an editor overlooked an important detail, Cameron jumped in and was pitch-perfect. When we left a newspaper office, Cameron would give me pointers, just as Zach had done on so many stops. As we traveled the state, there was always something to laugh about, and sometimes it seemed as if we were still in college. Most of all, Cameron and I both have a deep appreciation for how beautiful Texas is, and there were long stretches where neither of us said anything: We just stared out the window, literally in awe.

This was late in the campaign, and I had gotten used to sleeping in inexpensive motels and eating very inexpensive meals. I was broken in, you might say. But Cameron had not been traveling with me previously, so he wasn't broken in yet. One morning, on the rough side of a very rough town, we met for a quick (free) breakfast at the economy motel we had just stayed in. Cameron looked absolutely terrible, and I asked if he was okay. He let out a hearty laugh and said he was great, considering he had slept all night in a chair with a loaded pistol across his lap and his luggage piled high against the motel room door.

Another time Cameron pulled up to the valet of a very expensive restaurant in San Antonio, looked at me, and said, "Mike, I'm a businessman, not a politician, and I'm not going one more day without a good dadgum meal. I'll buy." The food was wonderful, and it was the first fine-dining experience I had had in weeks. Ironically, it gave me the worst indigestion, and it was the only time on the campaign trail that I felt sick. I asked Cameron to pull into a gas station somewhere in the middle of nowhere so that I could put something more familiar into my system and hopefully feel better. A gas station sandwich, basted in chemicals and sealed in plastic and chased down with a Bud Lite (Cameron was driving), did the trick.

As I was paying for the sandwich, I asked the middle-aged woman at the cash register if she was going to vote in the upcoming election. She said she didn't know there was one. I asked if she had ever heard the names Wendy Davis or Greg Abbott. She hadn't. I figured there was no point in discussing the comptroller race, or anything else for that matter, so I just bought the sandwich and the beer, and Cameron and I hit the road.

....

Election Day was drawing near, and I was beginning to relax: All the mysteries and uncertainties of campaigning had begun to resolve themselves. The debate was the only real challenge left.

I decided that we as a team would assume Hegar was bluffing and that he would cancel the debate at the last minute. Maybe it was wishful thinking on my part. I could easily see him stopping the negative press by agreeing to debate, letting half the voters cast their ballots in early voting, and then at the last minute canceling the debate, leaving me without enough time to campaign on his dodge.

So in the days leading up to the debate, I decided I would issue a daily press release entitled "I can't wait to debate" that would tee up one policy matter each day and lay out my point of view. Since the other statewide debates (governor and lieutenant governor) had come and gone and our debate was the only one left (Ken Paxton, needless to say, refused to debate Sam Houston), I had hoped the press would pick up on my series of press releases and make our debate a story. Then, if Hegar canceled, I could look back and say I'd done everything I could think of to keep Texans awake and interested in the comptroller race.

About this time, I noticed that Hegar had started saying on the stump that he would "work hard to make sure Texans had good-paying jobs." Of course, that means absolutely nothing, but it sounded good, and it reinforced the narrative—which, again, I don't for one second believe—that Republicans are better at creating jobs than Democrats.

One of my campaign themes was to show voters that the Republicans were not the pro-jobs party and to argue that Texas can do so much better than we're currently doing. So I really didn't like the fact that Hegar, who didn't seem to know much about anything except politicking, had started to vomit the Republican applause line about creating jobs. And I thought to myself that if I got the chance during the debate, I'd call him out on it.

....

As determined as I was to win, I started to contemplate how I would react to a loss. I was beginning to see the seventeen months of the campaign as building a foundation that would be valuable over the long haul whether I won or lost this particular race. If I were to lose, four more years to study the state, build relationships, and learn the finer art of political communication would put me in a much better position to lead. The challenge felt strangely familiar, as if I were career building (for example, trying to become a PwC partner) rather than politicking. The upcoming debate, for example, wasn't about winning the election as much as it was building skills and rising to the attention of people I needed next time around. That's something businessmen and -women know how to do, and I focused squarely on that task.

....

When the day of the debate finally arrived, I was relaxed and ready. I had engaged consultants to help me practice the finer points of televised political debates. I'd done nothing like it before. I knew Hegar's style well, and I expected him to drone on about family and sixth-generation Texan regardless of what the questions were. I figured I'd have to interrupt him, which is something I've never been good at. So I hired experts in televised debating, and our practice sessions were devoted to my interrupting a Hegar stand-in who was droning on and saying nothing. If I practiced it, I knew I could stay calm when I had to do it for real.

Hegar and I and our teams met at the TV studio about forty-five minutes before the debate. Glenn was so perturbed at the attacks I'd made on him that he wouldn't look me in the eye. I wasn't overjoyed at my attacks either, truth be told, because Glenn is a devoted family man. I, too, am a devoted family man, and I can't imagine my sons watching someone spend hundreds of thousands of dollars in an effort to discredit their old man. But Glenn put himself on the public stage, and he was now running for the wrong office and for the wrong reasons. When politicians do that, someone has got to go after them aggressively. Someone's got to throw them off balance and force them to defend themselves. Without robust competition, democracy breaks down.

Sitting with Glenn and uncomfortably pretending that we weren't at each other's throats, however, was a feeling I thoroughly detested. We were mic'd up, cameras focused and ready, and in a moment we'd be on live TV, where I knew I'd have to throw punches at some kid's dad. I felt angry that I needed to be there. I also knew that I better not show it; the consultants had been telling me that in a TV debate, you have to be the most likeable one. Smiling and connecting with voters was far more important than any substantive thing I might say.

Let's just get this over with, I thought as I tried to gin up a not-too-phony smile.

....

The debate wasn't really much of a debate. We had thirty minutes, and we just sat around a table and talked. The first question, why are you running for this office, took up as much as five minutes. The second question, regarding revenue forecasting, took up another five minutes. First one candidate answers, then the other. A third question came down the pike regarding tax collecting, and once again it was going to be one candidate, then the other.

Technically, I felt confident that I was doing a better job than Hegar. I answered substantively, and Hegar prattled on about sixth generation, and coming from a farming family, and his wife and kids, and good grief. But I also knew that if all I accomplished was to do a better job than my opponent in an otherwise boring thirty-minute tele-vised conversation, there wouldn't be anything memorable about it. Despite the fact that most Texans had voted and that the debate didn't really matter, all my friends and innumerable political operatives and donors were watching me.

So about two-thirds of the way through, I figured that we were being far too gentlemanly and that it was time to spice things up a bit. And when I had my chance, I threw a hard punch. I called Hegar out for wanting to triple the sales tax. It worked; Hegar wasn't prepared for a *mano a mano* exchange. I decided to strike him again, this time on his refusal to close the property tax loophole in exchange for campaign money from the big lobbyists. Again, he blanched, but he didn't have anything to come back at me with. In my closing remarks, I decided to hit him one last time by saying, "I find it comical that a career politician would lecture a thirty-year businessman on job creation."

As soon as I said that, our time was up. We took off our lapel microphones, we shook the moderator's hand, and we headed for the door. But I was so ashamed to be involved in politics at that moment—having to hit a family man on live TV—that I didn't want to shake Glenn's hand or acknowledge his team. I felt like a man running out of a burning building.

Zach and Cameron walked me to the car, and when we hopped inside and closed and locked the door, I turned and asked them, "Well, what did you think?" They were both very excited and started replaying the parts of the debate that they had liked the most. I found myself unable to recall a single moment, but I enjoyed feeding off their enthusiasm. We drove to a local beer garden where a small group of friends, family, and supporters had gathered. When I entered the room, the crowd erupted in applause, and soon I was getting my back slapped by all kinds of people. Evidently they'd liked my debate performance. I was delighted, even though I couldn't remember a thing.

I was so happy to see Suzanne at the beer garden that I gave her a big hug and a kiss. I can't believe how lucky I am to have such a close friend in Suzanne. This was one of the only campaign events she had attended over a long seventeen-month campaign, not because she's indifferent, but because she's very shy. She told me that she'd had to say a few words to the crowd before the debate, and I asked her how it went. She said it was okay, but a friend nearby said, "She did great!" I gave her another big hug, which I enjoyed more than she did, and then I took the podium and said a few not-so-memorable words.

With that, the campaign was effectively over. I had tackled every challenge and faced down every fear. I raised a respectable amount of money. I learned to make a stump speech. I got used to TV interviews. I survived a convention speech. And that night, I survived a debate on live TV. Most importantly, I held my head high as a Texas Democrat in a deep red state—because it was the right thing to do—and I stayed true to what I believe in.

31

....

Home Stretch

From the outset of the campaign, I'd had a hard time conceptualizing the end of it. I don't normally mind the unknown—in fact, I find it stimulating—but running a statewide campaign is different. For months, I had been working under a cloud of uncertainty and anxiety. I was delighted that Election Day was fast approaching and that, soon, all mysteries would be revealed.

A few days before Election Day, Zach received a note from Leticia's camp detailing all the campaign events she had coming up. She said I was welcome to join any or all of them. A little later that same day, Zach received a similar note from Wendy's campaign team. I thought this would be a terrific way to spend the last few days of the campaign.

Wendy and Leticia were bright, energetic, and sincere. They would have been terrific leaders. Too often, my Republican friends would call and tell me how much they didn't like either one of them—not enough of this or not enough of that. But they never put their criticism in the context of policy; it seemed to me they just didn't like them because they were playing for the opposing team.

Politics, I had learned, is mostly about identity. People identify with their party the same way a student identifies with his high school football team. When the other school's team comes to town, their bus might get pelted with eggs. When the players step off the bus, they might hear hisses and boos. The players might be perfectly likeable and honorable people. But their character doesn't matter as much as their affiliation. I had no idea, before I ran this race, that this was how politics worked.

I made appearances with Leticia in Houston, Brownsville, and McAllen, and I made appearances with Wendy in Houston and San Antonio. Wendy was flying between campaign stops in an airplane, Leticia traveled by motor coach, and I drove my Landslide. On two occasions, my team dropped me off on a street corner, and Leticia's bus picked me up. We then drove a couple of blocks to the event, where a popular Tejano band would be blasting a lively tune and revving up the crowd. The coach would make its dramatic appearance, pulling right up to and looming large over the podium, and Leticia and I and others in her entourage would jump off the bus and wave at the crowd. It was a real hoot.

Leticia's events were the most fun, thanks to the band, and thanks to the crowds, who would be wound up and ready to party. My job was to stand on the podium behind Leticia with all the other luminaries, and when my time came, to try to entertain and energize the crowd. The bit that always worked went something like this:

"Your Democratic slate looks like you, Texas! When you look at the Republican slate, do you see Texas? Do you see women?"

At that point the crowd would get it. "NO!" they would shout back.

"Do you see diversity?"

"NO!" even louder.

I'd pause and lower my voice for effect.

"Now just look at *your* slate. Do you see women?"

"YES!"

"Do you see diversity?"

"YES!!!"

"Your Democratic slate looks like Texas! It comes with women *and* men. It comes with *diversity*. And—"

Slight pause.

"*Your* Democratic ticket comes complete . . . with its own CPA!"

As corny as it sounds, it never failed to get a big laugh. I learned that when a crowd is revved up, they want to shout and they want to laugh. It's great fun for a stand-up comedian wannabe like me.

Wendy's events were completely different. She didn't have a warm-up band to get people's juices flowing. Instead, there was a phalanx of TV news crews, giving the event a much more serious tone. You could see police and security guards, and once there was a helicopter overhead. Wendy would work her way through the crowd, allowing one supporter after another to take their picture with her. She would pause from time to time to do a quick TV interview, and you could see her face and hair illuminated by ultrabright TV lighting. Her mouth would be moving, but you couldn't hear a thing, which added to the intrigue. When the speaking started, the local organizer or another politician would make an introduction, and then came Wendy's speech. Sometimes it was a "Let's go get 'em!" speech, but most of the time it was more dignified.

I was invited to speak only once at one of Wendy's events. Otherwise I just turned up to show support. And that was fine with me: Wendy was playing in the big leagues, and I was still in the minors.

Neither Wendy nor Leticia seemed the least bit fatigued or down about the fact that the polls at the very end didn't look good. I admired their endurance and their belief in themselves. I believed in my heart that they ought to win, and I kept thinking to myself (and saying to others) that this was what an upset looked and felt like.

....

I made my last trip to the Valley, and I decided to stop halfway and spend the night in my beloved Port Aransas. By now I was finished traveling with others. I am essentially a loner, and the hardest part of the campaign for me, by far, was always having someone (not part of my family) with me. So I headed south in Landslide—alone, thank goodness—and I checked into the same hotel in Port Aransas that I had been in three times already on the trail. It was near dusk, and after unpacking I drove to the beach and pulled out a canvas chair that I kept in the back of Landslide at all times just for this purpose. I settled in with a good book and started reading as the sun started its long set. There were very few people on the beach, and the weather was cool enough for a sweater. I figured I had about forty-five minutes to read while I watched the sun go down, all alone, on a huge Texas beach on a cool fall evening.

That visit to the beach only a few days away from Election Day was one of the best and most memorable moments on the campaign trail. I felt right with myself, and I knew that I would soon be reunited with friends and family after seventeen months of campaigning. That evening—and the next morning at 5:00 a.m., when I went back to the beach to watch the sun come up again—all I felt was a sense of pride that I'd had the courage to participate, in a big way, in the Democratic process.

I've always loved waking before dawn and hitting the road. This last campaign trip was no exception. In fact, I was almost giddy. I had gone down to Brownsville from Port Aransas, made my last campaign appearance, and I was headed home.

I picked up a mid-morning voice mail from a close friend whose son Bryan was gravely ill. He had collapsed on a training mission with the US Army, and my sons had gone to New York to sit by his bed. With great emotion, my friend let me know how thankful he was that Michael and Christopher had gone to see Bryan, how my sons were like brothers to him, and how much their visit had cheered him up. Perhaps it was the strain of being away from family and friends for so long, but tears filled my eyes as I listened to the voice mail, and I had to turn off the highway until I got over it. All Suzanne and I had ever wanted for our boys was for them to understand that joy comes from being good men. Well, they are very good men indeed, and it made me think how lucky Suzanne and I are.

I also thought about life after the election. At this point, I knew it was unlikely that I or the other Democrats would win, but it certainly wasn't impossible, and the idea of jumping into a large, complex, and important challenge such as serving Texas as comptroller was thrilling. But I worried about it as well. I worried about missing my family and friends, knowing how easy it is for a workaholic like me to get lost in his work. I also worried about money: Electoral success would mean leaving a lucrative consulting career, which would involve a financial sacrifice that would land on my extended family. The thing I worried about the most, however, was the prospect of somehow being the only Democrat to win. Rationally, I knew this wasn't going to happen, but the thought of being targeted for destruction by a massive, well-oiled, and in my opinion corrupt political machine was daunting.

If, on the other hand, I lost the election—as the polls now were saying I would—I could simply go back to consulting in the energy arena, which I find endlessly fascinating. I could spend time with friends and family, and I could enjoy my favorite pastime—sailing. And as a CPA, I would go back to being an honest broker, sleeping like a baby every night of the week knowing that I was a financial "cop on the beat." I would be able to say that I ran a worthwhile campaign, and I wouldn't have to go through life unhappy with politicians and ashamed that I hadn't had the courage to act.

As determined as I was to win, in short, I didn't mind the idea of losing one bit.

Our Texas Passion: Guns!

On the last leg of my last road trip on the campaign, I received a call from an old friend named Billy who lives in South Texas. He was calling to say that according to a voter guide, I wasn't a National Rifle Association (NRA) member. He pleaded with me to join right away, or else I was certain to lose the election.

I told Billy that I didn't see a reason to join. I own a gun, and I used to hunt, but now I enjoyed sailing, and I don't have time for both. (Billy knew all about my sailboat addiction; he was married to one of my PwC partners, and they all knew about me and sailing.) Still, he was adamant, even suggesting that he might not be able to vote for me if I didn't join the NRA right away.

I gave it some thought. In fact, I had been toying with the idea of joining, if for no other reason than to hear the NRA's point of view on gun violence and gun control. Most of what I know comes from reading the newspapers, and most of what's in the newspapers is the hair-on-fire nonsense you hear from politicians. I always like to hear all sides of a debate, and being an NRA member might help me do that. But I figured that if I joined now, someone would one day accuse me of joining just to create an appearance. Politicians do that all the time, and I never want to fall into that trap.

I explained myself to Billy. He accepted my reasoning, but he was certain that I was going to lose thousands of votes.

I couldn't help think how much easier politics would be if I just played the game.

....

I own a gun. I've always enjoyed guns. I was once an avid hunter, and I revere the US Constitution and our right to own guns. But I also know from firsthand experience how dangerous guns can be.

My father and I were hunting in the woods behind our house in Pennsylvania. I must have been thirteen years old, and I was carrying a single-shot Savage break-action 16-gauge shotgun. I'd had gun safety training, and I knew that you never walked through the woods with the "safety" in the off position, you never walked with your finger near the trigger, and you never

(Continued . . .)

let the muzzle of your gun point in the direction of another hunter (or your-self). It took all three safety protocols to be sure nobody got hurt, and I was fastidious with all three.

We came to a large boulder in the rugged terrain. Dad stepped over it easily, and he'd walked a few paces ahead of me by the time I reached it. I was much shorter than Dad, so stepping down from the boulder would be a little more difficult but not impossible. But as my foot touched the ground, my gun discharged. I was pointing my gun away from Dad, so I missed killing him by a few feet.

I could not believe what had happened. Despite my training, and con-scientiousness, my gun had accidentally discharged. I almost collapsed from the shock of it all, and my Dad and I set our guns down and knelt. Tears were streaming down my cheek as Dad led us in a prayer, thanking God that one of us hadn't died that day.

....

Guns are very dangerous, and the very sight of a gun is unsettling for some people. That's why Texans agreed many years ago on basic ground rules involving guns in public. They simply wanted to keep people safe and to show some decency toward people who feel uncomfortable around guns. We've lived in harmony with these gun laws for a long, long time, and few Texans (until very recently) spent much time thinking about them.

But out of nowhere, it seems, politicians in Texas started scaring voters (and rounding up votes) by screeching that gun rights are in jeopardy. Some-thing has to be done about it! The government is going to take your guns!

This, of course, is nonsense. Not one politician in my memory, Democrat or Republican, has ever threatened to actually take away people's guns. Ever. But hysteria, if you can foment it, works. Gun owners turn out in droves to vote for the candidate that won't take their guns, and political hacks fall all over themselves to prove that they alone can be trusted to preserve Second Amendment rights.

Good policy rarely emerges when actors are so willingly deceptive.

Gun violence in the United States and in Texas had been declining over many years, and it was not because gun laws became more strict. The decline in gun violence was linked to policing techniques and the overall health of our society (e.g., education and employment levels). If we are serious about reducing gun violence, we need to get serious about educating our young people, we need to make sure they have good-paying jobs when they graduate, and we need to invest in health services for the mentally ill. We need to continuously improve our criminal justice system, and (needless to say) we need to continuously improve our anti-terror capabilities. These are the essential ingredients in controlling gun violence, in my opinion.

That said, nearly every Texan I spoke to on the campaign trail believes we need expanded background checks for gun purchases so that criminals, mentally ill people, and terrorists have as difficult a time as possible getting their hands on a gun. But the "they're comin' to take our guns" crowd flies into a rage at the very thought of it, setting some politicians into heavy pandering mode. A constructive, fact-based dialogue becomes next to impossible.

While the 2014 campaign was under way, there was a debate over two new laws which, taken together, will accomplish little more than to create confusion and frustration. One law allows gun owners to carry handguns in holsters, as in the Old West (Open Carry), and the other requires public universities to allow guns on campus (Campus Carry). Both laws took effect in 2016.

Now, there's always the possibility that Open Carry and Campus Carry will backfire on the Republicans. If the state fails to attract business because families don't want to move to Texas, or if gun violence escalates because of it, then lawmakers had better be ready to respond quickly by amending or repealing the law. In particular, Campus Carry might very well impact public universities in a negative way if the best faculty and students go somewhere else in order to find a gun-free environment.

My biggest beef with the Campus Carry crowd has nothing to do with guns. It has to do with freedom. I suspect that many of those who demanded Campus Carry have never, and never will, set foot on the campus of a public university. Instead of leaving the gun policy to the college administration—a sensible thing to do in a free country—they impose their will on the entire institution, for reasons not even tangentially related to a well-regulated

(Continued . . .)

militia. It's a usurpation of the freedom that parents, students, faculty, and staff would otherwise have to manage their own affairs on their own campus.

I suspect that in the end, neither law will be of any real consequence, and I suspect we'll get used to both of them. That will be a sad day for the politicians who feed on hysteria, but no doubt they'll find other ways to keep the gun lobby well stoked, irritating the heck out of the rest of us.

....

During the debates over Open Carry, I had a conversation with a big old boy who worked at a restaurant in North Texas while I was waiting for a friend to join me for dinner. I asked whether his restaurant was going to allow guns, and he said no. "Not good for creating a family environment," he said.

"How do you personally feel about the law?" I asked.

"I don't really care," he said. "But in my view, people who open carry are really stupid."

I asked why, and he looked at me in a puzzled sort of way. I didn't think my question was stupid, but then again, I don't routinely carry a firearm. I suspect he could tell that I didn't.

"When a bad guy walks into a convenience store and starts shooting," he said, "who do you think he's going to shoot first? The guy with the gun! That's why I'm not going to open carry."

It was a good lesson in personal security, which I guess he thought I needed.

32

....

Election Day

When Election Day arrived, I was as calm, relaxed, and self-satisfied as I could be. We started as a team in the morning at a polling station near my home. I arrived a few minutes after the polls opened, ready to greet my neighbors on the big day. There wasn't a soul in sight. I waited for about ten minutes, and then a lone voter parked his car and came walking toward me as I was standing outside the "no candidates beyond this point" line. By the time he reached me, it was awkward for both of us because he knew I was going to make my pitch and he was going to have to react to it. We played our parts, and then he went inside the polling station.

Immediately, I walked straight to my car and said to the team that I was not going to spend the whole day doing *that*.

So we wandered over to a heavily trafficked polling place near downtown Houston, only to find a sea of politicians chasing every person who parked their car and headed to the polls. They were like swarms of mosquitos, and it was clear from the pained expression on voters' faces that they were not winning many votes. I said to the team, "Let's find something else to do."

We wandered over to the Harris County Democratic Party campaign headquarters to join a large number of volunteers who were working the phones to get out the vote. I was given a handful of call sheets, and I started making calls on my cell phone. Plenty of pictures were taken of me, the candidate, shoulder to shoulder with volunteers making calls. I enjoyed it and could have sat there all day, but Zach was just too restless, and after about thirty minutes, he urged us to find something else to do.

Then I had an idea. Why didn't we simply go hang out at the Hyatt in downtown Houston? There is a row of tables in the lobby where we could sit and drink coffee, and we could count on a steady stream of PwC partners and staff who would pass through the hotel as they headed for their cars. It was home turf for me for sure. The team agreed.

It turned out to be a fun afternoon at the Hyatt. I greeted lots of friends as they walked by, for more than two hours. Each time I would see someone I knew, they would charge up and talk to me, knowing that today was the big day. They were respectful and encouraging, and I enjoyed each and every conversation. In the back of my mind, I was thinking that I would either be comptroller-elect in a few hours, or I would be reentering the energy arena and working once again with these people. Both were perfectly acceptable outcomes at this stage of the game, and I was ecstatic that one or the other was right around the corner.

At one point Sam Houston called and asked if I wanted to join him at his office a few miles away and watch returns together. Sam and I had planned a party at a local watering hole that night, and our friends and supporters would be assembling for a fun evening. By custom, the candidate waits to make a big entry when the results are known. So it made sense that Sam and I would watch the returns together, then go to the party together.

We had our small teams with us, plus a few others, including the Texas Oracle, as we watched the returns come in.

With six percent of the precincts reported, the election was called for the Republicans.

I never understood why they called the elections with so few precincts in, but Sam's right-hand man explained that the early votes had already been counted, and they represented just under half of all the votes to be cast. That plus the six percent of precincts reported were enough to make the call. It looked as if we were going to lose by a whopping twenty points. Every candidate was getting roughly the same number of votes, on both tickets. It was a straight party vote for sure. There probably wasn't much Sam or I could have done to impact the outcome.

I turned to Sam, and he looked stricken. I knew instantly what he was thinking. For Sam, this was more than an electoral loss. Sam had just lost to a man who was going to be indicted for criminal wrongdoing, and who'd completely hid from public view. His opponent didn't campaign, as an honorable man should do; he manipulated the political machinery, and as a result, he had just become the state's top law enforcer. We were all stricken, Sam more than the rest, at how corrupt Texas politics had become.

I looked around the room and saw long faces on Cameron, Zach, and Demi as well. I wasn't quite sure what to say, so I simply stood and started toward the elevator.

But despite my empathy for Sam and my distaste for what had happened in his race, congenital cheerfulness came back to me before the elevator door had closed. As we rode down together, Sam's face regained its color, too, and I could see he was going to be just fine. We had done our best, and we had served Texas in a way that we could be proud of.

We reached ground level and started to our cars when Sam suddenly spun around and asked, "You planning to call Glenn Hegar and congratulate him?"

"I don't think so," I said. "What do you say to an opponent who didn't campaign?"

"Me either," was all Sam said.

....

About seventy-five people had assembled at our watch party, and most everyone knew by the time we arrived that we hadn't won. Still, it was a joyful scene, and I was happy to see everyone.

I must confess that the competitor in me felt a little awkward walking in and saying, in effect, "Hi, it's your old friend Mike, returned from a seventeen-month mission, and I failed!" It stung for a moment, but only for a moment.

By the time I had worked my way up to the stage, greeting people as I went, I was feeling genuinely wonderful. Suzanne and some very good friends had gathered where a microphone had been set up for speeches. Steve and Lisa Kelly, very close friends from Kingwood, were on hand. For ten years they've been joining Suzanne and me for dinner at a Mexican restaurant near our respective homes, every Friday night. That's some five hundred dinners, minus the handful of Fridays (but not many) we've missed over the years. Steve can read my mind, and he knew that I wouldn't be sad. His broad, congratulatory smile gave him away, and it was great to see both of them.

Suzanne gave me a big hug and a kiss, and I could see she was having a fun evening. She is unflappable; she would have been happy if I had won, but she was also plenty happy that I had lost. What Suzanne cares about in life, namely family and friends, has zero to do with winning or losing political campaigns. Meeting and marrying Suzanne back in the 1980s was by far the best thing that ever happened to me. Our sons Michael and Christopher were away at college, but they each sent a quick text along the lines of YOU DID GREAT, POPS! CONGRATULATIONS!

Other close friends had assembled, including Mark Goss and his wife Melissa. Mark was my best man at our wedding twenty-six years earlier, and we've been close for many, many years. In college we would talk for hours about politics, and like so many young businessmen we had fallen under the spell of Ronald Reagan. When I called Mark to tell him I was running as a Democrat, I braced myself, but I hadn't needed to. He was one of the first to say he understood. Mark is conservative, but he's got a fighter's reflex when it comes to corruption, and he supported me all the way.

When it came time for speeches, I kept mine simple:

> An experienced politician told me that you prepare two speeches for Election Day. Otherwise, it's bad luck.
>
> Having thought about it, I decided that win or lose, it's the same speech.
>
> We are trying to make history in Texas by bringing political competition to our state. Had we won, the work ahead of us would be just as enormous as it seems tonight. This will be a long, frustrating journey, but we owe it to each other to stay the course. Texas is the second largest state, but we are the fastest-growing

state, and that makes us the most important state in the world's most important constitutional democracy. The quality of our political lives in the United States is linked to the quality of our political lives in Texas. It is essential that we bring political competition to Texas. It is essential that we keep our shoulder to this wheel and make history, as we surely will, and turn Texas into a two-party democracy.

So, let's go home tonight and not set our alarms, because we've earned the luxury of sleeping in. But come 10:00 a.m. tomorrow, let's all get back into the game and keep working until we accomplish this essential objective.

The crowd warmly applauded, and with that, I brought my 2014 campaign to become Texas comptroller to a close.

....

Steve and Lisa drove us the twenty minutes it takes to get home from Houston late at night. We could have been driving home from an Astros game, except that I was more wound up than usual, and that's saying something. I sensed that Lisa was watching to see whether I was putting on a show, only to collapse in tears when Suzanne and I were alone. But I wasn't, and the four of us talked about how much fun we were going to have on a post-election weekend trip to Mexico we had planned a few days earlier.

Steve and Lisa dropped us off, and I went outside to sit and unwind while Suzanne went to bed. It was a balmy November evening with a light haze that obscured the stars. A few poked through, and I enjoyed seeing them. A good friend of ours, Steve Bowen, is a NASA astronaut who flew three Space Shuttle missions. Suzanne and I were his guests, along with our sons, at each of his launches in Florida, the first of which was a night launch.

Watching the Space Shuttle launch was a spiritual experience. The power is unfathomable, the sound waves making your clothes flap even though you're five miles away. With binoculars, you can see the boosters separate, and for another minute or two you can see a brilliant white dot getting smaller and smaller. Just a few minutes later the craft is flying eighteen thousand miles an hour, and your friend is strapped to it.

Every time I sit under the stars, I get lost thinking about what it must have been like for Steve to fly on the Shuttle. And sure enough, there I sat, fresh off a seventeen-month, multimillion-dollar, statewide campaign, alone to collect my thoughts, and all I could think about was how cool it must be to be an astronaut.

33

....

Listening Tour

When I awoke the next morning, there were many opportunities in front of me. I knew it would take some time to settle into a strategy for making the most of the years I have ahead of me. I called Will Hailer and asked if he had time to get together in Austin to debrief, and he invited me to meet him for lunch the next week. Meantime Suzanne and I had arranged to take our sons, her sister, and my young nieces and nephews to ride roller coasters at an amusement park in San Antonio. I love roller coasters, and there's nothing better than spending a few days with family in an amusement park scrambling your brains to commemorate some big event.

Will Hailer and I met in Austin over lunch a week later and compared notes. I told him that I was pleased with the support I had received from donors and the party and that I was not the least bit deterred by the outcome of the election. I made it clear that I have a long-term view of our need to make Texas politically competitive, and the only question I had now was what, specifically, I might do to help achieve that.

Will asked whether I would consider running for office again, and he suggested that if I did so, support would be there. I told him we'd know when it was time to raise money in 2018. In the meantime, I told him that I wanted to use the platform I had built to keep the pressure on Republicans to do right by Texans.

My reading of the tea leaves was that the Republicans were going to go quietly about their business of refusing to fund public education, taking us further into debt, ignoring the highway and water crises that are already on us, paying off campaign donors by cutting their taxes (and making hardworking Texans pay for it), and continuing to refuse any program that might help achieve a thriving and ascendant middle class. And they are going to disguise this whole anti-Texan program, with remarkable insincerity, as "the conservative agenda." And until the Democrats create real competition at the statewide level, the Republicans will get away with it.

That's why I told Will that I was going to stay in the fight.

....

Within a few days of our meeting, Will called and asked if I would be willing to go on a "listening tour" of the state. He said if I were willing, Texas Democratic Party Chairman Hinojosa would extend the invitation, and I would be charged with finding out what the Democratic Party faithful had to say about the election. It was my intention to launch an energy consulting firm right after the holidays, and the listening tour would delay its launch by at least three months. I knew that the listening tour wouldn't be full-time, however, which also meant that I could write this book and start calling on my business contacts to lay the groundwork for Collier Analytics, LLC. I said yes, but I set a hard deadline for completing the tour by February 1.

Throughout the course of December and January, I traveled around the state or sat in my home office participating in conference calls, listening to Democrats share their point of view about the party's loss, and more importantly, its trajectory. Our loss in 2014 was much wider than our loss in 2010, which in turn was much wider than the loss in 2006. If we were to continue as a franchise, we had to address that.

I was surprised at how generous people were with their kind remarks about my campaign. The TV commercials, which many activists had seen on YouTube, were a real hit, and I was pleasantly surprised at how many Democrats were urging me to run again in 2018.

But what pleased me the most about the listening tour was that I discovered a sense of pride and purpose among Texas Democrats that an electoral loss couldn't diminish. To stay committed to a cause after a defeat is the truest test of commitment. Democrats in Texas want to see fellow Democrats win because they are tired of being treated like second-class citizens by a Republican leadership that has become arrogant. Democrats can see the pain of one-party rule in a large and complex state, and they are chafing at the antidemocratic and corrupt measures Republican politicians use to remain in power.

When we finished the tour, I sat down at my computer and wrote a one-page letter to Chairman Hinojosa thanking him for inviting me to conduct the listening tour. Then I took about ninety minutes to write a short framework, thinking that I would expand it into a comprehensive series of findings and recommendations. But when I'd finished with the short version, I was pleased with it as it was. It was simple and, I thought, actionable.

I sent the report to the Texas Oracle, whose judgment had become invaluable to me. He offered a few edits but said I should let it fly. I sent it to a party staffer who had helped me with the tour, and he surprised me by circulating it to everyone he could think of. When it came back to me about ten days later, it was largely unchanged. I was very pleasantly surprised.

An Excerpt from the Collier Report to Gilberto Hinojosa

March 2015
To the Honorable Gilberto Hinojosa
Chairman, Texas Democratic Party

Dear Chairman Hinojosa,

In December 2014, you invited me to conduct a "listening tour" around the state of Texas to understand—based on conversations with party chairs, activists, volunteers, candidates, and elected officials—why the Democrats lost by double digits to Republicans in the 2014 election cycle, and to make recommendations as to how we might win in 2016 and beyond. I was honored that you asked me to do this, and I am pleased to write to you today with my findings.

As you know, I asked the Democratic Party to support my run for comptroller not because it was the surest route to success, but because the Texas Democratic

Party stands for the things I stand for: integrity and intelligence in government and respect for individuals and individual freedom. I am delighted to continue my work with you and members of the Texas Democratic Party around the state who so warmly received me some eighteen months ago.

With the help of TDP staff, I conducted conference calls and participated in meetings in Austin, Dallas, Houston, Beaumont, El Paso, and Montgomery County. I also spoke to Democrats in one-on-one conversations in San Antonio; rural North, West, and East Texas; and the Rio Grande Valley. Altogether, I heard from hundreds of Democrats that were a representative sample of our party's diversity across the state.

I encouraged participants to comment on our party's message and our field programs. I have included our local Democrats' thoughts on the election, as well as my own analysis and recommendations for the party going forward. I am in complete agreement with the very clear consensus that emerged from my conversations.

I conducted these conversations before voter data had been analyzed by TDP. That meant that our conversations were qualitative in nature. This report is qualitative, and not quantitative, for the same reason. And while I tried to keep the conversations focused on broad themes that can be implemented statewide, there were times when we discussed important caucus-specific issues, which I will discuss with you separately.

Chairman Hinojosa, I want to take this opportunity to thank you and everyone at the Texas Democratic Party, along with the party faithful, for throwing your shoulder to the wheel to help me succeed. We did not win the battle in 2014, but if we stay in the fight, we will win the war!

I look forward to discussing this letter, and these recommendations, with you at your earliest convenience.

Best regards,
Mike

....

A very clear consensus emerged from my conversations regarding what it means to be a Texas Democrat and what we must do to develop a winning message.

First, we need to narrow, and then sharpen, our message around the fact that *the Democratic Party is the unique, historic, and indispensable champion of the working and middle class.* We will motivate voters through our unwavering commitment to economic security for hardworking Texans. In this, the Democratic Party has an unimpeachable record of fighting for safe working conditions, fair employment practices, livable wages, access to affordable health care, access to excellent public education, support for college tuition, respect for diversity, and antipathy toward discrimination. Republican politicians in Texas, in contrast, have an indefensible record of bringing forward policies that work against the interests of the working and middle class. We should be vigorous and relentless in driving this point home.

Second, we should trumpet the fact that Democrats promote policies that result in economic expansion, creating real economic opportunities for everyone, not just for the sons and daughters of the well-to-do. Thus the **Texas Democratic Party is the true pro-business party**. We understand that we must invest in schools, roads, and water infrastructure without becoming addicted to debt and without abandoning our low-tax framework. This is the key to a thriving economy over the long term that will lift everyone's chance at a productive and successful life. Republicans falsely claim credit for the Texas miracle, when in fact they have given us terrible public schools, crippling congestion, inadequate water resources, and a mountain of debt. We should never miss an opportunity to drive home the point that our economy thrives despite these Republican policies, not because of them. We must constantly remind voters that it's the Democrats who offer policies that are genuinely pro-economic expansion and job growth and which promote a healthy and well-educated workforce for the future.

Third, **Democrats, not Republicans, can be trusted to keep taxes low for hardworking Texans**. Democrats will not tolerate corporate interests shifting the tax burden onto the backs of the people who actually live and work here, something the Republicans are very good at. Republicans are also very good at increasing tolls and fees (hoping Texans won't realize these are taxes) while they are leading us into a very deep hole of debt and dilapidation (the most insidious form of "tax," because debt and dilapidation become our children's problem). Democrats need to constantly remind voters that Republican politicians work very hard against the interests of ordinary Texans (even their own Republican supporters!) when it comes to tax policy, whereas Democrats will hold the line on taxes for the people who actually live and work here.

Finally, **Texas Democrats are men and women of faith**, just as surely as Republicans are. While Republicans claim for themselves the religious mantle, and brand us as anti-religious, Democrats of faith must not hide their light under a bushel. Democrats of faith must show that their religious beliefs lead them to empathy and compassion, traditional Texas values that have been abandoned by Republican politicians. Democrats of faith must also show that fidelity to the US Constitution and the rule of law, and therefore to individual freedom, is perfectly consistent with our religious beliefs.

To quote one loyal Democrat, these are the "kitchen-table issues" that matter to Texans, and we should focus on these relentlessly. Our "ownership" of these issues is not just spin; our track record of accomplishment over many decades is unassailable. And they are not transient principles or course corrections that might be seen as pandering. Democrats have always believed in, and delivered on, these promises. Our track record proves it, and Republican politicians will be unable to attack us, or defend themselves, when Texas Democrats find their voice.

There is an asymmetry in Texas politics. Republican politicians have the luxury of deliberately misleading their followers, which they do with great vigor and enthusiasm. In contrast, it's in the DNA of the Texas Democrat to deal rationally and honestly with matters of public policy. We allow this asymmetry, which should be a strategic advantage in our hands, to be turned against us by Republicans. We need to retake the initiative and make this asymmetry work for us. We need to continuously trumpet the good things Democrats have done over many decades for hardworking families, and we need to hammer the Republicans for using deception to achieve their political aims.

34

....

Just Wait

By the time the Republicans were being sworn in, in 2015, the price of oil had begun to collapse, and economic trouble for our state was clearly on the horizon. This is exactly what I'd worried about during the TribFest panel (only to be rebuffed by an "I know better than you" Republican who I think today looks darn stupid).

But the fact that the energy economy was losing speed and altitude, and with it jobs as well as state revenues, didn't stop the big corporations from throwing a $4.5 million inaugural bash for their Republican heroes, with parades and live bands and oceans of beer and millions of pounds of BBQ.[1] It was clear to me they were celebrating another four years of getting whatever they wanted from a junta they had just installed. Their $4.5 million party was chump change in comparison to the $1+ billion annual tax cut they got a few weeks later.

Sadly, the energy depression that followed was worse than anything Texas had seen in decades, and Republicans found themselves in a real pickle. They gave the big corporations that massive tax break, just as newly sworn-in Governor Abbott said they would, and soon they are going to find that there's not enough money for schools, roads, bridges, securing unsafe dams, and the rest. Politicians can't very well brag about the Texas miracle—not unless they want to offend all the good folks working in the oil business who have been laid off, and to expose themselves to the charge that oil, not Republican policies, is the real Texas miracle.

Say what you will about politicians, they're clever when it comes to spin. They stopped spinning the "Texas miracle," but they've started spinning the "Texas model," as in Texas politicians know how to do things right. There's even a whiff of "You ought to try it!" aimed at other states and at the country as a whole. But if we want to export the Texas model, we'd better fix it first, and there is no way that's going to happen while we remain in the iron grip of a political machine. We *must* have political competition in Texas.

Some say the Democratic Party is wasting its time in attempting to do this and our prospects for success are fading fast. That's what the Republicans want everyone to think, because a feeling of inevitability keeps voters at home on Election Day. But I've spoken to thousands of Texans: Democrats, Republicans, Libertarians—you name it. They are ready for change. They'll vote for Democrats in Texas when they are convinced the Democrats are focused on kitchen-table issues such as creating jobs and keeping taxes low and fair, while cherishing their freedom and the US Constitution. I would not have joined the Democratic Party otherwise. And the harder I work to get this message out, the more support I feel from Democrats and Republicans alike.

So to those who say there is no accounting for Texas—that our politics are awful and always will be—I say just wait.

EPILOGUE CHAPTER 1

....

The 2018 Contest Takes Shape

A quiet fellow from El Paso sat to my left, and together we faced a large conference table in a downtown Austin skyscraper. I knew his name, but I knew little about him. He was a pleasant fellow with a boyish, toothy grin and none of the stuffiness that comes with being a US congressman. For the next three hours, the youngster from El Paso listened patiently and didn't say a word as leaders of the Texas Democratic Party debated Donald Trump's recent election and what it meant for Texas.

Party Chairman Gilberto Hinojosa called the meeting. Former governor candidate Wendy Davis was there, as were US Congressman Joaquín Castro and his twin brother, Julian. Julian had just returned from Washington, DC, where he had served as secretary of Housing and Urban Development. Also in attendance were the former mayor of Houston, Annise Parker; Mayor Steve Adler (Austin); Senator Raphael Anchia; and former state representatives Trey Martinez Fischer and Alan Vaught.

The only folks in the room who had never held office were our host, businessman Jack Martin, and Crystal Perkins, the party's newly hired executive director. And, of course, me.

When Donald Trump won the 2016 election, I knew immediately that Democrats would do very well in the midterm elections. I also knew that Texans were reaching the boiling point over public education and property taxes. As I traveled the state, I became convinced that my ideas were powerful enough to sway voters. But I figured I would have to run for governor; only the governor could control the narrative and get the message out, right?

Another run for comptroller was out of the question. Glenn Hegar, who defeated me in 2014, had turned out to be exactly the kind of comptroller I knew he would be—one who carried water for the higher-ups but stayed completely away from policy. And voters were OK with that. So I'd decided to run for a more consequential position. Besides, folks—including the party's outgoing executive director, Will Hailer—were talking about me as a governor candidate.

So there I sat next to the kid from El Paso at a meeting meant to kick off the 2018 election season, hoping to get the nod to run for governor.

The nod never came.

We all liked each other and enjoyed comparing notes, but nobody wanted to get into the messy business of picking a 2018 slate. Instead, we talked wistfully and without real direction. By midafternoon, the meeting had run its course. That's when the quiet fellow from El Paso, Beto O'Rourke, cleared his throat and, out of nowhere—and totally out of sync with the topic at hand—said, "I have something I'd like to say."

We all turned to Beto.

"I have to run for Senate. I can't look my children in the eye ten years from now and tell them I didn't have the courage to do it. I told my constituents I would serve only two terms in the House, so I plan to do this. Joaquín, I hope you run, too. But I have to do this."

Congressman Castro, who everyone assumed would run for Senate, didn't seem the least bit fazed by Beto's outburst. Nobody did. Beto held the floor for about five minutes, and we all sat and listened respectfully. His sincerity and passion were remarkable. He talked about running for and winning the El Paso city council seat, listening to people, and being a regular guy. He said he'd done the same when he ran for Congress. That style—understanding voters' concerns and earning their trust through honest dialogue—would serve him well in the upcoming Senate race.

Beto's pitch was authentic, exuberant, even contagious. But could he really charm a state as big as Texas? Could anyone with precious little name recognition defeat Senator Ted Cruz, the most well-known politician in our state? Though it felt like a long shot to me, Beto seemed to be a one-of-a-kind politician. *Who knows*, I thought. *Maybe he'll make a splash.*

I left the meeting a Beto fan, but I figured Joaquín Castro, who had much more name recognition, would beat him in the primary. As for my plans—I was still set on running for governor.

A few weeks later, I drove to South Texas to meet with potential donors who might support my campaign. It was early 2017, and candidates would soon be maneuvering into position. While I was in the Rio Grande Valley, I called Chairman Hinojosa. He invited me to stop by, which I was very happy to do, and he took me on a little tour of his Brownsville office and the restored historic home across the street where he and his wife lived.

As we talked, Chairman Hinojosa asked if I had given any thought to running again in 2018. Needless to say, he was playing a subtle game because he (and everyone else) knew I'd been talking about running for governor. So I decided to play a subtle game too. I said I was open to running but wondering which office made the most sense. What did Chairman Hinojosa think I should do?

Chairman Hinojosa got right to the point—he urged me to run for lieutenant governor. We needed a firebrand at the top of the ticket to turn out the Democratic base, he reasoned. And the incumbent, Lieutenant Governor Dan Patrick, was very unpopular; I might beat him for that reason alone. He pointed out that Patrick might not run for reelection (Patrick had been angling for governor); in that case, I would be running against someone with low name recognition and little campaign money.

Of course, he said, lieutenant governor holds much more power than the governor. I could actually get things done in that role.

I sat for a moment, disappointed the nod wasn't for governor. But Chairman Hinojosa's logic was sound, and I am a team player. "Yes," I said. "I'll run for lieutenant governor." He immediately replied, "Thank you. I'm glad we got that straightened out."

As I made the six-hour drive from deep South Texas to Houston, I mulled over the commitment I'd just made. Could I raise the money and attract attention if I ran for lieutenant governor? After all, few

Texans know the lieutenant governor is the most powerful position in the state. What would happen if we ended up with a firebrand governor candidate who started a right-wing Republican stampede? What if we had no candidate at all? What if Beto ran for Senate and became a rock star? Would that energy lift everyone else? But what if he fell flat? Could a candidate for lieutenant governor motivate the base?

All these variables quickly exhausted me. Finally, I put it to rest with this simple decision: If the chairman of the Texas Democratic Party wanted me to run for lieutenant governor, then I'd run for lieutenant governor and not look back.

EPILOGUE CHAPTER 2

....

Launch Sequence and Mission #2

I had just taken a position with Duff & Phelps, a global financial services firm, and was building a merger and acquisitions practice in the energy arena. When I broke the news of my campaign, my employers were very supportive, structuring an arrangement that allowed me to campaign full-time while serving as a senior advisor to the company. Once that was in place, I started calling on donors who'd financed my 2014 campaign. They were "all in," and we started raising good money; the first $250,000 came in just a few days. I was off to a strong start.

Then something truly remarkable happened. Dozens of Texans with no political experience—good neighbors leading ordinary lives—started registering to run for office: US Congress, State Senate, Texas House, county commissioner, you name it. We had never seen anything like it. Many of the Democratic primaries were contested, some with multiple candidates. Donald Trump's election motivated terrific people to run for office. They didn't care about the odds; they just signed up and started campaigning because they were worried about their country.

And they campaigned on specific issues (like education, health care, etc.). They wanted to solve problems honestly and treat people with respect. This was precisely the recommendation I'd made to the party a few months before. Down-ballot candidates talking about "kitchen table" issues would get Democrats to the polls. I had a very good feeling about 2018.

Then, like a tornado, "Beto-mania" came out of nowhere. The kid from El Paso sure knew how to campaign. He didn't take money from PACs; Beto just hit the road in his pickup truck, switched on Facebook Live, and treated everyone to a fun, rollicking ride around the great state of Texas with a young, energetic, fun dude with a funny name. It was brilliant!

As our prospects brightened by the day, I had to deal with an unexpected challenge. Traditional donors stopped giving me money. Not all of them, but most. Too many good candidates needed resources, and donors like to spend their money where it will do the most good. My opponent had a formidable $15 million war chest, so Democratic donors chose to support local candidates in swing districts—races where their bucks would make a real bang against opponents without much money.

Like I said—I'm a team player. I wasn't the least bit surprised. Nor was I disappointed. Why? As long as donors supported Democratic candidates, I would benefit from their investment. But I still needed to blunt the impact of Dan Patrick's massive war chest.

So I decided to think strategically and make every dollar count. Figuring Patrick would carpet-bomb the state with last-minute TV ads, my only hope was to make those ads ineffective. So I did two things.

First, I riled up voters as much as I could over public education and property taxes. Patrick's record here was awful, and I hoped that public outcry would force his campaign to spend money defending him. Scott Milder, the Republican who had challenged Patrick in the primary and later endorsed my campaign, was a huge help because teachers paid very close attention to him (I'll talk more about Scott later).

Then, I assembled a cutting-edge digital team, the likes of which Texas politics had never seen. They skillfully targeted voters with messages, many of which thoroughly discredited Patrick before his barrage of TV ads ever hit the airwaves.

My digital team began with Courtney Grigsby, who discovered the two guys I came to call "the Gremlins." Ali Zaidi and Jared Hrebenar joined my team after high school; the two interns quickly earned my trust. Ali and Jared worked on my campaign between their college freshman classes; they and their boss, Courtney, were absolutely incredible. They could tell from their digital tracking that at least two million Texans planned to vote for me.

And we knew from that same digital tracking that our messages were resonating with voters. Patrick's polls revealed he was in trouble on education and property taxes, so he took the bait, spending millions of dollars on ads addressing both. And when our digital team's targeted audience saw those ads, they responded as we'd hoped: "Yep, there's Dan Patrick lying about education and property taxes, just like Collier said he would." Achieving those results was an unbelievable performance by some incredibly smart, loyal, and good people.

Patrick's huge war chest and my more limited campaign funds pushed me to hone my message. I condensed my platform into five simple, powerful commitments:

- restore retired teacher health-care benefits (the previous legislative session had made deep cuts);

- close the big corporate property tax loophole (discussed in the essay on page 120) and use that money to fund public education;

- expand Medicaid (it's a good deal for Texas);

- reform our criminal justice system; and

- end gerrymandering by adopting an independent redistricting commission.

No candidate for Texas lieutenant governor had ever been as specific. And no candidate—Democratic or Republican—had a plan as popular with Texas voters. All I had to do was get my message out. With very little money, I relied on Courtney and the Gremlins and their digital prowess. And they almost pulled it off!

My message was so effective that Dan Patrick, a radio entertainer by profession, a man who never shied away from political back and forth—he even weirdly challenged TV personality Geraldo Rivera to a debate—was afraid to appear on the debate stage with me. He knew I would absolutely tear him to shreds. I had command of the facts, I stayed on message relentlessly, and I was on the winning side of every issue. Patrick had cut public education by $660 million, he said "No!" to funding retired teacher benefits, he took campaign cash to keep the big corporate property tax loophole wide open, he blocked school and gun safety measures, he raised property taxes more than any lieutenant governor in history, he refused to hire a new state auditor (even though the last one quit three years earlier), he added $10 billion in new debt to the state's books, and he wasted everyone's time with a hateful bathroom bill that tanked Texas's business reputation.

Patrick knew a debate would cost him the election. But he didn't just avoid a debate. He avoided voters and reporters. I found this to be a miscarriage of democracy, though it didn't surprise me. The Dan Patricks of the world aren't interested in democracy; they crave power, democracy be damned. Though not surprising, it's a disgrace.

Patrick's refusal to come out of his campaign bunker and present himself to voters and reporters made my campaign pretty simple. I got up in the morning, did all that I could to get my message out, and went to bed. For more than a year, that was my life.

I referred to my campaign strategy as "high-tech, high-touch," an expression I borrowed from a management treatise I read years ago. The digital machine ran constantly; my job was to supply content. So I met as many Texans as I possibly could, sometimes driving for hours— me and Ol' Paint, my white Ford F-150—to see a few activists before turning around to head home. Our digital platform placed images and video from those interactions in front of thousands of Texans. Truth be told, I am so enthralled by my beloved Texas and so love the people who live here that I enjoyed all 100,000 miles of the campaign.

The best part, far and away, was shaking hands and talking one-on-one with folks before and after an appearance. I shook so many hands that my elbow and wrist were developing tendonitis. One evening in Beaumont, I shook more than six hundred hands! As I drove home, my hand on the steering wheel was swollen. Like politics of a bygone era, the 2018 race was all about meeting people—with the modern aspect of sharing those encounters through digital media. In contrast, my 2014 comptroller race had been all about raising money and buying TV commercials. I think high-tech, high-touch is the future of politics, and that suits me just fine.

Another major difference between campaigning in 2014 and 2018 was the voters' preference for authenticity and lack of interest in polished advertisements. In 2014, most people knew me from high-production-quality TV commercials, ads we ran at enormous expense. By contrast, in 2018 we produced only two such TV commercials—and they accomplished precious little. Would you believe that a simple video recorded by the Gremlins on an iPhone, showing me standing in front of a Jeep at a gas station late at night, a hamburger in one hand and milk in the other, saying, "I don't know where I am," outperformed polished ads that we put in front of voters?

When we wanted to talk to voters about water resources in Texas, I jumped into a swimming hole with my suit on. Why not? I've always had a zany side. We picked a Friday afternoon and there, in Georgetown—my hometown—I jumped into the San Gabriel River. The resulting digital ad performed better than most of our other advertising. Suffice it to say, campaigning in the new digital world is a whole lot more fun than the old days of phone calls, money raising, and Hollywood-style TV commercials.

EPILOGUE CHAPTER 3

....

If God Wills I Become
Lieutenant Governor . . .

Although I'd already run for statewide office, my name recognition at the outset of the 2018 campaign was very low. Texas, after all, is a very, very big state, and you can't imagine how much time and money it takes to build any sort of brand equity.

So, when Michael Cooper from Beaumont entered the Democratic primary, I was very worried. Our names are almost identical, and few people knew either one of us. Michael is a terrific person—tall, handsome, charismatic—and he's done some preaching. Few things terrify an accountant like me as much as competing for public office against someone like Mr. Cooper. Even so, we genuinely liked each other, and seeing him on the campaign trail was always a joy. As the primary unfolded, I knew that, with such similar names and low name recognition, anything could happen. I often said to my team (and to myself), "If God wills me to be lieutenant governor, then I'll be lieutenant governor. If not, then I won't."

It was a close primary, but I won. And Michael Cooper and I remained friends.

A much more remarkable primary story happened on the Republican side. Public education supporters recruited Scott Milder, Dan Patrick's primary opponent. Scott's a former city councilman from Rockwall; he and I met at a candidate forum in East Texas where our primary opponents were no-shows. As we shook hands on stage before the event, Scott and I instantly liked each other. We were in the race for the exact same reason: our belief in public education in Texas. And we both saw Dan Patrick as education's number one enemy.

Though Scott and I belonged to opposing political parties, the sincerity of our motives inspired us to pledge mutual support. We made several appearances together, enjoying each other thoroughly. Though Scott didn't win his primary, he commanded more than twenty-five percent of the Republican vote, a testament to his appeal and to Texans' desire for excellent public education. Before primary night ended, Scott crossed party lines and endorsed me. And we campaigned together until Election Day. No doubt Scott and I will remain comrades-in-arms in the fight for public education.

Perhaps the one new relationship that impacted me the most was with Pastor Charles Johnson, leader of Pastors for Texas Children and an enthusiastic supporter. We both see public education as a moral imperative, and we made many campaign appearances together. Pastor Johnson is an exuberant man with an unquenchable thirst for justice that is motived by his faith. As we grew closer, Pastor Johnson changed my heart and awakened a similar motivation in me (though I haven't yet found a way to tell him).

In the future, I expect to be in the trenches with Scott Milder, Pastor Johnson, and other devoted, pro-public education leaders like Troy Reynolds (Texans for Public Education) and Carolyn Boyle (Parent PAC). We won't cease fighting for public education until Texas has the best public schools in the nation.

Perhaps the most pleasant surprise of the campaign came when Suzanne was surfing the net and discovered a thirty-second commercial of me talking about compassion. I was stunned; our campaign hadn't created it. I wondered, *Who did?* I looked closely and recognized the video was recorded in a barbecue joint in Goldthwaite, Texas, where I'd spoken to a small group of Democrats. Unbeknownst to me, a fellow named Brock Cravy was filming as I spoke from the heart about bringing compassion back to public policy. Brock turned that moment into a commercial people really responded to.

Well, if folks liked hearing me talk about compassion, I decided I would happily oblige. I was raised in the Christian faith by a Catholic father and a Methodist mother, and that upbringing and resulting value system mean so much to me. It's why I found such joy traveling the state and preaching the gospel of compassion. On the stump, I'd forcefully say that separation of church and state is fundamental to freedom, and my audience would burst into applause. Then, I'd tell them I was raised Catholic, I read the Bible, and I had found compassion and empathy in that ancient book. Often, I'd recite this verse: "Whatsoever you do to the least of thy brethren, that you do unto me." That pretty much sums it up for me. My audience would always show their support with enthusiastic applause.

As I warmly reflect on how Christian values played an increasingly important role in my campaign experience, the abortion issue remains a major frustration. Unlike the 2014 election cycle (which was all about abortion), the issue almost never came up in 2018. I certainly had no plans to bring it up because it creates enormous difficulties for Democratic candidates. Obviously, Republicans will stampede if you campaign on a pro-choice platform. Not so obviously, but importantly, many Democrats will stay home too; in Texas, many Democrats are Catholic.

The fact that nobody was talking about abortion should have been good for my campaign, right? Not necessarily. Thousands of pro-public education voters wanted to vote for me but felt unable to do so because of the abortion issue. One otherwise supportive Texan told me that if she cast a vote for a Democrat, she would not be able to go to Heaven.

The fact is, my calling is to reduce the need for abortion services through education, contraception, and adoption—because that's what works! Passing anti-abortion laws doesn't reduce the need for abortion services. Nor does demeaning women or taking away their decision rights. Although I didn't have the chance to debate Dan Patrick, I longed for the opportunity to say what I thought needed to be said: The lieutenant governor does not have the power to outlaw abortion. Even if he did, it wouldn't change a thing. The lieutenant governor does, however, have the power to reduce the need for abortion services—through education, contraception, and adoption. And that's what we should be working on. It's frustrating beyond description.

EPILOGUE CHAPTER 4

....

Broken Hearts and Unyielding Resolve

Not long after I formally announced my decision to run for lieutenant governor, a gunman entered a church in Sutherland Springs, opened fire, and killed two dozen Texans in their place of worship. It was devastating. For the first time, I felt the utter bankruptcy of releasing a statement offering thoughts and prayers and nothing more. I decided that as lieutenant governor, I would move aggressively to address gun violence. After a tragedy like Sutherland Springs, I was not going to face voters with little more than thoughts and prayers.

Within six months of the church massacre, tragedy struck at Santa Fe High School. A gunman killed a dozen Texans, many of whom were students. I felt a visceral motivation to act, so I organized a press conference with representatives from American Federation of Teachers and Moms Demand Action. Together, we called for a special legislative session to appropriate funds for school safety and take up the issue of gun safety.

My opponent's response to the Sutherland Springs and Santa Fe tragedies? He offered thoughts and prayers. Patrick went on to blame video games and godlessness for America's mass murder epidemic; he then blocked any meaningful discussion of gun safety. It was disgraceful.

Clearly, we need to invest more in school counselors and trained psychologists. We need adults who can develop relationships with students and address difficult situations before—not after—a crisis develops. And we need sensible gun laws, like background check systems that work and "red flag" laws that allow authorities to temporarily remove weapons, following due process, if someone presents a danger to themselves or the community. Implementing these two steps, each perfectly consistent with the Second Amendment, would change Texas's politics around gun safety dramatically. When I came out forcefully for these two measures, I did not receive any pushback from anyone. Texans are ready.

A wonderful woman named Rhonda Hart, whose daughter, Kimberly, died in the Santa Fe High School shooting, reached out to me during the campaign. Rhonda transformed her grief into an unshakable resolve to see Texas take up school and gun safety in earnest. She and I became friends; I'm a parent too, and whenever I was with Rhonda, I couldn't imagine her pain. That empathy, and my desire to do something more than offer thoughts and prayers, fueled my resolve. It enabled me to work hard, driving ten hours in one day to make five campaign appearances, sleep in a Holiday Inn Express somewhere in the middle of nowhere, and get up and do it again and again for months. When I think about the folks who wanted me to win (and there were many), Rhonda always comes to mind first. To know Rhonda and what my campaign meant to her is to understand where my energy and drive came from.

EPILOGUE CHAPTER 5

....

The Galileo of Texas!

A few hundred years ago, a wiz with a telescope proved the earth revolves around the sun. Folks thought Galileo was crazy; after all, the Catholic Church had been telling everyone for centuries that the sun revolved around the earth! How dare Galileo use facts to dispute a notion as old as time.

Well, I'm not a wiz at anything, but I do have years of experience analyzing complex financial systems. When I demonstrated to Texans that Republicans have been raising property taxes for years, I felt like the Galileo of Texas. "No way, Mike!" I'd hear. "Republicans don't raise taxes; Democrats do!"

The truth is, the Republicans running Texas are responsible for our property tax crisis. See Article III, page 5, note 3, paragraph 2, sentence 2, of the state's 2018–2019 budget: "Property values, and the estimate of local tax collections on which they are based, shall be increased 7.04 percent in tax year 2017 and 6.77 percent in tax year 2018." The previous budget says the same thing, except the increases were 4.56 percent in tax year 2015 and 6.18 percent in tax year 2016.

In total, the state budgets passed by these so-called conservative Republicans raised property taxes 26.88 percent over four years.

Now, some in the media howled—that can't possibly be right! No Republican would ever raise taxes! Surely "shall be increased" must mean something other than "shall be increased"! Anyway, these were just words, that's all. Besides, the state doesn't actually collect property taxes.

I was quick to correct them. The Texas comptroller visits each appraisal district to make sure property values do, in fact, increase with the market. I also pointed out that, in the face of rising home values, the Texas Education Agency sent a letter to Texas school districts telling them not to lower their tax rates or they might lose state aid. When the state says property taxes "shall be increased," there's no question—they meant it!

Besides, the Texas Constitution is crystal clear: The legislature is responsible for all aspects of school funding, whether it collects the money or delegates that task to local school districts. When the constitution says the state is the responsible party, blaming school districts for raising taxes (which Republicans consistently do) is pure hooey.

But this, I think, is the most astonishing part. Those so-called conservatives running the state routinely and deliberately raise school property taxes every year. Why? Because they have no choice! The state of Texas can no longer pay its bills. And that's due to three consequential decisions the legislature made over the years, decisions that have seriously compromised our revenue systems.

- In 1991, they froze the motor fuel tax at $0.20 per gallon; purchasing power has fallen by two-thirds, or more than $5 billion per year (see page 141).

- In 1997, they passed the equal and uniform law, which allows owners of large commercial and industrial properties to underpay their taxes by $4 billion per year (see page 120).

- In 2006, they replaced the old business franchise tax with the new business margin tax, which created a $5 billion annual structural deficit (according to then Texas comptroller Carole Keeton Strayhorn).

But wait—it gets worse! To make ends meet, the state began borrowing money; today, we owe more than $100 billion. Texas school districts owe $120 billion. That means debt service at the state level is $2 billion per year and at the school district level, more than $6 billion per year.

When you add it all up, we've blown a $20 billion-plus per year hole in our budget (and that's before inflation). Texas is in a fiscal death spiral! No wonder the lawmakers turn to local property taxes—it's the only thing they can do to raise money! The legislature pulls it off by laundering local property tax dollars through the school funding mechanism, hence the state budget language: Property taxes "shall be increased."

The actual budget mechanics work like this. At the start of the budget process, the state sends economists out to predict how much property values will grow. With that information, estimates are made as to how much tax revenue will flow into local coffers. Budget writers then figure out what state money is needed to hold flat total spending (for example, per-student spending). And voila! Property taxes go way up, and Texans don't get anything in return. We're paying more, so the state gets away with paying less—and that's how we make ends meet after blowing holes in our revenue systems. And it's only going to get worse.

On the campaign trail, I talked only about closing the 1997 equal and uniform statute because it's massive, it's well documented—and closing the loophole would not raise taxes. It would merely enforce the law. I talked about it everywhere I went; in fact, I've been talking about closing the equal and uniform loophole in interviews, speeches, conversations, opinion pieces, this book, everything, for five years! And I keep waiting for someone—anyone—to say it's "fake news." After all, I'm essentially accusing our state's top leaders of a conspiracy to let owners of large commercial and industrial properties cheat the rest of us by $4 billion per year (that's $5 billion today, when you consider inflation).

As this update goes to print, not once in all these years has anyone shown me that I'm wrong. No politician, no pundit, no college professor, no appraisal district chief, no reporter, no large property owner, no county commissioner, no schoolboard trustee. *No one.*

A Dallas TV station decided to put together an investigative report on the subject. I and many others were interviewed, and near the end of the campaign, when the reporter issued his piece, he sided with me.

Calling these budget shenanigans a conspiracy is not hyperbole. The Texas Constitution states that properties subject to taxation must be taxed in proportion to their value. However, the equal and uniform statute lets the owners of large commercial and industrial properties set their appraisals below market. That, in my opinion, makes it illegal. And Republican politicians do everything in their power to sweep this under the rug (including taking huge campaign contributions to do so). Just read the 2016 report written by the Senate Select Committee of Property Tax Reform and Relief. The committee held meetings all over the state and spoke to hundreds of Texans about property taxes. The report is silent as to commercial and industrial properties. Except it's not *completely* silent. A Democratic senator on the committee appended a letter stating that testimony regarding commercial property valuations had been omitted from the report.

Need more?

In 2016, the Legislative Budget Board wrote a report, The Government Effectiveness and Efficiency Report, which clearly states that equity appeals under the flawed equal and uniform statute cause reductions in school funding and increases in homeowner property taxes.

It's a conspiracy. Period. And Texans are waking up to it. Before long, lawmakers will start talking about it—but they'll only offer confused (and confusing) data and deliberate obfuscation. They have not and they WILL NOT close that loophole, thank you very much. They can prove me wrong, but I know I'm right.

Desperate to win reelection, Dan Patrick looked Texans in the eye and said he lowered property taxes, which is complete rubbish. Texans saw their property tax bill go up, not down. Small businesses were hit the hardest. Year by year, it's getting worse, and the culprit is state fiscal policy. And all the Dan Patricks of the world can do is lie. What a complete disgrace.

Lying about property taxes wasn't the only whopper Dan Patrick told during the campaign. He told retired teachers they could trust him "forever"—even though he had just slashed their health-care benefits. He told active teachers he'd fought for a $10,000 raise; in fact, he'd blocked increased funding for public education. Then, he promised teachers he'd try again but refused to say where he'd get that funding (which means it's not going to happen).

And that's the part of Texas politics that's broken. Because we lack effective political competition, politicians can lie through their teeth and get away with it. And that's why I got involved in Texas politics in the first place.

A side note: Shortly after the election, a Texas Democratic Party official asked me to keep an open mind about running for the US Senate in 2020. Since I outperformed all other Democrats (including Beto O'Rourke) in the majority of Texas counties, perhaps I'm the right person to challenge Senator John Cornyn. At least, that's the theory.

But I'm not inclined to do it. Why? Because my heart is in Texas, and my passion is Texas public education. There are plenty of good people to run for US Senate.

But I will say this: The Galileo analogy applies to national policy just as surely as it applies here in Texas. Like Galileo looking through a new lens and seeing the heavens as they truly are, Americans recently saw what so-called conservatives have in mind for ordinary Americans. Their short-lived control of the entire federal government right after Donald Trump was elected revealed this unmistakable ambition: to provide massive tax cuts for the already rich, let the deficit explode, and then use the deficit as a pretext for cutting Social Security, Medicare, and Medicaid. Through manipulation of federal finances, so-called conservative politicians—including Texas's own senators, Ted Cruz and John Cornyn—are trying to cut Social Security, Medicare, and Medicaid benefits, which millions of hard-working Americans from both parties rely on.

And just like Texas politicians, national politicians conceal their unfair policies in a cloak of spin and nonsense. They pound their chest and brag about tax cuts without ever saying that the already rich got most of them. They say their tax cuts will create jobs, but they don't dare point out that tax cuts for working- and middle-class families would have created perhaps even more jobs. And they preach the evils of "entitlements," hoping their voting base won't figure out that so-called entitlements are the very programs they'll need to survive in retirement.

I am every bit as passionate about federal tax policy and its brutal unfairness to working- and middle-class families as I am about how Texas tax policy is weakening our state. The Democratic nominee for US Senate, whoever that person might be, can count on my help informing working- and middle-class Texas families that a vote for these policies is a vote against their own economic self-interest.

EPILOGUE CHAPTER 6

....

Tremendous Progress

With the Gremlins' digital campaign machine up and running, word about me and my platform spread quickly. Everywhere I went, life-long Republicans would tell me they were going to vote for me. Teachers (active and retired), people who were paying property taxes, and just about anyone who heard my message were pulling for me. There I was, running a substantive campaign, making promises that would make my state a much better place to live and raise a family—promises I knew I could keep—and it was wonderful.

The downside to running an all-digital campaign? People who aren't in your target market don't know anything about you. It's not like traditional campaigning, where everyone, even voters who will never vote for you, sees you on TV. And reporters—well, they only write about candidates with massive war chests. So even though our digital tracking told us we were making terrific progress, newspapers had almost nothing to say. When they did write about me, they told their readers I didn't stand a chance (enduring the naysaying was by far the hardest part of the campaign.)

At a fund-raising event, a major donor wanted to know why he hadn't seen anything about my campaign. One of the Gremlins quickly shot back, "Oh, we're campaigning all right; just not at you. We have your vote—it's your neighbor we're working on." Digital campaigning is that precise.

If the newspapers weren't writing about me, at least they had Beto to write about, and that stirred up plenty of interest in the election. I don't use the word "admire" very often, but I can say I admire Beto. He proved to be every bit as authentic as I thought he would be when we sat together at that Austin meeting. I wasn't sure anyone could charm a state as big as Texas, but not only did he pull it off, he charmed the entire nation! Beto is not a calculating politician, but he is smart. He calls it exactly as he sees it, he communicates brilliantly through storytelling, and he possesses natural charisma. We all learned a lot from Beto! And we're all hoping he runs again.

There were also plenty of wonderful stories written about excellent down-ballot candidates, several of whom won and all of whom contributed to Democrats' success in 2018. I hope those who came up short stay in this fight.

Not much was written about Lupe Valdez, who won the nomination for governor in a close runoff against Andrew White, former Texas governor Mark White's son. Sadly, we lost Governor White in early 2017. Andrew had entered the race to honor his father's memory and bring his problem-solving mindset back to Texas politics. I enjoyed getting to know Andrew very much. He's a terrific person and has a lot to offer Texas.

As for Lupe, it turns out she was fiery, fun, and effective on the stump. I also found her to be warm, sincere, and compassionate in person, someone I was proud to campaign with. The daughter of migrant workers, Lupe pulled herself up by her bootstraps, ultimately becoming sheriff of Dallas County. She never talked about giving people a handout; she talked about giving people a hand-up! Her job—defeating an incumbent Republican governor with a $40 million war chest—was the hardest one. But she fought with grit and determination, and we all fell in love with her.

As Election Day drew near, our digital tracking suggested we might very well win. Newspapers and political pundits, however, remained utterly dismissive. Our analytics told us Patrick was in trouble. And he was pouring millions of dollars into TV commercials, telling us we were right. But reporters and talking heads, with their remarkably thin grasp of the situation, completely missed those signs.

One well-known (and now seriously discredited) pundit insisted I was never a factor in the lieutenant governor race. I guess he thought Patrick was buying TV time all over the state and draining his war chest just to impress the neighbors. Political pundits don't yet understand modern campaigns.

Despite the lack of coverage, all the state's newspapers that endorsed 2018 candidates endorsed me: *The Dallas Morning News, Houston Chronicle, San Antonio Express-News, Corpus Christi Caller-Times, San Angelo Standard-Times, Waco Tribune-Herald, Longview News-Journal, Marshall News Messenger,* and *Bryan-College Station Eagle.* Having this support was a huge relief. Had those endorsements gone to my opponent, it would've damaged my reputation in the business world.

The day before Election Day, I was jolted by a call from the Texas Department of Public Safety. They wanted to meet and discuss security. I wasn't afraid for my safety, but I felt a sense of remorse. I worried that I was putting Suzanne—my wife and best friend—through an ordeal. She hasn't the slightest interest in drawing attention to herself, and I could tell how worried she was about the public spotlight. But there was no mistaking her desire to see Democrats (including her husband) win big after Donald Trump's election. The daughter of a former US diplomat, Suzanne has lived all over the world. She hates bigotry, she reveres democracy, she practices compassion, and she is angry as a hornet that, thanks to Donald Trump, racism in America is on the rise. So even if winning the election meant an uncomfortable adjustment, we both knew this had to be done.

On election night, all the local and state candidates who were in Austin came to the watch party at the Driskill Hotel. The Driskill is where, some thirty-five years earlier, my long-lost college friend, Chuck Doty, told me I would never run for office. The Driskill is where, five years earlier, I'd held my first meeting with my first consultant, Jason Stanford, to talk about the comptroller race. Now, the Driskill was my "war room," where family and friends could watch election returns as hundreds of Democrats partied in the adjoining concourse.

Guests and revelers began arriving at 6:30 p.m. I was directed to make a grand entrance at 8:15 p.m.; that allowed time to shake hands until the polls closed (7:00 p.m.), find a place to throw on a suit and tie, and get to the Driskill. Cameron Chandler—or, as I call him, the Texas Oracle—joined me for poll duty (I've known Cameron since our Longhorn Band days when we marched together; he's my political alter ego), and by 7:30 p.m., we found ourselves in a UT campus parking garage. Cameron maneuvered his car into a corner for privacy, and just as I might have donned my band uniform for a 1980s-era game-day road trip, I quickly changed clothes. The irony was just too rich.

Around 7:45 p.m., Cameron and I were ready and waiting when my phone rang. It was the Gremlins, breathless with news; returns from a key battleground county had just come in, and I was in the lead—and I needed to come to the Driskill right away. The feeling was electrifying.

But there are 254 counties in Texas. As results continued to come in, our lead slowly gave way. The euphoria that greeted me when I arrived at the Driskill turned to tears. Though I hurt for all the people who were crying, I wasn't the least bit sad or upset. Texas is a huge state and these things take time. We'd made great strides. I had proven the pundits wrong—I'd lost by only 4.9 percentage points, which is closer than any Democrat had come to defeating the incumbent lieutenant governor in more than twenty years.

I won urban areas handily and did well in fast-growing suburbs, places where we'd invested in digital messaging. But there were hundreds of counties where I just hadn't had the time or money to communicate my message. We know from our tracking that another $2 million in campaign money could very well have moved 250,000 voters from the Patrick column to the Collier column for the win. To be clear, donors contributed generously to down-ballot candidates, to Beto, and to some extent, to me, and all of that effort put me within striking range of becoming Texas lieutenant governor. You know the saying: No football team ever lost a game, they just ran out of time! That's exactly what happened to me on November 6, 2018. So I'm not the least bit unhappy.

When I joined the Democrats in 2013, I knew I'd have a long, difficult, uphill struggle. I didn't leave the Republican Party because I found an easier path to victory! My decision was a matter of principle, and I am not fazed by the loss. I've made hundreds of terrific friends all over Texas. We are in this fight together, and we are fighting for things we believe in. My endurance has yet to be tested.

EPILOGUE CHAPTER 7

....

Now What?

Despite Democrats winning two US congressional seats, several seats in the Texas legislature, and countless county administrative and judge positions, Republicans still control the state. Will Democrats' significant success be a wake-up call for the GOP? Or will they double down on their failed policies?

Sadly, I predict it will be the latter. A leopard doesn't change his spots.

And here is what it will mean for Texas. The big corporate property tax loophole will remain open. Our state's revenue crisis won't get solved. Our public schools will, therefore, have less money. Teacher retirement benefits will not be restored; in fact, they might be cut further. Property taxes will continue to increase. Texas will take on more debt and likely face a credit downgrade. Interest expense will increase, more Texans will lose health care, and our transportation and water infrastructure problems will remain largely unsolved. We won't expand Medicaid, even though thirty-seven other states have concluded it's a good deal. Nothing will be done to stop gun violence in our schools and communities. There will be no criminal justice reform. And after the 2020 census, we'll see a fresh round of extreme gerrymandering designed to shield the Republican political machine from accountability.

I pray I'm wrong, but I suspect I'll be proven right. When these predictions come true, Texans will be determined to drive change. I have time now to reach the voters I haven't reached already. If my health is good and if donors get behind me, I believe I can win in 2022. The state of Texas dearly needs political competition! My love for this state, and the people in it, are what keep me in this fight.

In the meantime, I hope folks continue to join me in this quest to save Texas politics! As I said earlier, it's not looking so improbable, is it?

APPENDIX

....

Newspaper Endorsements

I was proud to have the following Texas newspapers endorse me in both my 2014 campaign for comptroller and 2018 campaign for lieutenant governor:

Houston Chronicle
The Dallas Morning News
San Antonio Express-News
San Angelo Standard-Times
Corpus Christi Caller-Times
Longview News-Journal
Bryan-College Station Eagle
Waco Tribune-Herald
Marshall News Manager

Three newspapers that endorsed me in 2014—*Beaumont Enterprise, Austin American-Statesman*, and *Fort Worth Star-Telegram*—did not endorse either candidate in the race for lieutenant governor. No newspapers endorsed Lieutenant Governor Dan Patrick in his reelection bid.

You might ask, if so many major newspapers in the state got behind me, why did I lose? Former Houston mayor Bill White said it best when he warned that in politics today, the outcome of an election reflects the overall sentiment toward the candidate's party, and that sentiment is very hard to influence if you are running down-ballot (e.g., for an office like comptroller).

Said another way, party machinations—more so than qualifications or policy preferences—drive the outcome of the vast majority of elections in modern American politics.

Would I have lost in a state with two highly competitive political parties? We'll never know, but there is no doubt in my mind that qualified candidates need to step up and "buck the system," so that machine politicians know they work for the people, not the party.

That's a key difference between America and dictatorships like China and Russia, where one party calls all the shots. Every hack politician is loyal to the party first, to the people second. That could happen in American if we ever let our guard down.

My Republican friends think I'm crazy to work as hard as I do to help the Democratic Party in Texas become competitive. They are out getting rich, and I'm not—which, frankly, can be depressing at times. But I dearly love my country and my state, the freedoms we enjoy, and our Constitution, and it shouldn't be that hard to figure out what propels me on this improbable quest.

"For Lt. Governor: Mike Collier"

—Houston Chronicle[1]

Though running as a Democrat, Collier is a former Republican and much about him resembles one of Texas' most respected lieutenant governors, Republican Bill Ratliff. Like the East Texas statesman, elected by his Senate colleagues in 2000, Collier is earnest almost to the point of boring, seemingly unencumbered by the partisanship and ego that often taint the process, and while we can't say if he'd ever be knighted by his colleagues as Ratliff was with a nickname as lofty as "Obi-Wan Kenobi," we can say Collier is a smart guy.

So smart, in fact, that his fellow Houstonian Dan Patrick wouldn't dare debate him. . . . We give our full-throated endorsement to Mike Collier for lieutenant governor, not just because we oppose Patrick's petty, divisive and cynical approach to the job, but because we refuse to accept that in just 20 years, Texas' most powerful legislative office can't be won by a person who puts people before politics, a statesman in the spirit of Ratliff.

"We Recommend Mike Collier for Lt. Governor"

—Dallas Morning News[2]

[W]e recommend Democrat Mike Collier, 57, a corporate accountant from Humble and a former Republican, over Lt. Gov. Dan Patrick, a Republican. Collier could provide strong fiscal leadership and a collaborative tone conducive to addressing the state's complex challenges. . . .

Collier promises to pursue three top priorities: closing corporate tax provisions that allow some companies, unlike homeowners, to pay less than fair market value; expanding state Medicaid coverage to draw down additional dollars from the federal government; and establishing an independent commission to reduce the impact of partisan gerrymandering. He also would use some dollars from the rainy day fund to shore up teacher retirement pensions. . . . Collier is temperamentally moderate and a consensus-seeker. Lowering the temperature in the state Senate and getting back to issues that matter is something all Texans should embrace.

"Collier Best Pick for Lt. Governor"

—San Antonio Express-News[3]

Public school financing is among the top issues facing this state if it is to have the workforce it needs to remain economically competitive. This Editorial Board recommends Democrat Mike Collier — who Patrick so far has refused to debate—for lieutenant governor. . . . On immigration, Collier questions the value of redirecting Department of Public Safety resources to South Texas to allegedly enhance border security. And he correctly notes that the Legislature's sanctuary cities bill, which penalizes local jurisdictions whose law enforcement supposedly doesn't cooperate with immigration authorities, is unneeded and sows distrust of the police in immigrant communities. Patrick supported both these measures.

Collier's solution to the state having the highest number of uninsured in the nation, partly, is expanding Medicaid under the Affordable Care Act. Patrick opposes this. And we note that while GOP leadership generally opposes the ACA—with the attorney general actively trying to derail pre-existing condition protections and other provisions — it has failed to come up with any meaningful solution of its own.

Collier has ideas. Patrick's tenure has been marked by divisiveness and punting—particularly on school finance. We recommend Collier. And, as in other races, we find the incumbent's refusal to debate troubling—and telling.

"CPA Mike Collier for Comptroller"

—Corpus Christi Caller-Times[4]

If the state comptroller were a non-elected professional, sensible Texans would hire what they've never voted into that office—an accountant. Democrat Mike Collier—CPA and former oil company chief financial officer—would be a shoo-in. And the Republican nominee, state Sen. Glenn Hegar, a farmer—nothing wrong with farmers—would be irrelevant.

Hegar is an example of a recurring mistake voters make—a politician seeking a promotion to comptroller to then what?

Collier is believable when he says comptroller wouldn't be a steppingstone for him. He's easy to envision as a comptroller. Lieutenant governor? That would require some imagination. He has never run for office, says he wants to take the politics out of this one and—call us naive—we take him at his word.

Collier says his outrage at the grossly inaccurate comptroller's estimate of 2011 started him on this path. Even we financially knowledge-deficient non-accountants smelled the fishiness of Comptroller Susan Combs's estimated $27 billion deficit at the time—and said so. Revenue from the oil boom already was flowing rapidly into the Rainy Day Fund, which Gov. Rick Perry declared off limits for budget-balancing.

The Legislature, including Hegar, accommodated him with a $5.4 billion cut in education funding. Hegar declared that he was proud of it.

Collier called him out for having done so, which Hegar answered by claiming to have been taken out of context, which prompted a PolitiFact review, which found Collier's statements true. Unequivocally, contextually true.

Collier proposes quarterly revenue estimates, which would help lawmakers and the public know where Texas stands financially. He praises Combs for one thing—transparency—but says all she did was dish out mountains of unexplained data. He proposes explaining what it means—a task he's uniquely qualified to do.

He also would emphasize the comptroller's watchdog role. For example, he wouldn't be shy about explaining how the Rainy Day Fund can be used responsibly—especially when ideologues declare it off limits.

Collier says if the comptroller's office were run the way he wants to run it, it wouldn't generate many headlines for the person in charge. As much as we love headlines, we agree. Electing him would be good for Texas's financial health.

"Pick Political Novice Mike Collier for Texas Comptroller"

—*Fort Worth Star-Telegram*[5]

There are few jobs in Austin for which political inexperience might be considered an asset. State comptroller is one of them, and the political outsider who deserves the position is Democrat Mike Collier.

While he's politically green, Collier has gained a bounty of relevant experience from his three-decade career as a Certified Public Accountant—first at Exxon, then at PriceWaterhouseCoopers, before serving as CFO in an oil company he helped build.

Collier says his motivation to run came after the botched 2011 revenue estimates by outgoing Comptroller Susan Combs, which indirectly lead to a $5.4 billion cut in education funding, some of which has been restored. Providing more accurate financial projections and quarterly fund balance estimates top Collier's agenda.

He also proposes restoring the Texas Performance Reviews to the comptroller's office to increase accountability of state agencies, and would continue to improve upon efforts to bring more transparency to the state's finances.

The 53-year-old Houston businessman, who told the *Star-Telegram* Editorial Board that he has no designs on higher office, has also said that he'd like to "leave politics out of it" (the office, that is). It's an approach that is tough to argue with, since the job of comptroller— the state's CFO, treasurer and accountant—should transcend politics.

In contrast, the Republican candidate, state Sen. Glenn Hegar, 43, is every bit the politician. The lawmaker and farmer from Katy has served in the Legislature for more than a decade, where he chaired the Sunset Advisory Commission and worked to eliminate wasteful spending.

While he's certainly a political animal, Hegar, 43, is still a credentialed competitor. He wants to make the state's financial information more accessible and to improve the agency's accuracy as a revenue estimator.

But Hegar's proven strength is as a politician, and Texans would more likely benefit from a candidate whose strength is in numbers.

Collier and Hegar recently scheduled their first and only debate for Oct. 29.

Libertarian Ben Sanders and Green Party candidate Deb Shaffo also are seeking the office.

The *Star-Telegram* Editorial Board recommends Mike Collier for comptroller of public accounts.

Notes

Chapter 1: My Texas History

1. "Alexander Haig," *Time*, April 2, 1984.

Chapter 4: Okay, Maybe I Am Crazy (Angry?) Enough

1. Jay Root, "Dewhurst, Straus, Perry See Opportunity for Tax Relief," *The Texas Tribune*, January 9, 2013, https://www .texastribune.org/2013/01/09/taxes-going-down-top-leaders-say/.
2. James Moore, "Rick Perry Versus the Schoolchildren of Texas," HuffPost Politics, the blog, *Huffington Post*, January 6, 2013, http://www.huffingtonpost.com/jim-moore/rick-perry-education_b_2421776.html.
3. Erica Grieder, "Texas Has an Unexpected 8.8 Billion Surplus," *Texas Monthly*, January 21, 2013, http://www.texasmonthly.com/ politics/texas-has-an-unexpected-8-8-billion-surplus/.
4. Dave Montgomery, "Perry Praises Texas School Funding as 'Phenomenal,'" *Fort Worth Star-Telegram*, January 9, 2013, http:// www.star-telegram.com/living/family/moms/article3833583.html.
5. W. Gardner Selby, "Rick Perry Says Texas Education Spending Increased a Phenomenal 70 Percent as Enrollment Escalated 23 Percent," *PolitiFact Texas*, January 16, 2013, http://www .politifact.com/texas/statements/2013/jan/16/rick-perry/rick -perry-says-texas-education-increased-phenomen/.
6. Chandra Villanueva, "Sizing Up the 2014–2015 Texas Budget: Public Education," The Center for Public Policy Priorities, August 22, 2013, http://forabettertexas.org/images/ED_2013_08_PP_ publicedbudget.pdf. A graph on p. 2 shows spending at $10,611 in 2002, and at $9,624 in 2014 in constant 2013 dollars.

7. Ross Ramsey, "Combs Spurs a Political Stampede," *The Texas Tribune*, June 3, 2013, https://www.texastribune.org/2013/06/03/combs-spurs-political-stampede/.

8. Matthew Waller, "Four Republicans Seek State Comptroller Seat," *San Angelo Standard-Times*, August 20, 2013, http://www .gosanangelo.com/news/four-republicans-seek-state-comptroller -seat-ep-306170426-355446381.html.

9. Hans Peter Mareus Neilsen Gammel, *The Laws of Texas, 1822– 1897, Volume 1*, 1898; http://texashistory.unt.edu/ark:/67531/ metapth5872/, accessed February 1, 2016, University of North Texas Libraries, The Portal to Texas History, http://texashistory .unt.edu; crediting UNT Libraries, Denton, Texas.

10. National Education Agency, "Rankings & Estimates; Rankings of the States 2004 and Estimates of School Statistics 2005," June 2005, Table H-4: "State & Local Govt. Expenditures for all Education, 2001–02, Per $1,000 of Personal Income in 2002($)," p. 53, http:// www.nea.org/assets/docs/HE/05rankings.pdf.

11. National Education Agency, "Rankings & Estimates; Rankings of the States 2014 and Estimates of School Statistics 2015," March 2015, Table H-4: "State & Local Govt. Expenditures for All Education, 2011–12, per $1,000 of Personal Income in 2012($)," p. 53, http:// www.nea.org/assets/docs/NEA_Rankings_And_Estimates-2015-03 -11a.pdf.

12. National Education Agency, "Rankings & Estimates; Rankings of the States 2004 and Estimates of School Statistics 2005," June 2005, Table H-11: "Current Expenditures for Public K–12 Schools per Student in Fall Enrollment, 2003–04($)," p. 55, http://www .nea.org/assets/docs/HE/05rankings.pdf.

13. National Education Agency, "Rankings & Estimates; Rankings of the States 2014 and Estimates of School Statistics 2015," March 2015, Table H-11: "Current Expenditures for Public K–12 Schools per Student in Fall Enrollment, 2013–14($)," p. 55, http://www.nea.org/assets/docs/NEA_Rankings_And_Estimates -2015-03-11a.pdf.

14. Lindsey Wanner, "SAT Scores by State 2014," *Commonwealth Foundation*, December 22, 2014, http://wwwcommonwealth foundation.org/policyblog/detail/sat-scores-by-state-2014.

15. Morgan Smith, "Texas Posts Top High School Graduation Rates, Again," *The Texas Tribune*, August 5, 2014, https://www.texastribune.org/2014/08/05/texas-posts-top-high-school-graduation-rates-again/.

16. Valerie Strauss, "Texas GOP Rejects 'Critical Thinking' Skills. Really," *The Washington Post*, July 9, 2012, https://www.washingtonpost.comblogs/answer-sheet/post/texas-gop-rejects-critical-thinking-skills-really/2012/07/08/gJQAHNpFXW_blog.html.

17. "Republican Party of Texas, Report of Permanent Committee on Platform and Resolutions as Amended and Adopted by the 2014 State Convention of the Republican Party of Texas," https://www.texasgop.org/wp-content/uploads/2014/06/2014-Platform-Final.pdf; "2012 Republican Party of Texas Report of Platform Committee," http://s3.amazonaws.com/texasgop_pre/assets/original/2012Platform_Final.pdf.

18. Texas Education Agency, "2015–2016 Student Enrollment, Statewide Totals," accessed May 1, 2016, https://rptsvr1.tea.texas.gov/cgi/sas/broker.

19. Texas Charter Schools Association, "Fast Charter Facts," data based on the TEA 2014 Comprehensive Biennial Report on Texas Public Schools, http://www.txcharterschools.org/news-events/charter-faq/.

20. Private School Review, "Texas Private Schools," accessed May 1, 2016, http://www.privateschoolreview.com/texas.

21. Private School Review, "Texas Private Schools by County," accessed May 1, 2016, http://www.privateschoolreview.com/texas.

22. Ibid.

23. Georgetown University, Georgetown Public Policy Institute, Center on Education and the Workforce, "Recovery: Job Growth and Education Requirements Through 2020," June 2013, accessed May 1, 2016, https://cew.georgetown.edu/wp-content/uploads/2014/11/Recovery2020.SR_.Web_.pdf.

24. "Notable Quotes of Sam Houston," The Sam Houston Memorial Museum, Huntsville, Texas, http://samhoustonmemorialmuseum.com/history/quotes.html.

Chapter 7: Bracing for Launch

1. Susan Combs, Texas Comptroller of Public Accounts, "Biennial Revenue Estimate, 2012–2013 Biennium, 82nd Texas Legislature," January 2011, http://www.texastransparency .org/State_Finance/Budget_Finance/Reports/Biennial_Revenue _Estimate/bre2012/96-402_BRE_2012-13.pdf; Ross Ramsey, "Comptroller Estimates Available Revenue," *The Texas Tribune*, January 10, 2011, https://www.texastribune.org/2011/01/10 /comptroller-estimates-available-revenue/.

2. Susan Combs, Texas Comptroller of Public Accounts, "The 2012–13 Certification Revenue Estimate," December 12, 2011, http://www .texastransparency.org/State_Finance/Budget_Finance/Reports /Certification_Revenue_Estimate/cre1213/CRE2012-13.pdf.

3. Susan Combs, Texas Comptroller of Public Accounts, "Biennial Revenue Estimate, 2012–2013 Biennium, 82nd Texas Legislature," January 2011, http://www.texastransparency .org/State_Finance/Budget_Finance/Reports/Biennial_Revenue _Estimate/bre2012/96-402_BRE_2012-13.pdf.

4. Erica Grieder, "Texas Has an Unexpected 8.8 Billion Surplus," *Texas Monthly*, January 21, 2013, http://www.texasmonthly .com/politics/texas-has-an-unexpected-8-8-billion-surplus/.

Chapter 9: Hazing the Rookie

1. Michael B. Sauter, "States Spending the Most on Education" (also includes info on states spending the least), *24/7 Wall St.*, May 31, 2013, http://247wallst.com/special-report/2013/05/31/states-that -spend-the-most-on-education/; Kids Count Data Center, a Project of the Annie E. Casey Foundation, "Economically Disadvantaged Students, 2012–13," data provided by Texas KIDS COUNT at the Center for Public Policy Priorities, http://datacenter.kidscount .org/data/tables/8224-economically-disadvantaged-students? loc=45&loct=2#detailed/2/any/false/1124/any/16743,16744; Suzanne Macartney, "Child Poverty in the United States 2009 and 2010: Selected Race Groups and Hispanic Origin," US

Census Bureau, American Community Survey Briefs, November 2011, https://www.census.gov/prod/2011pubs/acsbr10-05.pdf; Department of Education, ED Data Express, "Percent Limited English Proficient Students, 2013–14," accessed May 1, 2016, http://eddataexpress.ed.gov/data-element-explorer.cfm/tab/data/deid/4/; TCTA, Texas Classroom Teachers Association, "Teachers Deal with the Prevalence of Poverty," updated April 25, 2014, accessed May 1, 2016, https://tcta.org/node/13805-teachers_deal_with_the_prevalence_of_poverty; Lawrence Hardy, "The Costs of Immigration," American School Board Journal, April 2012, http://www.asbj.com/MainMenuCategory/Archive/2012/April/0412pdfs/The-Costs-of-Immigration.aspx.

2. Jessica Barnett, "SAT Scores by State 2013," Commonwealth Foundation, October 10, 2013, http://www.commonwealthfoundation.org/policyblog/detail/sat-scores-by-state-2013.

3. Susan Owen, "Texas' Change in Highway Miles Not No. 1 When Adjusted for State Size, Population," PolitiFact, January 28, 2014, http://www.politifact.com/texas/statements/2014/jan/28/rick-perry/texas-change-highway-miles-not-no-1-adjusted-size/.

4. Gordon Dickson, "Texas Road Debt: $23 Billion," Fort Worth Star-Telegram, September 14, 2014, http://www.star-telegram.com/news/traffic/your-commute/article3873168.html.

5. "10 States with Enormous Debt Problems: Report," Huffington Post, August 28, 2012, http://www.huffingtonpost.com/2012/08/28/state-debt-report_n_1836603.html; Sue Owen, "Texas Near Top in Local Debt per Capita," PolitiFact, December 6, 2013, http://www.politifact.com/texas/statements/2013/dec/06/debra-medina/texas-near-top-local-debt-capita/.

6. Robert T. Garrett, "Census: Texas Still No. 1 in Rate of Uninsured," Dallas Morning News, Trail Blazers Blog, September 16, 2016, http://trailblazersblog.dallasnews.com/2015/09/census-texas-still-no-1-in-rate-of-uninsured.html/; Elizabeth Mendes, "Texas Uninsured Rate Drifts Further From Other States," Gallup, March 8, 2013, http://www.gallup.com/poll/161153/texas-uninsured-rate-moves-further-away-states.aspx.

7. "Teenage Pregnancy in the United States," Wikipedia, last modified May 14, 2016, https://en.wikipedia.org/wiki/Teenage_pregnancy _in_the_United_States; Carrie Feibel, "Teenage Pregnancy in Decline, But Texas Still #1 for 'Repeat' Teen Births," Houston Public Media, May 30, 2013, https://www.houstonpublicmedia .org/articles/news/2013/05/30/43916/teenage-pregnancy-in -decline-but-texas-still-1-for-repeat-teen-births/.

8. Leslie Lee, "Worth It: Weighing the Costs of Implementing the State Water Plan and the Consequences of Doing Nothing," Texas Water Resources Institute, *TXh2o* Winter 2013, http://twri.tamu .edu/publications/txh2o/winter-2013/worth-it/.

Chapter 11: Discovering Texas, One Phone Call at a Time

1. United States Department of Labor, Bureau of Labor Statistics, "Regional and State Employment and Unemployment: August 2008," released September 19, 2008; see Table 3: "Civilian Labor Force and Unemployment by State and Selected Area, Seasonally Adjusted," http://www.bls.gov/news.release/archives /laus_09192008.pdf.

2. United States Department of Labor, Bureau of Labor Statistics, "Regional and State Employment and Unemployment: August 2013," released September 20, 2013; see Table 3: "Civilian Labor Force and Unemployment by State and Selected Area, Seasonally Adjusted," http://www.bls.gov/news.release/archives /laus_09202013.pdf.

3. Sheryl Jean, "Economic Snapshot: Is Texas the New California?" *Dallas Morning News*, December 9, 2015, http://interactives .dallasnews.com/2015/ca-biz-relocation/.

4. Eric Schnurer, "The Secret to Cutting Government Waste: Savings by a Thousand Cuts," *The Atlantic*, July 2, 2013, http://www .theatlantic.com/politics/archive/2013/07/the-secret-to-cutting -government-waste-savings-by-a-thousand-cuts/277458/.

5. Mitch Mitchell and Anna M. Tinsley, "Perry's Medicaid Plan Would Pass on $76 Billion in Federal Funds for Texas," *McClatchy DC*, July 10, 2012, http://www.mcclatchydc.com/news/politics -government/article24732598.html.

6. Billy Hamilton Consulting, "Expanding Medicaid in Texas: Smart, Affordable and Fair," a report analyzing the state and regional impacts of extending Medicaid under the Affordable Care Act; prepared for Texas Impact and Methodist Healthcare Ministries of South Texas, Inc., January 2013, https://texasimpact.org/sites /default/files/resource-files/Smart%20Affordable%20and%20 Fair_FNL_FULL.pdf.

7. Aman Batheja, "Rick Perry Calls for $1.6 Billion in Business Tax Cuts," *The Texas Tribune*, April 15, 2013, https://www.texastribune .org/2013/04/15/perry-calls-16-billion-business-tax-cuts/.

8. Texas Health and Human Services Commission, "2008–2009 Report on Residual Uncompensated Care Costs," accessed May 1, 2016, http://www.hhsc.state.tx.us/reports/2011/Rider-40 -0111.pdf.

9. Billy Hamilton Consulting, "Expanding Medicaid in Texas: Smart, Affordable and Fair," a report analyzing the state and regional impacts of extending Medicaid under the Affordable Care Act; prepared for Texas Impact and Methodist Healthcare Ministries of South Texas, Inc., January 2013, https://texasimpact.org/sites /default/files/resource-files/Smart%20Affordable%20and%20 Fair_FNL_FULL.pdf.

10. Texas Association of Business, "Expanding Medicaid Managed Care in Texas—The Right Dosage for Texas Recipients," April 10, 2015, tmp_59_4-10-2015_35708_.pdf.

11. Robert T. Garrett, "Census: Texas Still No. 1 in Rate of Uninsured," Trail Blazers Blog, *Dallas Morning News*, September 16, 2015, http://trailblazersblog.dallasnews.com/2015/09/census -texas-still-no-1-in-rate-of-uninsured.html/.

Chapter 15: The Republican Candidates

1. "Victoria Moseley's Interview with Senator Glenn Hegar," published April 18, 2014, https://www.youtube.com/watch?v=3cuiyOwycYk.

2. Bob Price, "Why Does Texas Comptroller Susan Combs Support Sen. Glenn Hegar," *Texas GOP Vote*, December 31, 2013, http://www.texasgopvote.com/economy/why-does-texas-comptroller-susan-combs-support-sen-glenn-hegar-006221.

3. "Glenn Hegar Admits He's Unqualified for Comptroller," Glenn Hegar, speaking to the Greater Fort Bend County Tea Party on January 23, 2014, published on February 5, 2014, https://www.youtube.com/watch?v=xwVyMQV37UY.

4. Terrence Stutz and Robert T. Garrett, "Lieutenant Governor Candidate Dan Patrick Knows Struggles of Going Broke," *Dallas Morning News*, September 19, 2013, http://www.dallasnews.com/news/politics/headlines/20130919-dan-patrick-walked-away-from-large-business-debts.ece.

5. Paul Burka, Erica Grieder, Sonia Smith, and Brian D. Sweany, "The Best and Worst Legislators 2013; The Worst: Senator Dan Patrick," *Texas Monthly*, July 2013, http://www.texasmonthly.com/list/the-best-and-worst-legislators-2013/the-worst-senator-dan-patrick/.

6. Aman Batheja, "Hegar Amends Filing to Include Wife's Income," *The Texas Tribune*, February 26, 2014, https://www.texastribune.org/2014/02/26/hegar-amends-financial-filings-include-wifes-incom/.

7. Kate Alexander, "Glenn Hegar Wins GOP Comptroller Primary After Harvey Hilderbran Bows Out of Runoff," *Austin American-Statesman*, March 7, 2014, http://www.statesman.com/news/news/state-regional-govt-politics/glenn-hegar-wins-gop-comptroller-primary-after-har/nd77q/.

Chapter 16: The Collier-Brigham-Smith #1

1. Marshal Ferdinand Jean Marie Foch, message to Marshal Joseph Joffre during the First Battle of the Marne, September 8, 1914.

2. Robert T. Garrett, "Hegar, Who Once Urged 'Just Do It' on Property Tax Abolition, Now More Cautious," Trail Blazers Blog, *Dallas Morning News*, March 20, 2014, http://trailblazersblog.dallas news.com/2014/03/hegar-who-once-urged-just-do-it-on -property-tax-abolition-now-more-cautious.html/.

3. Ross Ramsey, "A Tax Notion That Conceals a Math Problem," *The New York Times*, March 27, 2014, http://www.nytimes .com/2014/03/28/us/a-tax-notion-that-conceals-a-math-problem .html?_r=0.

4. Brenda Bell, "Appeals Shift Tax Burden," *Austin American-Statesman*, September 28, 2013, http://www.mystatesman.com /news/news/appeals-shift-tax-burden/nZ9mP/.

5. Erica Grieder, "The Senate Passed a Property Tax Reform!" *Texas Monthly*, Burka Blog, May 1, 2015, http://www.texasmonthly .com/burka-blog/the-senate-passed-a-property-tax-reform/.

Chapter 18: Meeting with the Tea Party

1. Texas Comptroller of Public Accounts, "Biennial Property Tax Report," Tax Years 2012 and 2013, Texas Property Tax, December 2014, http://comptroller.texas.gov/taxinfo/proptax /pdf/96-1728-12-13.pdf.

2. Susan Owen, "Texas' Change in Highway Miles Not No. 1 When Adjusted for State Size, Population," *PolitiFact*, January 28, 2014, http://www.politifact.com/texas/statements/2014/jan/28/rick-perry/ texas-change-highway-miles-not-no-1-adjusted-size/; US Department of Transportation, Federal Highway Administration, "Highway Statistics 2001: State Highway Agency-Owned Public Roads—2001," Table HM-81: "Rural and Urban Miles; Estimated Lane Miles and Daily Travel," http://www.fhwa.dot.gov/ohim/hs01/hm81.htm; US Department of Transportation, Federal Highway Administration, Policy and Governmental Affairs, Office of Highway Policy Information, "Highway Statistics 2012: State Agency-Owned Public Roads—2012," Table HM-81: "Rural and Urban Miles; Estimated Lane-Miles and Daily Travel," October 2013, http://www.fhwa.dot. gov/policyinformation/statistics/2012/hm81.cfm.

3. Texas A&M Transportation Institute and INRIX, *2015 Urban Mobility Scorecard*, August 2015, http://d2dtl5nnlpfr0r.cloudfront .net/tti.tamu.edu/documents/mobility-scorecard-2015.pdf.

Chapter 19: Convention Madness

1. "Republican Party of Texas, Report of Permanent Committee on Platform and Resolutions as Amended and Adopted by the 2014 State Convention of the Republican Party of Texas," https://www.texas gop.org/wp-content/uploads/2014/06/2014-Platform-Final.pdf.
2. Demos and the Center for Public Policy Priorities, "Texas' Investment in Higher Education Lags Behind Student Needs and Workforce Demands," accessed May 2, 2016, http://www.demos .org/sites/default/files/publications/Texasbrief-Final_0.pdf.
3. "Republican Party of Texas, Report of Permanent Committee on Platform and Resolutions as Amended and Adopted by the 2014 State Convention of the Republican Party of Texas," https://www.texas gop.org/wp-content/uploads/2014/06/2014-Platform-Final.pdf.
4. Ibid.

Chapter 20: The Watchdog Tour

1. Stephen Goss, Alice Wade, J. Patrick Skirvin, Michael Morris, K. Mark Bye, and Danielle Huston, "Effects of Unauthorized Immigration on the Actuarial Status of the Social Security Trust Funds," *Social Security Administration Actuarial Note*, Number 151, April 2013, https:// www.ssa.gov/oact/NOTES/pdf_notes/note151.pdf.
2. Paul J. Weber, "Texas Approves $800 Million for Border Security," *PBS NewsHour*, The Rundown, June 16, 2015, http:// www.pbs.org/newshour/rundown/texas-approves-800-million -border-security/.
3. "Dan Patrick—Washington Has Failed Us," published on October 8, 2014, https://www.youtube.com/watch?v=yfZ9eDA2daQ.
4. Colin Campbell, "Rick Perry: There Is 'A Very Real Possibility' ISIS Forces Have Crossed US-Mexican Border," *Business Insider*, August 21, 2014, http://www.businessinsider.com/rick-perry-isis -forces-crossing-us-mexican-border-2014-8.

5. Journeyman Pictures, *Inside ISIS and the Iraq Caliphate*, published on July 2, 2014, https://www.youtube.com/watch?v=yvE-ZYTziTU.

Chapter 21: Late Summer Doldrums

1. "Glenn Hager [*sic*] Part 1 of 2 by Montgomery County Tea Party, Texas," published December 31, 2013 (see 45:00), https://www.youtube.com/watch?v=Fp9XimysFfc.

2. "Victoria Moseley's Interview with Senator Glenn Hegar," published April 18, 2014 (see approx. 3:40), https://www.youtube.com/watch?v=3cuiyOwycYk.

3. "Glenn Hager [*sic*] Part 1 of 2 by Montgomery County Tea Party, Texas," published December 31, 2013 (see 5:30), https://www.youtube.com/watch?v=Fp9XimysFfc.

4. Ibid. (see 6:17).

5. SB 1342, Texas Senate Bill "Relating to Evidence of Inequality of Appraisal in Judicial Appeals of Appraisal Review Board Orders," http://openstates.org/tx/bills/83/SB1342/; I'm told it died in committee.

6. Brenda Bell, "Appeals Shift Tax Burden," *Austin American-Statesman*, September 28, 2013, http://www.mystatesman.com/news/news/appeals-shift-tax-burden/nZ9mP/.

7. The folks who lined up against the bill are in the legislative record, and each gave money to Hegar per the Texas Ethics Commission campaign finance records.

8. "Victoria Moseley's Interview with Senator Glenn Hegar," published April 18, 2014 (he talks about it a little over halfway through the interview), https://www.youtube.com/watch?v=3cuiyOwycYk.

9. W. Gardner Selby, "Mike Collier Says Opponent Glenn Hegar 'Is Proud of'" Legislated Cuts in Public School Funding," *PolitiFact*, September 5, 2014, http://www.politifact.com/texas/statements/2014/sep/05/mike-collier/mike-collier-says-opponent-glenn-hegar-was-proud-l/.

10. Aman Batheja, "Hegar Amends Filing to Include Wife's Income," *The Texas Tribune*, February 26, 2014, https://www.texastribune.org/2014/02/26/hegar-amends-financial-filings-include-wifes-incom/.

11. Texas Ethics Commission campaign finance records.

12. PwC, "Texas Enacts Permanent Franchise Tax Rate Reduction," Tax Insights from State and Local Tax Services, June 17, 2015, http://www.pwc.com/us/en/state-local-tax/newsletters/salt -insights/assets/pwc-exas-enacts-permanent-franchise-tax-rate -reduction.pdf.

Chapter 23: To Get Along, Just Go Along

1. David Barer, "A Brief History of the Texas Water Plan," *StateImpact*, May 28, 2013, https://stateimpact.npr.org /texas/2013/05/28/a-brief-history-of-the-texas-water-plan/.

2. Texas Public Policy Foundation, "Richard Fisher @ Texas at a Turning Point," April 16, 2014, published on April 28, 2014 (see his remarks starting at 39:58), https://www.youtube.com /watch?v=H2bKsGyacm4.

3. American Society of Civil Engineers, "2012 Report Card for Texas' Infrastructure," http://www.infrastructurereportcard.org/wp-content /uploads/2013/02/2012-Texas-Report-Card-FINAL.pdf.

Chapter 26: Corruption

1. Susan Combs, Texas Comptroller of Public Accounts, to Formula One World Championship Limited, May 10, 2010, copy in the author's possession.

2. Stef Schrader, "Does this 2010 Letter Mean Texas Has to Pay to Host Formula One After All?" Black Flag, December 28, 2015, http://blackflag.jalopnik.com/does-this-2010-letter-mean-texas -has-to-pay-to-host-for-1749973825.

3. Recital number 11 of the Agreement between the City of Austin and Circuit Events Local Organizing Committee, copy in the author's possession.

4. Attorney General Greg Abbott to the Honorable Jerry Patterson, Commissioner of the Texas General Land Office, May 18, 2012, copy in the author's possession.

5. Attorney General Greg Abbott to Land Commissioner Jerry Patterson, August 17, 2012, copy in the author's possession.

6. Steffi Probst, "Scratch Marks on a Clean Slate?" Risk Advisory, July 12, 2012, http://news.riskadvisory.net/2012/12/scratch-marks-on-a-clean-slate-german-public-officials-and-corruption/.

7. "F1 Boss Bernie Ecclestone Pays to End Bribery Trial," *BBC News*, August 5, 2014, http://www.bbc.com/news/world-europe-28656050.

8. Affidavit (F22) of Stephanie Richmond, November 6, 2013, 261st Judicial District, Travis County, 3fourTexas MGP, L.L.C., v. Circuit of the Americas, LLC, and Steve Sexton, No. D-1-GN-12-002781; Nolan Hicks, "$250M in State Funding for F1 Track in Question," *San Antonio Express-News*, September 13, 2014, updated September 15, 2014, http://www.expressnews.com/news/local/article/250M-in-state-funding-for-F1-track-in-question-5753674.php.

9. From Austin Tighe of Feazell & Tighe, LLP, to Jack Hohengarten, Assistant Attorney General, Attorney General of Texas, January 6, 2014, copy in the author's possession.

10. From Assistant Attorney General Jack Hohengarten to Austin Tighe of Feazell & Tighe, LLP, January 27, 2014, copy in the author's possession.

11. Tim Eaton, "Comptroller Candidate Takes Aim at Circuit of the Americas Subsidy," *Austin American-Statesman*, October 2, 2014, http://www.mystatesman.com/news/news/comptroller-candidate-takes-aim-at-circuit-of-the-/nhZ4w/.

12. Patricia Kuo, "Formula One Cancels $1.8 Billion Loan after IPO Postponed," Bloomberg, June 15, 2012, http://www.bloomberg.com/news/articles/2012-06-15/formula-one-said-to-cancel-1-8-billion-loan-after-ipo-postponed.

13. Lauren McGaughy, "Scathing Audit Rakes Governor's Office Over Texas Enterprise Fund," *Houston Chronicle*, September 25, 2014, http://www.houstonchronicle.com/news/politics/texas/article/Scathing-audit-rakes-governor-s-office-over-Texas-5781567.php.

14. John Keel, State Auditor's Office, "An Audit Report on The Texas Enterprise Fund at the Office of the Governor," September 2014, SAO Report No. 15-003, https://www.sao.texas.gov/reports/main/15-003.pdf.

15. Jonathan Selden, "Jury: Rancher Shortchanged for SH130 Land," *Austin Business Journal*, October 30, 2006, http://www .bizjournals.com/austin/stories/2006/10/30/daily2.html.

16. Aman Batheja, "Debt Issues Tied to SH 130 Could Impact Toll Projects," *The Texas Tribune*, October 23, 2013, https://www .texastribune.org/2013/10/23/threat-toll-road-default-could-hurt -future-project/.

17. Ibid.

18. Jamie Lovegrove, "SH 130 Toll Road Operator Files for Bankruptcy," *The Texas Tribune*, March 2, 2016, https://www .texastribune.org/2016/03/02/sh-130-toll-road-files-bankruptcy/.

Chapter 27: The Down-Ballot Boys

1. Manny Fernandez, "Grand Jury Indicts Texas Attorney General, Ken Paxton, on Felony Charges," *The New York Times*, August 1, 2015, http://www.nytimes.com/2015/08/02/us/grand-jury-indicts -texas-attorney-general-ken-paxton-on-felony-charges.html.

Chapter 28: All in the Family

1. "What is HB2?" Texas Policy Evaluation Project, July 2014, https:// www.utexas.edu/cola/txpep/_files/pdf/HB2%20Fact%20Sheet- 7July14.pdf; Morgan Smith, Becca Aaronson, and Shefali Luthra, "Abortion Bill Finally Passes Texas Legislature," July 13, 2013, *The Texas Tribune*, https://www.texastribune.org/2013/07/13 /texas-abortion-regulations-debate-nears-climax/.

2. Guttmacher Institute, "Fact Sheet—State Facts About Abortion: Texas," June 2015, https://www.guttmacher.org/fact-sheet/state -facts-about-abortion-texas.

3. "Texas Hospital Association's Testimony in Opposition to Section 2 of House Bill 2 by Jodie Laubenberg, Relating to the Regulation of Abortion Procedures, Providers, and Facilities, Providing Penalties, House Committee on State Affairs," July 2, 2013, http://graphics8. nytimes.com/science/texas_abortion_testimony.pdf.

Chapter 29: My Fifteen Minutes of Fame

1. For the curious, the ad, published on October 13, 2014, is available online here: https://www.youtube.com/watch?v=MbXE_pVzyy0.

Chapter 30: The Debate

1. Marissa Barnett, "Comptroller Race: $120,000 in Late Money to Hegar," *Dallas Morning News*, Trail Blazers Blog, November 3, 2014, http://trailblazersblog.dallasnews.com/2014/11/comptroller -race-120000-in-late-money-to-hegar.html/; Andrew Wheat, "Are Big Donors Abandoning Attorney General Ken Paxton?" *Texas Observer*, April 29, 2016, https://www.texasobserver.org /big-donors-abandon-ken-paxton/; Patrick Svitek, "Lopsided Money Race on the Eve of Comptroller Debate," Texas Politics Blog, *Houston Chronicle*, October 29, 2014, http://blog.chron .com/texaspolitics/2014/10/lopsided-money-race-on-eve-of -comptroller-debate/.

2. Per the campaign finance report for the period September 26– October 25 as filed with the Texas Ethics Commission.

Chapter 34: Just Wait

1. Christopher Hooks, "At Greg Abbott's Inaugural Blowout, A Governor Is Born," *Texas Observer*, January 20, 2015, https://www.texasobserver.org/greg-abbotts-inaugural-blowout -governor-born/.

Appendix: Newspaper Endorsements

1. From "For Lt. Governor: Mike Collier," *Houston Chronicle*, October 20, 2019, https://www.houstonchronicle.com/opinion /recommendations/article/For-Lieutenant-Governor-Mike-Collier -Dan-Patrick-13323753.php.

2. From "We Recommend Mike Collier for Lt. Governor," *Dallas Morning News*, October 17, 2018, www.dallasnews.com /opinion/editorials/2018/10/17/recommend-mike-collier -lieutenant-governor.

3. "Collier Best Pick for Lt. Governor," *San Antonio Express-News*, October 20, 2018, https://www.mysanantonio.com/opinion/editorials/article/Collier-best-pick-for-lieutenant-governor-13321861.php

4. "Endorsement: CPA Mike Collier for Comptroller," *Corpus Christi Caller-Times*, October 20, 2014, http://www.caller.com/opinion/editorials/endorsement-cpa-mike-collier-for-comptroller-ep-628709106.html.

5. "Pick Political Novice Mike Collier for Texas Comptroller," *Fort Worth Star-Telegram*, October 14, 2014, http://www.star-telegram.com/2014/10/14/6200525/pick-political-novice-mike-collier.html.

About the Author

For many years, Mike Collier was a partner in the worldwide accounting firm of PricewaterhouseCoopers, where he provided audit and financial consulting services to companies in the energy industry. Mike also served as the chief financial officer of a Texas oil company. Today, Mike is a consultant in Houston, working with private equity firms investing in growing Texas companies.

Mike started his career at Exxon and later moved to the audit practice of Price Waterhouse, where he earned his CPA license and worked in the Austin, Dallas, New York, and Houston offices. Mike graduated from Georgetown High School, in Central Texas, and received an undergraduate degree in Petroleum Land Management and an MBA from the University of Texas at Austin. He and his wife Suzanne have been married for almost three decades, and they have two sons who graduated from Kingwood High School before also going to UT.

Mike was the Democratic nominee for Texas State Comptroller in 2014 and remains active in helping Democrats win elections and create healthy political competition in Texas.